PRE-OWNED ASSETS:
CAPITAL TAX PLANNING
IN THE NEW ERA

AUSTRALIA
Law Book Co.
Sydney

CANADA and USACarswell
Toronto

HONG KONG
Sweet & Maxwell Asia

NEW ZEALAND
Brookers
Wellington

SINGAPORE and MALAYSIA
Sweet & Maxwell Asia
Singapore and Kuala Lumpur

PRE-OWNED ASSETS: CAPITAL TAX PLANNING IN THE NEW ERA

EMMA CHAMBERLAIN AND
CHRIS WHITEHOUSE

with BARRY McCUTCHEON

LONDON
SWEET & MAXWELL
2004

First Edition 2004

Published in 2004 by
Sweet & Maxwell Limited of
100 Avenue Road, London NW3 3PF
(http://www.sweetandmaxwell.co.uk)
Typeset by Interactive Sciences Limited, Gloucester
Printed in Great Britain by
MPG Books Ltd, Bodmin, Cornwall

A CIP catalogue record for this book
is available from the British Library

ISBN 0-421-89560-8

PREFACE

The days when tax avoidance was viewed as a game played out between taxpayer and Revenue subject to well established rules of conduct have long since gone. The growth of a tax avoidance industry promoting schemes that were frequently artificial; rarely anything other than complex and which displayed a high level of ingenuity in using the legislation against the intention of its promoters has unsurprisingly provoked a fierce reaction from Government and Revenue. We now live in an age when fire will be fought with fire and the old certainties are no more. No longer is it possible to say that legislation to stop tax avoidance will not affect past schemes or that tax is only payable if the case falls within the clear words of the legislation.

The subject matter of this book—the Pre-Owned Assets Charge —offers a case study in tax avoidance and the reaction against it. IHT avoidance, widespread and often "artificial", has been met by a novel charge: rather as Canning called into being a New World to redress the balance of the Old, so income tax has been summoned to cover up the cracks in IHT. From the original announcement on 10 December, Ministers have not wavered from two principles: firstly that this novel solution was going to happen (in modern terminology it was "non negotiable") and, secondly, that a major objective was to bring back within the tax net past transactions. In some cases, such transactions had been carried out over 17 years ago. Objections based on retrospective taxation were to be fiercely resisted. Within these parameters the consultation process was then distinguished by great willingness on the part of Ministers and the Revenue to amend and clarify the original detail and to exclude "hard" cases. (Typically these were situations when the new charge would be unnecessary since the taxpayer would in any event suffer an IHT charge or where the reservation of benefit legislation was not intended to apply.)

While the Revenue and Government's willingness to entertain amendments as the Schedule passed through Parliament was wholly admirable, the resultant mutilation of the original Finance Bill legislation was not pretty to behold and Sch.15 is unsurprisingly something of a mess. Further, such legislation "on the hoof" inevitably carries within it the seeds of its own destruction and is unlikely to stop the spiral of avoidance/anti-avoidance legislation. Perhaps good will eventually emerge if it encourages a future Government finally to address the reform of death duties. Inheritance tax has been in a sorry state since the wholesale mutilation of Capital Transfer Tax by Tory Governments in the 80s. This book has been written with the intention of explaining the new legislation and considering how it affects existing arrangements and its impact upon future tax saving strategies.

For a number of taxpayers the introduction of the POA charge will lead them to rue ever having sought to avoid IHT. To deal with such cases it is unfortunate that the legislation does not afford a complete fiscal unscrambling. Realisation of the mess that they have ended up in will lead some taxpayers to question the scheme that they had purchased (usually for much fine gold!). Signing papers without appreciating their full impact may well lead to a trickle of cases before the courts seeking to set the whole thing aside on the basis of mistake[1].

There is, however, another side to the coin. Rising property values not accompanied by corresponding adjustment to the IHT rates brought many taxpayers into the IHT net during the late 90s for the first time. This fuelled a demand for an "arrangement" that would prevent a large portion of the property value being taken up in a windfall tax charge. It was a desire to share this increased prosperity (if that is the correct word to describe a property boom) with children and family that fuelled the glut of IHT schemes. Nothing has been done to deal with the real sense of injustice resulting in a flat rate tax of 40 per cent once the £263,000 nil rate band has been used up.

The POA charge is an aggressive response to such schemes which is unlikely to be wholly successful in dousing the fires of discontent. As such it is likely to be viewed in the future as merely a further step in the ongoing tussle between a cash strapped Exchequer and reluctant taxpayers. It was more a knee jerk reaction than a well thought out response to the fundamental problem which lies in the structure of IHT.

In producing the book against a tight schedule the authors are greatly indebted to Catherine Aldred at 5 Stone Buildings and to the production team at Sweet & Maxwell.

The law is stated at October 1, 2004.

EMC
CJW
BMcC

---

[1] See for example the recently reported case of *Wolff v Wolff* 6/9/04 Ch. D.

CONTENTS

PART IV: PLANNING IN PRACTICE: PROACTIVE PLANNING

APPENDIX 1: THE LEGISLATION

APPENDIX 2: MATERIAL ISSUED BY THE INLAND REVENUE

TABLE OF CASES

TABLE OF STATUTES

PART 1: SETTING THE SCENE

This Part outlines the reasons for the introduction of the Pre-Owned Assets Regime and provides a general introduction to Inheritance Tax and to the reservation of benefit legislation.

CHAPTER 1

INTRODUCTION

The Finance Act 2004 (FA 2004) s.84 and Sch.15 introduced an **1–01** entirely new tax charge known as "the pre-owned assets" charge ("the Regime"). The Regime charges individuals to income tax on an annual basis in respect of benefits they enjoy—or, in some cases, are capable of enjoying—from certain kinds of property which they have owned at some time after March 17, 1986. The charge is intended to perform two functions: first, as a fine on individuals who have escaped the clutches of the IHT reservation of benefit provisions by what the Revenue regards as unacceptable means; and second, as a warning to individuals thinking about trying to escape from the clutches of IHT that they run the risk of other such fines being introduced in the future.[1] It will be helpful to consider why the Government came to the view that such a radical course was in order.

Inheritance Tax and the Finance Act 1986

It all goes back to the Finance Act 1986, which, apart from **1–02** rechristening Capital Transfer Tax as Inheritance Tax, introduced both the potentially exempt transfer ("PET") regime and the reservation of benefit rules. Unlike the CTT regime, which did not allow tax free gifts in excess of the nil rate band threshold but had no reservation of benefit rules, the PET regime was intended to encourage timely giving by allowing lifetime gifts to be IHT free provided that the donor survived seven years. However the donor had to give up all benefit from the gift. One could give freely, but the gift had to be without any strings which allowed, or might allow, the

---

[1] It is also possible to see the Regime as a (rather arbitrary) wealth tax, but the authors think it operates more as a fine than as a wealth tax.

donor to enjoy the gifted property in the future (and nor must the taxpayer **in fact** benefit from the gifted property).[2]

Not surprisingly, ever since the introduction of the PET regime and the reservation of benefit provisions, tax advisers have been busy—in the Government's view, far too busy—devising methods by which individuals could make PETs of property which, without infringing the reservation of benefit provisions, they still continued to enjoy or to have the potential to enjoy. This, of course, was only to be expected. Normally when new anti-avoidance legislation is introduced there is a cat-and-mouse game between taxpayers and the Revenue with the Revenue incrementally cracking down on loopholes and gambits until the legislation is sufficiently watertight to achieve its end. This is how matters initially proceeded with the reservation of benefit rules.

Ingram—the Revenue's first defeat

1–03 The Revenue's first significant defeat was in the *Ingram* case,[3] following which they introduced, in the traditional manner, narrowly targeted anti-avoidance legislation in relation to disposals made after March 8, 1999. The Revenue and some tax advisers are still debating the effectiveness of this legislation in certain areas (see the discussion of reversionary leases in Chapter 15) but if matters had stopped there the Pre-Owned Assets charge would probably never have been introduced.

Eversden—the straw that broke the camel's back

1–04 The *Eversden* case—discussed in more detail below[4]—was first decided in the taxpayer's favour by a Special Commissioner in 2001. Prior to that decision, the planning technique which the Revenue challenged in *Eversden*, and which was capable of being used in a variety of circumstances, had been employed on a relatively limited basis but the Commissioner's decision obviously encouraged others to do so as well. The Revenue appealed and Lightman J., in 2002 also found for the taxpayer. This led to a number of "*Eversden*" schemes being developed, marketed and implemented. Matters were made

---

[2] The relevant legislative provisions are in Appendix I.

[3] The *Ingram* case and "*Ingram* arrangements" are considered in Chapters 2 and 14.

[4] See Chapters 2 and 16.

even worse for the Revenue when the Court of Appeal in 2003 unanimously upheld Lightman J.'s decision.

This forced the Revenue's hand and the Finance Act 2003 introduced anti-avoidance provisions designed to defeat *Eversden* schemes implemented by disposals made after June 19, 2003. Needless to say, advisers scrutinised these new anti-avoidance provisions with a view to identifying any remaining loopholes. Their motivation for doing so was perhaps even stronger than usual: by now taxpayers had become accustomed to circumventing the reservation of benefit provisions and almost expected to continue to be able to do so. After all, their advisers had always come up with something in the past—why should they not do so now? Advisers, for their part, had found devising ways round the reservation of benefit provisions a remunerative area. There was clearly a continuing demand. All that was needed was a product.

The authors—yes, they must admit it—also carefully studied the new anti-avoidance provisions, attempted to devise new approaches and examined the approaches put forward by others. Having done so, we concluded that in fact the new provisions did their job rather well and that the various attempts being suggested for outflanking them were, on the whole, unlikely to succeed. Others, however, reached different conclusions. Rather as a barren field—the tax planning landscape immediately after June 19, 2003—can suddenly explode into a carpet of colourful wild flowers, so a whole series of "post-*Eversden*" schemes—discussed in Chapter 16—appeared to brighten the lives of clients intent on having access to property which they had given away.

As the Revenue was well aware, "*Eversden* schemes" were **1–05** merely one of a number of IHT "arrangements" on the market and which were designed to circumvent the reservation of benefit rules. Of these, the so-called Home Loan (or Double Trust) Scheme had been widely marketed[5] and in addition chattel gifts and leaseback, reversionary leases, and cash gifts were employed. The Revenue was also aware that the new anti-*Eversden* legislation was under close scrutiny and that, almost inevitably, *Eversden* Mark II schemes would appear. In the Standing Committee debates[6] on the introduction of the Regime, Ms Dawn Primarolo, the Paymaster General, stated that the Revenue had tried twice to tighten up the reservation of benefit rules and that "it has encouraged more ingenious schemes"; the implication being that the Revenue thought or, at any rate, feared that these "more ingenious schemes" were effective. Hence, as a result it is thought of Ministerial prompting, the Revenue decided to adopt an entirely new *technical* approach. Further, having been shocked by the perceived scale of IHT avoidance, they decided

---

[5] It has been suggested that as many as 30,000 of these have been implemented.

[6] *Hansard*, Standing Committee Debates, May 28, 2004, col.256.

that not only must a shot be fired across taxpayers' bows, but also a shot must be fired *into* taxpayers' bows, *i.e.* that a wholly new *philosophical* approach was needed.

Too much of a bad thing

1–06 The need for a new philosophical approach was made crystal clear by Ms Dawn Primarolo in her opening remarks to the Standing Committee concerning the need for the pre-owned assets charge. Having referred to the figures mentioned above—30,000 taxpayers, billions of pounds of assets (*not* tax)—she said (the italics are the authors):

> "Faced with such figures, the Committee will not be surprised to hear that the Government decided to take action. *It is not enough to tackle new arrangements and future avoidance.* The Government wanted to send a clear message that artificial avoidance of that kind is not acceptable. Those who devise and market such schemes, and the people who take advantage of them, *need to understand that and not assume that* avoidance *is risk-free.* Such schemes have grown so rapidly because they are regarded as a one-way bet. The essential point is that nothing really changes. For example, let us consider somebody who wants to ensure that the house they live in is not part of their taxable estate, but they want to remain living there. They see their adviser, sign a series of papers and pay a substantial fee, even though there might be a relatively small amount of work in it. The client goes home, the paperwork is filed and the arrangements are designed to unscramble when the client dies and have no lasting effect. The only real effect is inheritance tax savings that can run into hundreds of thousands of pounds or more. Given that perception of risk and rewards, it is not surprising that people and advisers have found such schemes increasing attractive. *The clause gives notice that that is a false perception.*
> People who have used such schemes, or who contemplate others like them in the future, are right to think that they will get any inheritance tax saving that their scheme is able to assure, *but they are wrong to think that that protects them against any future tax charge. That is at the heart of the changes under schedule 15.*" [7]

This is an important statement, in a number of ways. First and foremost, it states the Government's new philosophical approach —taxpayers can now find that they are to be fined for having avoided IHT—and makes it clear that this "is at the heart" of the new legislation. Secondly, it greatly oversimplifies the characterisation of the kind of arrangements people entered into. While it is probably fair to say that people who entered into *Eversden* arrangements did not substantially alter their affairs, that was certainly not true of other arrangements, notably so-called "*Ingram*" schemes which had significant capital gains tax consequences. This is an important point if,

---

[7] *Hansard*, Standing Committee Debates, May 28, 2004, col.238.

as Dawn Primarolo stated, the kind of schemes which were objectionable were those which involved no real change in the taxpayer's situation. Thirdly, although one can have some sympathy with the view that avoidance of IHT had reached such proportions that a solution was required which would put a lot of people altogether off the idea of trying to avoid the tax, that does not justify the particular solution that she proposed. This is because any solution should not only do what it sets out to do (*viz.* prevent IHT avoidance), but should also satisfy other criteria among which are: first, it should not catch individuals who are not successful tax avoiders; second, it should not complicate excessively an already over complicated system; third, it should not impose excessive compliance requirements and fourth there should be some certainty about its effects and whether the taxpayer is in fact subject to the charge under the Regime at all. In short, the solution must be technically efficacious and perceived to be "fair". If it is not, its philosophical justification becomes irrelevant.

Implementing the Regime

The Chancellor's Autumn Statement of December 10, 2003 **1–07** announced that measures would be taken to tackle tax avoidance including the avoidance of IHT.[8] On the following day, a consultation document ("The Tax Treatment of Pre-Owned Assets") was published.[9] For the first time it was made clear that what was being proposed was an income tax charge on (broadly) the benefit derived from the continued use of assets by a former owner. As a consultation document it was flawed: instead of an analysis of the problem and a number of suggested solutions it merely gave scanty details of a brand new tax charge. Little wonder that all those who contributed to the exercise urged the Government to adopt a different solution.[10] The die had already been cast, however, as had been made clear in the press release of the previous day which referred to the charge being introduced by legislation in the Finance Bill 2004 with consultation being confined to "the detailed workings of this measure."

There is no evidence that at this stage any one had sat down and thought through the implications of the proposed income tax charge: instead it has all the hallmarks of someone's "bright idea" which was

---

[8] See Appendix II for this press release.
[9] Contained in Appendix II.
[10] Most obviously to amend the IHT legislation on gifts with reservation to stop up the loopholes.

seized upon by a government which had become irritated beyond measure by the activities of the tax avoidance industry.

A technically misconceived approach

1–08 The starting point in evaluating the Regime technically is to realise that it is built on shaky foundations, because it involves the grafting of a minicode—the Regime—onto another minicode—the reservation of benefit rules—which was itself ineptly grafted onto the basic IHT legislation. It will be surprising if this does not produce problems for both the taxpayer and the Revenue.

The consequences of the inept grafting of the reservation of benefit rules onto the IHT legislation is already a matter of public record. Two examples suffice: first, *Eversden* schemes which took advantage of the inadequate integration into the reservation of benefit rules of the IHT exemptions for transfers of value and the effect in that context of s.49(1) of the Inheritance Tax Act 1984; and secondly, the fact that no one can predict with any certainty the effect for the reservation of benefit rules of what should be a straightforward transaction, namely the settling by an individual of property on trusts under which he retains an interest in possession.[11]

The grafting of the Regime onto the IHT legislation generally, and the reservation of benefit rules in particular, can only lead to problems. Innocent taxpayers may fall within the ambit of the Regime because it does not adopt the approach used in the past to combat tax avoidance—*viz.* introducing narrowly targeted provisions. Instead it operates by taxing anything that is not expressly excluded from its ambit; for example, any disposal of land whether sale, gift or exchange, is caught where the taxpayer continues to occupy the land **unless** it falls within a specific exemption. Since it is obviously difficult to successfully exclude every type of innocent transaction, the scope for collateral damage on innocent taxpayers is considerable notwithstanding the Revenue's best efforts.[12] Amendments to the Regime—dealing with both ingenious schemes and wronged taxpayers—are inevitable.

So far as compliance is concerned, this is likely to be a significant problem, as is explained later.[13]

One cannot help but think that narrowly targeted IHT anti-avoidance legislation would have been a better option. It is true that tax planners have over the years developed various approaches to

---

[11] See 16–18.

[12] For some examples of this collateral damage see Chapter 26 (equity release schemes) and Chapter 6 (intangibles).

[13] See Chapter 13 (administration).

outflank the reservation of benefit provisions, but this was only to be expected in the years following the ill-thought out introduction of those provisions. Narrowly targeted anti-avoidance provisions—the Revenue's traditional approach—had closed off most of the loopholes and, in the authors' view, the remaining ones could have been dealt with in the same way leaving everyone knowing more or less where they stood. The possibility of the legislation hitting unintended targets would have been minimal. That approach, alas, has not been adopted.

A rush to implement

The problems caused by the misconceived approach of the Regime **1–09** have been exacerbated by its rushed implementation. The original proposals in the Consultation Document were substantially amended by the time that the 2004 Finance Bill was published, whilst no fewer than 45 amendments were made at Committee Stage of the Bill, and a further 18 at Report Stage. While the Revenue has been admirable in its willingness to consult on detail, the fundamental problem remains: by taxing everything not expressly excluded innocent transactions will be caught.

Howling protests

It is seldom that a proposal has met with such a hostile response from **1–10** all sides. For a particularly trenchant attack, see "Is Anyone Out There Listening?" by John Tallon, Q.C., *Taxation*, June 24, 2004.

Broad structure—the "Holy Trinity" approach

The broad structure of the Regime in Sch.15 is to establish a separate **1–11** charging system for each of three different kinds of property:

- Land (see paras 3–5).
- Chattels (see paras 6–7).
- Intangible property comprised in a settlor—interested settlement (see para.8).

Certain conditions, which vary according to the type of property concerned, must be satisfied before the Regime can apply. In the case of land and chattels certain transactions (called "excluded trans-actions") are outside the charge (see para.10). Even if the conditions are satisfied, there are a number of exemptions which may prevent the Regime from applying (see para.11).

Two tier structures: three into two will go

1–12 It is important to note at the outset that more than one charging system can apply to an arrangement. Assume that X lives in a house owned by a company all the shares in which are owned by a discretionary trust of which he is the settlor and under which he can benefit. The Regime is capable of applying to two assets: first, the house in which X lives under the para.3 charge on land; and secondly, the shares in the company, under the para.8 charge on settled intangible property. It is true that there are provisions to prevent double taxation arising in such a case, but the point to bear in mind is that each situation must be carefully analysed to arrive at its consequences under the Regime.

Guiding principles

1–13 The Regime is based on the following guiding principles:

- the value of property which is subject to IHT should not be subject to the Regime;
- property and transactions which are outside the IHT net either by reason of qualifying for favoured IHT treatment or by reason of what the Revenue regards as "acceptable" IHT planning should not be caught by the Regime; and
- land, chattels and settled intangible property not caught in the IHT net and to which no favoured treatment is given by the Regime are subject to the Regime.

No motive test

1–14 It is worth mentioning at this juncture that there is no motive test under the Regime, *i.e.* taxpayer cannot escape the ambit of the Regime by establishing that the arrangement was not implemented with a view to avoiding IHT but was instead entirely motivated by other considerations.

Equity release schemes

A good illustration of the absence of any motive requirement is **1–15** afforded by these arrangements. Take the example of Mrs A who owns her house worth £250,000. She has no other significant assets, so IHT saving is not an issue: all she is concerned about is ensuring that she can go on living in her house and has cash to fund her living expenses and to pay for improvements that might be required. With this in mind she might:

(a) sell the entire house to her children at full market value and rely upon them to allow her to continue in occupation;

(b) sell part of her house at full market value either to her children or to a commercial provider with the right to continue in occupation (a so-called equity release scheme); or

(c) borrow on the security of the house either from a commercial provider or from her children.

Is the Regime capable of applying to Mrs A in any of these circumstances? It is irrelevant that she is not motivated by a wish to avoid IHT since, as noted, the Regime takes no account of motive. All that is required is a disposal and occupation. Nor will the so-called *de minimis* exemption necessarily help given that the value of the occupation benefit is likely to exceed £5,000.[14]

Bizarrely on the above facts, the Regime will not apply to her if she does (a) or (c) but will apply to her if she does or has done (b). In the case of (a) this is an excluded transaction and in the case of (c) no disposal of her land has taken place at all. However, in the case of (b) there are no exemptions.[15]

Unscrambling a home loan scheme

The absence of any motive requirement will be significant in the **1–16** following case. Assume that Mr A set up a double trust arrangement some years ago so that his house is currently owned by Trust 1 in which he enjoys an interest in possession. Then trustees of that trust are indebted for (say) the full value of the house to the trustees of a separate trust which A had established for his children.[16] Fearful that

[14] The *de minimis* provision is considered at Chapter 9.
[15] See further, Chapter 26.
[16] Home Loan Schemes (or double trust arrangements) are considered in detail in Chapter 17.

he will be caught by the Regime, Mr A arranges to buy the house back from the trustees for its current value. The purchase is financed by a commercial loan from the X Bank. Mr A's intention in effecting the repurchase is to unscramble the structure which he had set up to avoid IHT and the assumption is that once he owns the property outright the Regime will not apply. Whilst commonsense (and fairness) would suggest that this should indeed be the case, the definition of an "excluded liability" makes no allowance for arm's length arrangements and so the protection afforded by para.11(1) is limited to the extent of that liability.[17]

Statutory links with IHT

1-17   Although the Regime is freestanding, it is intimately linked with IHT in a number of ways:

   (a)   not only is property which is comprised in an individual's estate for IHT purposes outside the scope of the Regime, but so is other property not comprised in the individual's estate but from which property which is comprised in his estate derives its value (see para.11(1)). This prevents the same value being subject both to IHT and to the Regime;[18]

   (b)   subject to certain qualifications, property which would fall to be treated as property subject to a reservation in relation to the individual is outside the scope of the Regime so that the same property is not subject to both IHT and to the Regime (see para.11(5)(a)). Furthermore, it is open to a person to opt out of the Regime in relation to property by electing to subject himself to the reservation of benefit rules in relation to that property. He thus has the choice of the lesser of two evils;[19]

   (c)   the territorial scope of the Regime is framed by reference to the territorial scope of IHT in some respects—there are notable mismatches—and the IHT deemed domicile provisions apply;[20]

   (d)   favoured treatment given to posthumous transactions is linked to the IHT favoured treatment given to such transactions so this remains a fruitful area for planning;[21]

---

[17] The definition of "excluded liability" in Sch.15, para.11(7) is considered at 17–13. See also Chapter 7 (exemptions).

[18] An important restriction—when there is an excluded liability "affecting the property has been mentioned at 1–16, above and is considered in detail at 17–12.

[19] See Sch.15, 21–23: this election is considered in detail in Chapter 11.

[20] See Sch.15, Chapters 12 and 20.

[21] See Sch.15, and Chapter 16.

(e) certain reliefs and exemptions are framed by reference to IHT reliefs and exemptions; and

(f) a number of IHT definitions apply for purpose of the Regime.

Definitions

The following terms are defined (as for IHT) as follows: **1–18**

(a) "interest in land" has the same meaning as in Ch. 4 of Pt VI of the 1984 Act;[22]

(b) "land" is defined as for IHT;[23]

(c) "property" has the wide IHT meaning in s.272 of the 1984 Act and so includes rights and interests of any description other than a settlement power;[24] and

(d) "settlement" and "settled property" have the same meanings as in the 1984 Act.[25]

As will be seen, the use of some of these IHT definitions may give rise to problems.

"Chattel" and intangible property" are defined as follows:

(a) "chattels" means any tangible moveable property (or, in Scotland, corporeal moveable property);[26] and

(b) "intangible property" means any property other than chattels or interests in land.[27] "Intangible property" is thus a default term in that it applies to all property other than chattels and interests in land and includes cash.

Associated operations

The IHT associated operations provisions[28] are of limited relevance **1–19** under the Regime. They apply in relation to the "excluded liability"

---

[22] See Sch.15, para.1.
[23] *ibid.*
[24] *ibid.*
[25] *ibid.*
[26] *ibid.*
[27] *ibid.*
[28] See IHTA 1984, s.268.

provisions, but otherwise do not apply for the purposes of the Regime (though they can be indirectly relevant in that they may apply for the purposes of determining whether or not property is subject to a reservation). In particular, although the Regime uses the term "disposition" it does not adopt the extended IHT definition of that term whereby a disposition includes a disposition effected by associated operations.[29] Indeed, as a general rule the Regime uses the term "disposal" rather than "disposition".

Valuation

1–20 The value of any property is the price which the property might reasonably be expected to fetch if sold in the open market at that time, but that price shall not be assumed to be reduced on the ground that the whole property is to be placed on the market at one and the same time.[30] This is the same as the basic IHT rule.[31] Note, however, that unlike IHT, the Regime does not contain any specific rules for valuing property. As we will see, this may cause compliance difficulties if say, a half share in the property is being gifted or someone only occupies part of a property.[32]

Starting date retrospectivity and "retroactivity"

1–21 The only time limit as to the application of the Regime is that it does not operate in respect of arrangements put into effect before March 18, 1986, which is also the cut-off date for the application of the reservation of benefit provisions.[33]

Strenuous representations were made that the Regime was retrospective and should catch only arrangements put into effect after December 9, 2003, (December 10, 2003 being the date on which it was announced that the Regime was to be introduced). The matter was raised in the Standing Committee debates with opposition amendments seeking to restrict its operation to the date when the reservation of benefit rules took effect, or failing that, when the *Ingram* anti-avoidance legislation took effect or, failing that, when

---

[29] See IHTA 1984, s.272.

[30] Sch.15, para.15; see also the rules concerning "excluded liabilities" in paras 11(6) and (7).

[31] See IHTA 1984, Pt VI.

[32] See 16–38 and *CIR v Arkwright* [2004] EWHC 1720 (Ch); [2004] S.T.C. 1323 for certain valuation issues and Chapter 3 for a discussion of the charge on land.

[33] Sch.15, paras 3(2)(a), 3(3), 6(2)(a), 6(3) and 8(2).

the *Eversden* anti-avoidance legislation took effect. These amendments were all rejected by the Government.

In the Standing Committee debates[34] Dawn Primarolo resisted the view that the Regime was retrospective on the basis that although it affected structures put into place before its introduction, it imposed a charge only on benefits enjoyed after April 5, 2005. The Regime, she asserted, was therefore retroactive, but not retrospective.

The Revenue acknowledged that unwinding arrangements effected prior to the introduction of the Regime may be difficult, if not impossible. The Regime accordingly provides taxpayers with the ability to "opt out" and, in effect, into IHT *viz*. This is discussed in Chapter 11.

The point was made in the Standing Committee debates that, given that transactions that took place as long ago as 1986 could be caught under the Regime, taxpayers would be faced with considerable difficulties in tracing down relevant information. The Paymaster General dismissed such concerns on the basis that such taxpayers would have had to keep records for IHT purposes. While this may be correct insofar as the circumstances of the donor taxpayers are concerned, transactions entered into by donees in respect of which they were under no obligation to keep any records can also be extremely important for Regime purposes and the difficulties involved in retrieving such information may be very great; see 3–21 and Chapter 13.

Human rights

The Finance Act 2004 carried with it a statement by the Chancellor **1–22** under s.19(1)(a) of the Human Rights Act 1998 that in his view the provisions of the Act were compatible with the Convention rights. In the House of Commons debates it was mentioned that a group of "eminent lawyers" were considering taking the introduction of the Regime to the European Court of Justice.[35]

The Joint Committee on Human Rights in Parliament was requested to investigate the matter and in June 2004 produced a report on Sch.15 considering whether its provisions were compatible with the Human Rights Act 1998. The Committee criticised the fact that the explanatory notes did not contain any express consideration of the Human Rights implications of the Bill and examined concerns that the provisions amounted to retrospective taxation and were therefore in breach of Art.1 to the ECHR Protocol.

[34] *Hansard*, Standing Committee A, May 28, 2004, col.261.
[35] *Hansard*, Finance Bill debates, July 7, 2004, col.876.

Article 1 gives the right to peaceful enjoyment of possessions and provides that no-one shall be deprived of his possessions "except in the public interest". However, it is expressly provided that this shall not impair the right of the state to secure the payment of taxes. Thus any interference with property rights to secure the payment of taxes must strike a balance between public interest and the protection of an individual's fundamental rights. Retrospective legislation might be regarded as requiring a clearer public interest. The Committee recognised that for such interference to be lawful it must also satisfy the requirements of accessibility and enforceability, *i.e.* the law must be intelligible and enable the individual to organise his affairs knowing with reasonable certainty the consequences of his actions.

The Committee accepted that the charge was not directly retrospective in that it was not levied in respect of the benefit enjoyed in previous years albeit it does impose a prospective liability in respect of future benefits by reference to past arrangements. The Committee concluded that the provisions were sufficiently accessible and foreseeable and that the interference was proportionate,[36] *i.e.* it struck a fair balance between the demands of the general interest of the community and the individual's fundamental rights.[37]

However, this view was reached on the premise that the income tax charge was only imposed in respect of a benefit derived from continued use of assets which have been disposed of in order to avoid liability to inheritance tax and therefore the tax cannot be characterised as an arbitrary confiscation. This is by no means the case and one could certainly argue that the imposition of income tax on innocent non-tax avoidance arrangements is an arbitrary imposition. Furthermore, the Committee seemed to imagine the Regime was clear in its application—it did not discuss the very real compliance issues for the taxpayer arising out of the ambiguity and uncertainty of the Regime in a number of areas.[38] Further, the occupier of the property or user of chattels could be left without any ability to pay income tax under the Regime for the privilege of continuing in occupation. While the taxpayer can elect into the inheritance tax regime, this does not put him in the position that he would have been if he had never entered into the transaction and raises the possibility

---

[36] See, *e.g. National Provincial Building Society v UK* [1997] S.T.C. 1466, where it was held that a taxation measure which had been enacted with retroactive effect did not violate Art.1 because the interference was justified.

[37] The Committee criticised Sch.15 merely on the basis that the benefit of the exclusions in para.10 should not be confined just to spouses but should be extended to homosexual couples and thus the Act discriminated on the grounds of sexual orientation.

[38] For a discussion of some of these uncertainties see, for example, Chapter 13 and 3–19 *et seq.*

of double inheritance tax charges on the same property without any relief.[39] Again this was not discussed.

The charge to income tax

The charge to income tax was originally to be under Sch. D, Case VI, **1–23** but, as a result of the rewritten legislation, under the Income Tax (Trading and Other Income) Bill it is assumed the charge will be under Ch.V, Pt VIII of the Bill.

Authors' approach

Given the structure of the Regime, the best approach is first to **1–24** consider how chargeable occasions may arise and then against that background, review the provisions which take property out of the Regime entirely. Before doing so, however, it will be appropriate to review briefly some key IHT rules.

---

[39] See for example the discussion in *Eversden* planning at 16–34. Recent Labour Governments have a poor record in introducing retrospective tax legislation: consider the introduction of the revised public access requirement for conditionally exempt property in 1998 (an area on which a case has been taken to the Commissioners) and the anti flip flop capital gains tax legislation in 2002.

CHAPTER 2

IHT AND RESERVATION OF BENEFIT

2–01 The Regime is intended to prevent taxpayers from circumventing the reservation of benefit rules and so avoiding the payment of IHT. In certain key areas it operates by reference to the reservation of benefit provisions. Accordingly, it will be helpful to consider a few essential IHT provisions briefly, before analysing the Regime.

Inheritance tax generally

2–02 Inheritance tax can be charged on an individual during his lifetime and on his death. Various exemptions and reliefs are available to prevent certain kinds of transactions from giving rise to a charge. For example, gifts between spouses are normally outside the scope of IHT,[1] as are certain family maintenance dispositions[2] and gifts of modest amounts.[3] Some of these exemptions and reliefs are effectively incorporated into the Regime and where that is done the terms of the IHT exemption or relief will be discussed.

The charge on death

2–03 IHT charged on death is intimately linked with the reservation of benefit provisions. It is therefore important to understand exactly how this charge operates. IHT is chargeable on a person's death as if immediately before he died he made a transfer of value and the value

---

[1] IHTA 1984, s.18.
[2] IHTA 1984, s.11.
[3] IHTA 1984, s.19 (annual exemption); s.20 (small gifts) and s.21 (normal expenditure out of income). In the latter case the exemption can be used to make substantial IHT savings given that there is no prescribed ceiling on the payments: see *Bennett v IRC* [1995] S.T.C. 54.

18

transferred thereby was equal to the value of his estate at that time.[4] For this purpose a person's estate is the aggregate of all the property to which he is beneficially entitled, except that immediately before his death his estate does not include excluded property.[5] Since for IHT purposes a person entitled to an interest in possession in settled property is treated as beneficially entitled to the property in which his interest subsists, on the death of such a person the settled property will form part of his estate and be subject to IHT.[6]

Reservation of benefit[7]

The fundamental provision in the reservation of benefit minicode **2–04** which determines whether an individual has reserved a benefit is s.102(1), the essential part of which is as follows:

> "... this section applies where, on or after 18th March 1986, an individual disposes of any property by way of gift and either—
>
> (a) possession and enjoyment of the property is not bona fide assumed by the donee at or before the beginning of the relevant period; or
> (b) at any time in the relevant period the property is not enjoyed to the entire exclusion, or virtually to the entire exclusion, of the donor and of any benefit to him by contract or otherwise;
>
> and in this section 'the relevant period' means a period ending on the date of the donor's death and beginning seven years before that date, or, if it is later, on the date of the gift."

For this purpose, by the Finance Act 1986, Sch.20, para.6(1)(c), a benefit which a donor obtained by virtue of associated operations of which the disposal by way of gift is one, shall be treated as a benefit to him by contract or otherwise.

Notice two key points. First, that what activates the provisions is a "**gift**" made by an individual. There is no definition of gift which will presumably bear its normal meaning as a transfer of property with donative intent. In any event, the use of "gift" as the triggering event distinguishes the reservation of benefit minicode from the rest of the IHT legislation where the key event is the making of a transfer of value. It is thought that in certain circumstances there can be a transfer of value for IHT purposes which is not a gift and this dichotomy may be exploited by taxpayers.[8]

---

[4] IHTA 1984, s.4(1).

[5] IHTA 1984, s.5(1).

[6] IHTA 1984, s.49(1). Primary responsibility for payment of the tax is on the trustees of the settlement.

[7] The legislation—in FA 1986 as amended in 1999 and 2003—is contained in Appendix I.

[8] For a fuller discussion of this, see 16–14.

Second, that what can trigger the rules once a gift has been made, is that the property is not enjoyed to the entire exclusion of the donor. This can mean *de facto* enjoyment. Notice that once a gift has been made it is never safe for the donor to enjoy benefits in the property (*i.e.* there is no seven-year period after which the slate is wiped clean).

Let-outs

2–05 The legislation provides that certain disposals by way of gift which would otherwise result in property being subject to the reservation of benefit provisions are taken outside the ambit of those provisions. For example, s.102(5) of the Finance Act 1986 takes a disposal of property by way of gift which qualifies for the IHT spouse exemption outside the provisions.[9] Some of these let-outs are effectively incorporated into the Regime so that a transaction which qualifies for favoured treatment under the reservation of benefit provisions generally also does so for the purposes of the Regime.[10] Where this is the case, the let-outs from the reservation of benefit provisions are discussed in detail.

Where the conditions in s.102(1) are satisfied, the property in question is *prima facie* "property subject to a reservation" and so caught by the reservation of benefit provisions. In certain cases, anti-avoidance legislation has the effect that property may be caught even though these requirements are not satisfied. Conversely, there are various ameliorating provisions that mean that even if s.102(1) requirements are satisfied or the anti-avoidance provisions are *prima facie* infringed there is not necessarily a reservation of benefit problem.

The donor's spouse

2–06 One point should be noted in passing concerning the scope of the provisions, namely that there is nothing in s.102(1) which makes property which the donor's spouse (but not the donor) is capable of enjoying or from which she benefits "property subject to a reservation" in relation to the donor.[11] On the contrary, the legislation

---

[9] It was this exemption which was exploited in the *Eversden* case, discussed in Chapter 16.

[10] A good example is "sharing arrangements" considered in detail in Chapter 22.

[11] A benefit to the donor's spouse is relevant under FA 1986, Sch.20, para.7. Also, the fact that the donor's spouse has a right may have adverse implications for the donor under FA 1986, s.102A.

confers favourable treatment on some gifts to spouses. This approach is also adopted for the purposes of the Regime.[12]

Ingram *and* Eversden

Two IHT cases—*Ingram* and *Eversden*—are particularly important **2–07** for the purposes of the Regime and it will be helpful to review them briefly.

THE *INGRAM* CASE[13]

Lady Ingram owned real property which she wished to give to her **2–08** children and grandchildren subject to retaining the right to occupy the property during her life. To achieve this she transferred the property to her nominee. The next day, acting on her directions, he granted her a 20-year rent free lease and on the following day transferred the property, encumbered by the lease, to trustees who immediately executed declarations of trust whereby the property became held for the benefit of her children and grandchildren, to the exclusion of Lady Ingram.

Following her death, the Revenue issued a determination that, under the reservation of benefit rules, the property was deemed to be comprised in her estate immediately before she died. The House of Lords found unanimously for Lady Ingram's executors. The lease was valid, but even if it was not, the property given away was the encumbered reversion. Their Lordships stressed that it was important to identify precisely what property had been given away by the donor and what (if anything) he had retained. Continued enjoyment of the latter did not amount to a reservation in the former (arrangements of the type adopted in this case are known as "shearing" operations). Not long after the House of Lords' decision, anti-avoidance legislation, intended to nullify the effect of the decision in relation to land was introduced (now FA 1986, s.102A—C[14]).

THE *EVERSDEN* CASE[15]

In 1988 Mrs S settled the family home, which she then owned, upon **2–09** trust to hold the same for herself as to 5 per cent absolutely and as

[12] See 5–03.
[13] [1999] S.T.C. 37 (HL) and see 14–02.
[14] Discussed below at 2–10 and 14–09 and contained in Appendix I.
[15] [2003] S.T.C. 822 (CA).

21

to 95 per cent upon the trusts of a settlement under which her husband, Mr S, was the life tenant. After his death the trust fund was to be held upon discretionary trusts for a class of beneficiaries which included Mrs S.

During their joint lives Mr and Mrs S occupied the family home—Mr S under the terms of the settlement, and Mrs S by virtue of her retained interest as a tenant in common. After Mr S's death in 1992 Mrs S continued to occupy the family home. In 1993 the trustees sold the house and, out of the proceeds, including Mrs S's 5 per cent share, acquired a replacement property and an investment bond. Thereafter Mrs S had a 5 per cent interest in the replacement property and the bond. She died in 1998 having, in the interim, been in sole occupation of the replacement property, but having received no benefit from the bond.

The Revenue argued that the entirety of the replacement property (and the bond) should, under the reservation of benefit provisions, be included in her estate immediately before she died by reason of her enjoyment of it.

The Court of Appeal unanimously rejected the Revenue's appeal. The case was argued solely on the application of s.102(5) of the Finance Act 1986 which provided that a disposal of property which was a spouse exempt transfer was outside the scope of the reservation of benefit rules. The Revenue sought to restrict the size of gift to which the spouse exemption applied by arguing there was a mismatch in the legislation between "gift" and "transfer of value". Although when Mrs S created the settlement she may have made a transfer of value to her husband of her 95 per cent interest, for the purpose of the reservation of benefit provisions she also made a series of gifts consisting of the equitable interests given to the various beneficiaries under the settlement and the exemption in s.102(5) was confined to the gift (of the life interest) which she made to her husband.

Carnwath L.J., with whom Brooke L.J. and Nelson J. agreed, rejected the Revenue's argument. *Ingram* was concerned solely with the nature of the interest retained by the donor and was decided in a different context. The same applied to the *Perpetual Trustee*[16] case. Neither was concerned with and neither addressed the position of successive interests forming part of a gift into a settlement. Carnwath L.J. held that it was not possible to introduce conceptual subtleties into s.102(5) without distorting the language.

Given s.49(1), Mrs S had clearly made a transfer of value of the whole of the settled property to her husband and to him alone. Section 102(5) applied to that transfer, and so Mrs S did not reserve a benefit. There was nothing in s.102 to modify the effect of s.49(1).

---

[16] *Comr for Stamp Duties for New South Wales v Perpetual Trustee Co Ltd* [1943] A.C. 425, PC.

If this caused problems then he concluded that they were for Parliament to correct.[17]

The Revenue heeded Carnwath L.J.'s comments and the Finance Act **2–10** 2003, s.185 duly introduced ss.102(5A)–(5C) into FA 1986 in order to reverse the Court of Appeal's decision. These provisions have effect in relation to disposals made on or after June 20, 2003. *Eversden* schemes put in motion before then were thus unaffected by the new provisions.

Section 102(5A) provides that s.102(5)(a) (the spouse exemption) does not apply if or, as the case may be, to the extent that the four conditions are satisfied:

(1) the property becomes settled by virtue of the gift;

(2) by reason of the donor's spouse (who is referred to as "the relevant beneficiary") becoming beneficially entitled to an interest in possession in the settled property, the disposal is or, as the case may be, is to any extent within the spouse exemption because of s.49(1);

(3) sometime after the disposal during the donor's lifetime the relevant beneficiary's interest in possession comes to an end; and

(4) on the occasion when the interest in possession comes to an end, the relevant beneficiary does not become entitled to the settled property or to another interest in possession in the settled property.

For this purpose: (i) the disposal of an interest is treated as the termination of that interest; and (ii) references to any property or to an interest in any property include references to part of any property or interest.[18]

Section 102(5B) then provides that to the extent that s.102 applies by virtue of s.102(5A), s.102 has effect as if the disposal by way of gift had been made immediately after the relevant beneficiary's interest in possession came to an end.

These anti-avoidance provisions were thus targeted directly at *Eversden* schemes. Tax planners were not slow in responding and a number of schemes were put forward as "Eversden Mark II

---

[17] For a fuller discussion see 16–10 *et seq.* The effect of s.49(1) has been considered at 2–03.

[18] FA 1986, s.102(5C).

23

Schemes." These schemes, the longer term implications of the *Eversden* case and the position under the Regime are considered in detail at Chapter 16.

Application of reservation of benefit provisions generally

2–11 Whether the reservation of benefit provisions apply in a particular case is generally outside the scope of this book, but the application of the provisions in certain cases in connection with the Regime is discussed in various contexts. When the provisions do apply, they have two consequences.

Clawback on death: s.102(3)

2–12 Section 102(3) provides that if, immediately before the death of the donor, there is any property which in relation to him is property subject to a reservation then, to the extent that the property would not otherwise form part of the donor's estate at that time, that property shall be treated as property to which he is beneficially entitled. This is important in two ways.

Interests in possession

2–13 First, the fact that s.102(3) does not operate with respect to property which **already** forms part of the deceased's estate immediately before he dies is hardly surprising because the reservation of benefit provisions are designed to prevent individuals from enjoying property which has ceased to form part of their estate. If it is already part of their estate, there is no reason to apply the reservation of benefit provisions to it. This exclusion from the operation of s.102(3) does mean that s.102(3) will not operate with respect to, *e.g.* settled property in which the deceased had an interest in possession immediately before he died[19] unless that property was excluded property.[20] As will be discussed below, this may be significant and open up certain tax planning opportunities.

[19] IHTA 1984, s.49(1).
[20] IHTA 1984, s.5(1).

Section 102(3) is not itself a charging provision. It merely provides **2–14**
that the deceased was beneficially entitled to the property in question.
The charge on death is then imposed on the property comprised in a
person's estate, not on property to which he is beneficially entitled.[21]
However, in many cases the point is not important, because the
general rule is that a person's estate is the aggregate of all the
property to which he is beneficially entitled.[22] That rule however, is
subject to one important qualification, namely that, immediately
before a person's death his estate does not include any excluded
property. So, where the property which is subject to a reservation is
excluded property no charge will be imposed on a person's death in
respect of it, notwithstanding that under s.102(3) he was treated as
beneficially entitled to it immediately before he died. Whether or not
property subject to a reservation is excluded property can in some
cases be a difficult question in theory though, as matters stand, not in
practice.[23]

The position in respect of non-settled property is straightforward.
Assume X, who is not domiciled in the UK for IHT purposes, dies
having reserved a benefit in respect of a house in Florida. As non-UK
situs property the house treated as owned by X, is excluded property
and no problems arise. If on his death X had been domiciled or
deemed domiciled in the United Kingdom when he died the property
would not have been excluded property.

Change the facts and assume that the house was owned by a
settlement which X had created when he was domiciled outside the
UK. If he dies domiciled abroad the position will be exactly as it was
in the first example. But what if X dies domiciled in the United
Kingdom, *e.g.* under the IHT deemed domicile rules?[24] In that case
the question which arises is which rules apply for determining
whether or not the house is excluded property for the purposes of the
reservation of benefit rules. If the fact that the house is settled
property is ignored, the house will be prevented by X's domicile
from being excluded property. If, on the other hand, account is taken
of the fact that the house is settled property and the rules for
determining whether or not settled property is excluded property are

---

[21] IHTA 1984, s.4.

[22] IHTA 1984, s.5(1).

[23] Excluded property is defined in IHTA 1984, s.6 and, in the context of settlements
and interests in settled property, see *ibid*. s.48.

[24] See IHTA 1984, s.267. For a consideration of the IHT domicile rules, see 8–05
et seq.

applied, the house will remain excluded property notwithstanding that X has become domiciled in the United Kingdom.[25]

For many years it was Revenue practice to adopt the latter approach and this was reflected in the *CTO Advanced Instruction Manual*. In late 2001 the Revenue amended the Manual in a way that indicated they had the position under review. In the event, possibly because of the Government's general review of the taxation of foreign domiciliaries, nothing has yet come of this review and it is the authors' understanding that the Revenue's old practice continues.[26]

Exemptions

2–15 The fact that s.102(3) operates to claw back property into the deceased's estate does not necessarily mean that such property will be subject to IHT on the deceased's death. Such a result will be avoided if the property devolves on the deceased's death in such a way that it qualifies for a relief such as business property relief. However, it is very doubtful whether property subject to a reservation can ever qualify for the IHT spouse exemption on death.[27]

Cessation of reservation: s.102(4)

2–16 Section 102(4) provides that if, at any time before the end of the "relevant period"[28] any property ceases to be property subject to a reservation, the donor is treated as having at that time made a disposition of the property by a disposition which is a PET.

Business relief and agricultural relief

2–17 In certain cases the rules governing the availability of business property relief and agricultural property relief are relaxed so that

[25] IHTA 1984, s.267 provides that non UK situs property comprised in a settlement is excluded property provided that the settlor was non UK domiciled when he made the settlement.

[26] See also *Private Client Business*, 2002, pp.3–4 "False Start in Change to Revenue IHT Excluded Property/Reservation of Benefit Practice" and 2003, pp.313–315 "Reservation of Benefit, *Eversden* Anti-avoidance, a Modest Proposal and a False Start".

[27] See 16–40.

[28] "The relevant period" means a period ending on the date of the donor's death and beginning seven years before that date or, if it is later, on the date of the gift: FA 1986, s.102(1).

property which is subject to a reservation may qualify for relief on the basis that if a notional transfer by the donee can include the donor's ownership and occupation periods in determining whether relief is due.[29]

A possible misunderstanding

2–18 The reservation of benefit rules sometimes give rise to a misunderstanding, the view being mistakenly taken that where an individual reserves a benefit he is (for IHT purposes) treated as though he had never given the property away. This is incorrect. The rules operate by clawing the property back into his estate immediately before he died, or by providing for a notional PET if he ceases to reserve a benefit but they do not operate by deeming the property never to have left his estate.

It accordingly follows that:

(i) As a matter of general law the property is comprised in the estate of the donee so that IHT will be payable on his death.

(ii) There is no CGT uplift on the death of the donor even though the reservation of benefit rules result in an IHT charge on the property.[30]

(iii) It is the donee who is primarily liable to pay any IHT owing on the reservation property resulting from the death of the donor.[31]

AVOIDING THE RESERVATION OF BENEFIT RULES

2–19 Inevitably taxpayers will seek to reduce their estates for IHT purposes by making PETs of property whilst at the same time wishing to retain benefits (*e.g.* use or income) from the property gifted. In some cases the taxpayer may be content simply to know that he will be able to obtain benefits from the gifted property if the need arises.

It is a testimony to the success of such arrangements that the Government has felt it necessary to introduce the pre-owned assets

[29] FA 1986, Sch.20, para.8 and see 27–05.
[30] See Taxation of Chargeable Gains Act 1992, s.62 for the CGT rules on death.
[31] IHTA 1984, s.200(1)(c); 204(9); 211(3) and see Chapter 13.

charge. What therefore were the arrangements entered into by tax payers which have led to this new tax?

2–20 **The Home Loan (Double Trust) Scheme:** which is probably the single most important reason for the legislation.

2–21 **The use of cash gifts:** an apparent weakness in the reservation of benefit legislation is that whilst there are tracing provisions which may apply if the original property given is switched into a new property, these rules do not appear to apply to a gift of cash. Hence if Albert were to given his son Sidney £100,000 which Sidney uses to purchase a house for occupation by Albert it is not considered that there is any reservation of benefit in the house.[32] Not surprisingly, the Regime therefore includes detailed provisions to catch cash contributions. They will still escape inheritance tax but instead suffer the POA charge.

2–22 **Reversionary lease arrangements:** these are considered in Chapter 15. It is widely thought that they were not caught by the anti-*Ingram* legislation provided that **either** the property had been owned more than seven years before the arrangement was entered into **or** that it had been purchased for full consideration at any time. Particularly difficult issues may arise in relation to self-assessment if the taxpayer is not certain whether he is within the Regime or not.[33]

2–23 **Chattel schemes:** these avoided the reservation rules either by a shearing arrangement or by satisfying the full consideration exemption. They are considered in Chapter 18.

2–24 *Ingram* **land schemes:** these have been caught by the reservation of benefit legislation since 1999 but pre–1999 arrangements are a target of the Regime.[34]

2–25 *Eversden* **schemes:** similar motivation. New schemes are within the 2003 legislation but "revenge" on past schemes has an attraction.[35]

---

[32] See Chapter 25—cash gifts.

[33] See Chapter 13—administration For example if he pays income tax now and then on his death it is found that there was a reservation of benefit so that he was never within the Regime, does he get his income tax back?

[34] See Chapter 14—*Ingram* arrangements.

[35] See Chapter 16—*Eversden* planning.

PART II: HOW THE LEGISLATION WORKS

This part considers in detail the Pre-Owned Assets legislation in FA 2004, Sch. 15. In this Part references to paras are to the provisions of Sch. 15. There are three distinct charging regimes as follows:

- land (para.3);
- chattels (para.6); and
- intangible property held in a settlor interested trust (para.8).

In addition, certain transactions are excluded from the charge on land and chattels (these are considered in Chapter 5) and there are a number of blanket exemptions from the charge (see Chapter 7). The income tax charge may also be avoided if an election is made under paras 21 or 22 to subject the property to the reservation of benefit rules—in effect to bring it back into the IHT net—and this is considered in Chapter 11.

CHAPTER 3

THE PARA. 3 CHARGE ON LAND

WHEN THE PROVISION APPLIES

Paragraph 3 applies when, in any year of assessment, an individual **3–01**
occupies any land, whether alone or together with other persons and
either of two conditions is met.

Occupation

The threshold test is thus one of **occupation**. The word is not defined **3–02**
and accordingly will bear its normal meaning of "taking possession". The authors consider that this requires the taxpayer to use or
be physically present in the property for at least part of the year. On
this basis:

  (i) more than one property may be occupied (*e.g.* a main
      residence and second home);

 (ii) a property may be occupied by a person if his possessions are
      stored there; and

(iii) a mere right to occupy which is not exercised does not
      amount to occupation.

An important point following from "occupation" requiring physical
use of the property is that a person receiving or entitled to receive
rents from a property is not in occupation.

It does not matter on what basis the individual occupies the land.
For instance it may be mere *de facto* occupation; or under a
gratuitous licence; or under a rack rent lease. All that is relevant in
relation to this threshold test is the fact of occupation.

This raises difficult issues where, for example, an infirm donor, in
principle caught by the Regime, has the right to occupy the whole but

only occupies a very small part of the house, never venturing into more than (say) three rooms. In these circumstances, will he be taxed on only a proportion of the appropriate rental value? Apparently not, since the legislation makes no provision for such an apportionment.[1]

3–03   Notice also that the legislation refers to the occupation of relevant land whether alone or with other persons. Even if the occupation is non exclusive there is no express reduction in the rental value.[2]

Nor is it clear how the rules would apply if the disposal was of (say) Gruesome Grange but the occupation was of merely the Lodge and did not affect the main house.[3]

There are also problems in reaching the correct valuation in the event that there is shared ownership of the land which could cause problems under self-assessment.[4]

The disposal condition

3–04 The first condition, the "disposal condition",[5] is that:

(a)   at any time after March 17, 1986 the individual owned an interest

(i)   in the land; **or**
(ii)   in other property the proceeds of the disposal of which were directly or indirectly applied by another person towards the acquisition of an interest in the land, **and**

(b)   the individual has disposed of all, or part of, his interest in the relevant land or the other property, otherwise than by an excluded transaction.

Paragraphs 3(2)(a)(i) and (b) cover direct acquisitions, *i.e.* cases where X previously owned and disposed[6] of the land which he now

---

[1] This is a matter that may be dealt with in the Regulations or guidance notes although it is not mentioned in the Consultation Document.

[2] See however, 3–10 onwards for a further discussion of how the chargeable amount on which the taxpayer pays income tax is reached.

[3] If the disposal was of the Grange including the Lodge then it is thought—however unfairly—that it is **all** the land that is taken into account. However:
(i)   if the Lodge is a wholly separate property arguably only that part of the gifted property should be taken into account; and
(ii)   in practice the Revenue would apply the reservation of benefit rules in such a case so that only the Lodge would be caught: the same approach may be adopted in the Pre-Owned Assets legislation.

[4] See 3–11.

[5] See Sch.15, paras 3(2)(a) and (b).

[6] Otherwise than by an excluded transaction.

occupies. Paragraphs 3(2)(a)(ii) and (b), on the other hand, cover representative acquisitions, *i.e.* cases where the land in question was acquired by someone other than X using the proceeds from the disposal (by whatever person) of property previously owned by X. So, if X gives Y Blackacre and Y sells Blackacre and buys Whiteacre, the disposal condition in para.(a)(ii) and (b) is satisfied.

The contribution condition

The second condition, the "contribution condition",[7] is that at any **3–05** time after March 17, 1986 the individual has directly or indirectly provided, otherwise than by an excluded transaction, any of the consideration given by another person for the acquisition of:

(a) an interest in the land; **or**

(b) an interest in any other property the proceeds of the disposal of which were directly or indirectly applied by another person towards the acquisition of an interest in the land.

Limb (a) of this condition covers directly funded acquisitions, and will generally involve cash gifts, *i.e.* where X provides Y with the funds to acquire Blackacre.[8] It also covers exchanges where, *e.g.* A gives Greenacre to B who then exchanges it for Brownacre. This would not be a representative acquisition because the *proceeds* of Greenacre are not being applied towards Blackacre. Limb (b) covers indirectly funded acquisitions, *i.e.* where X provides Y with the funds to acquire Blackacre, which Y acquires and subsequently sells, using the proceeds of sale to acquire Whiteacre.

New interests

For these purposes, a disposition which creates a new interest in land **3–06** out of an existing interest in land is to be taken to be a disposal of part of the existing interest.[9] The draftsman has deliberately introduced the term "disposition" for this purpose, in contradistinction to

---

[7] Set out in Sch.15, para.3(3).
[8] It is thought that a loan of money (even on commercial terms) amounts to the provision of consideration.
[9] Sch.15, para.3(4).

"disposal", but it is difficult to see to what effect. In particular, the extended IHT definition of "disposition"[10] does not apply.

Interaction of disposal and contribution conditions

3–07 As will be seen below,[11] the legislation provides for five excluded transactions in relation to the contribution condition, and five excluded transactions in relation to the disposal condition. Four of the excluded transactions which apply to the contribution condition also apply to the disposal condition but there is one excluded transaction which is only applicable to the contribution condition and one excluded transaction which is only applicable to the disposal condition. It may therefore be important to know which of the two conditions is relevant. The question is most likely to arise in cases where the owner of the land acquired it from someone other than the person who occupies it.

At first glance, it might be thought that there is a considerable overlap between representative acquisitions and funded acquisitions, but in practice the contribution condition in para.3(3) will normally be confined to cases where X has provided cash to fund the direct or indirect acquisition. This is on the basis that para.3(2)(a)(ii) of the disposal condition contemplates the application of *the proceeds* of the disposal of property, and the disposal of cash (whether of sterling or any other currency) by way of consideration will not produce any such "proceeds".[12]

THE CHARGE

3–08 Where para.3 applies to the individual in respect of the whole or any part of a year of assessment, an amount equal to "the chargeable amount" is treated as his income and is chargeable to income tax.

Definitions

3–09 There are seven definitions that have to be considered before one can determine the taxable benefit on which the individual will pay income tax! These are:

[10] This is in IHTA 1984, s.272.
[11] See Chapter 5.
[12] See 3–03. Consider, however, the Home Loan Scheme (discussed in Chapter 17) where the disponer lends trustees money to buy his house. Both conditions would appear to be satisfied.

1. the chargeable amount: being the appropriate rental value less certain payments made;

2. the appropriate rental value: being R x DV/V;

3. the rental value (R) being the rent which would have been payable if the property had been let at an annual rent equal to the annual value;

4. the valuation date;

5. DV being the value at the valuation date of the interest disposed of;

6. V being the market value of the relevant land at the valuation date; and

7. annual value: being broadly the rent that would be obtained from a standard residential letting of the entire land.

Each of these will be considered in turn.

The chargeable amount

For any taxable period—*i.e.* any year of assessment or part thereof **3–10** during which para.3 applies[13]—the chargeable amount is the "appropriate rental value", less the amount of any payments made by the individual in pursuance of any legal obligation to the land's owner in respect of his occupation.[14] The relevance of such payments is discussed below.

The appropriate rental value is defined as such proportion of the rental value (R) as is found by the following formula:

$$R \times \frac{DV}{V}$$

The DV definition varies slightly according to whether it is the disposal condition or contribution condition which is in point.[15] However, in all cases regard is to be had to certain considerations. Of these the least involved is "**the valuation date**" which, in relation to a taxable period, simply means such date as may be prescribed[16] and one can assume will, at least initially, be April 6, 2005.

[13] Sch.15, para.4(5).
[14] Sch.15, para.4(1).
[15] This is considered further at 3–12 along with the meaning of DV and V.
[16] Sch 15, para.4(5). By para.4(5)(a), regulations may in relation to any valuation date provide for a valuation of the land or any interest therein by reference to an earlier valuation date to apply subject to any prescribed adjustments. See Chapter 12 for further information.

The definition of the "rental value" of the land for the taxable period is the rent which would have been payable for that period if the property had been let to the individual at an annual rent equal to the annual value.[17] This leads on to the meaning of "annual value".

Annual value

3–11 The annual value is the rent which might reasonably be expected to be obtained on a letting from year to year if:

(a) the tenant undertook to pay all taxes, rates and charges usually paid by a tenant, **and**

(b) the landlord undertook to bear the costs of the repairs and insurance and the other expenses (if any) necessary for maintaining the property in a state to command that rent.

For this purpose, the rent is taken to be the amount that might reasonably be expected to be so obtained in respect of a letting of the land and is to be calculated on the basis that the only amounts that may be deducted in respect of services provided by the landlord are amounts in respect of the cost to the landlord of providing a service other than the repair, insurance or maintenance of the premises.[18] Accordingly the calculation of rent for these purposes will be based upon that payable under a relatively standard form residential tenancy. In the event that the individual makes some payments in respect of his occupation these may be deducted from the appropriate rental value in arriving at the chargeable amount.[19]

It is important to bear in mind that the Pre-Owned Asset charge will not apply if the taxpayer is in occupation of the land for "full consideration in money or money's worth". This exemption is dealt with at 7–17.[20]

---

[17] FA 2004, Sch.15, para.4(3). By para.4(5)(b), regulations may, in relation to any year of assessment, provide for a determination of the rental value of any land by reference to any earlier year of assessment to apply subject to any prescribed adjustments.

[18] FA 2004, Sch.15, paras.5(1)–(3).

[19] See 3–07.

[20] Note that whilst the rent calculation is spelt out in some detail for para.3 purposes the same is not true of the full consideration let-out to reservation of benefit. The two may very well be different—see Chapter 7.

As noted above the appropriate rental value is found by multiplying **3–12** the rental value for the taxable period by the fraction:

$$\frac{\text{value at the valuation date of the interest in the land disposed of (DV)}}{\text{value of the land at the valuation date (V)}}$$

i.e. R x DV/V

Example:

Assume that X effected an "*Ingram*" scheme by giving away the freehold interest in a land subject to a lease over it which he reserved to himself. At the valuation date the land is worth £1,000,000 and the encumbered freehold is worth £600,000. Assume the rental value is £50,000. This is then reduced as follows:

$$£50,000 \times \frac{£600,000}{£1,000,000} = £30,000$$

The appropriate rental value is therefore £30,000. Assuming X pays nothing for his occupation then £30,000 is also the chargeable amount. If X paid £5000 under a legal obligation, the chargeable amount would be reduced to £25,000.

The legislation broadly defines DV as the value at the valuation **3–13** date of the interest disposed of. However, the DV value may not be easily ascertainable.

Example:

Tony and Rebecca are married and own property as tenants in common in equal shares. Tony carried out an *Eversden* scheme in 1999 such that he gave his half share away to Rebecca on interest in possession trusts and part of that interest has now been terminated in favour of the children.[21] Tony will suffer an income tax charge from April 6, 2005 but what is the value (the DV) of the interest he gave on trust for his wife? Is it an arithmetical one half share or discounted to allow for the fact that she is in occupation and retains one half? Until the DV has been established Tony cannot self-assess.[22]

---

[21] See Chapter 16 for a consideration of *Eversden* schemes.
[22] See Chapter 16 for further comments.

Cash sales at an undervalue ("non exempt sales")

3–14 The legislation also caters for sales of the *whole interest in the land* at an undervalue so as to reflect the fact that the proceeds from the sale may be comprised in the value of the vendor's estate. It does so by providing that where the disposal of an interest in land is a "non-exempt" sale, the annual rent is reduced to take account of the undervalue.

"Non-exempt sale" is somewhat bewilderingly defined in relation to a disposal by a person of his interest in land as a sale which, although it was not an excluded transaction, was a sale of his *whole* interest in the property for a consideration paid in money in any currency.[23] This exemption is intended to cover sales at an undervalue. (Sales for full consideration will normally be excluded transactions—see 5–08 onwards.) The definition of non-exempt sale is, however, flawed because it only covers sales of the whole interest not sales of part (for any value) and it does not cover exchanges of property but only cash sales.[24]

In the case of non exempt sales the annual rent is reduced to take account of the undervalue by multiplying the annual rent by the following fraction[25]:

$$\frac{\text{the "appropriate proportion" of the value at the valuation date of the interest in the land disposed of}}{\text{value of the land}}$$

The "appropriate proportion" is:[26]

$$\frac{\text{value of the interest in land at the time of the sale (MV) } less \text{ the amount paid (P)}}{\text{value of the interest in land (MV) at the time of sale}}$$

Example:
Assume X sold for £800,000 land worth £1,000,000 and that the rental value is £50,000. The appropriate proportion is:[27]

$$\frac{£1,000,000 - £800,000}{£1,000,000 \text{ (MV)}} = \tfrac{1}{5}\text{th}$$

---

[23] Sch.15, para.4(4).
[24] These points are discussed further at 3–15, onwards.
[25] Sch.15, para.4(2)(a).
[26] Sch.15, para.4(4).
[27] MV-P / MV.

The rental value is then multiplied by the following fraction:

$$\frac{£200,000}{£1,000,000} \times 50,000 = £10,000$$

Cash limitation

This non exempt sale relief is expressly made available only to cash **3–15**
sales, though why this should be so is not clear.[28] This limitation is
capable of producing some unfairness. For example, no relief will be
available in respect of an exchange. Assume X transfers Blackacre
worth £1,000,000 to Y in consideration of Y transferring to X
Whiteacre worth £800,000 and X continues to occupy Blackacre.
The annual value of Blackacre, without any reduction, is £50,000. In
fairness this should be reduced to £10,000, but no such reduction will
be available. Instead, X will pay tax on £50,000 and *prima facie* be
liable for IHT on the value of Whiteacre which forms part of his
estate.

It might be argued that as Whiteacre is part of X's estate, it derives
its value from Blackacre and thus the exemption in para.11(1)(b)
applies such that there should be a reduced income tax charge on X's
occupation of Blackacre.[29] However, it seems difficult to construe
para.11(1) in this way.[30]

The position is unclear where there is a part exchange at an
undervalue with a cash adjustment, *i.e.* instead of Y transferring
Whiteacre worth £800,000 to X he transfers Greenacre worth
£300,000 to X and also pays X £500,000. It is to be hoped that in
such a case the annual rent would fall to be reduced to take account
of the payment of the £500,000.

Property limitation—sale of whole interest

Unlike an arm's length sale which is an excluded transaction under **3–16**
para.10(1), a transaction can only qualify as a non-exempt sale if it
is a sale of the whole interest; the disponer cannot retain any right or
interest over the land.[31]

---

[28] It may be that, given that transactions as long ago as March 1986 are relevant, the
Revenue wished to avoid valuation difficulties.

[29] See 7–07.

[30] For a fuller discussion, see 26–03.

[31] Compare the wording in 10(1)(a).

Example:

A retains a lease for 15 years and sells the freehold reversion to B for what he believes to be full consideration. It turns out that the price paid by B is an undervalue and therefore the sale is not an excluded transaction. However, it is not a non-exempt sale (because the sale is of part only) and therefore none of the purchase price received by A can be taken into consideration. Again, this is capable of producing unfairness.[32] Do the provisions on non-exempt sales have any practical application?

Take the example above: because A has not sold the freehold reversion for full consideration he is caught by the reservation of benefit rules. Therefore the Regime cannot apply due to the para.11(5)(a) exemption so A is outside the charge anyway.[33] It appears that the rationale behind non-exempt sales lies in the Revenue's interpretation of the reservation of benefit rules on sales at an undervalue. If A sells his house to B for £100,000 and it is worth £150,000 and A continues to occupy to property then the Revenue argues (apparently on a concessionary basis) that there has been a reservation of benefit in £50,000 only —the undervalue element. To the extent that there is a reservation of benefit, there is therefore no POA charge on £50,000. POA remains a possibility on £100,000 which is not subject to a reservation of benefit (*i.e.* two thirds of the value of the property). However, the provisions in Sch. 15 on non-exempt sales mean that the cash paid *is* taken into account when calculating the charge and thus on the above facts there would in the end be no POA charge.

3–17 The rules will not be relevant in relation to pre-1999 *Ingram* schemes where, for example, X carved out a lease for himself and then sold the freehold at an undervalue. Nor to reversionary lease schemes which might involve some sort of sale at an undervalue. In both cases the non-exempt sale provisions would be of no assistance because the disponer has not disposed of his entire interest in the land. He cannot retain any interest at all if he is to receive the benefit of the non-exempt sale provisions.

In summary, the non-exempt sale provisions are unlikely to have any application because such transactions have to be a disposal of the entire interest in land and being at an undervalue will generally involve a gift with reservation. Therefore the Regime cannot apply to them and the rationale for introducing the provisions seems misconceived.

---

[32] The possible application of the non exempt sale provisions in the context of Home Loan Schemes is considered at 17–16. Arms length sales which are excluded transactions are discussed at 5–08 onwards and equity release schemes and sales generally are discussed in Chapter 26.

[33] See para.11(5)(a) and Chapter 7.

Funded acquisition

Where the disposal condition is that the individual funded the **3–18** acquisition as discussed in 3–07, above, the appropriate rental value is found by multiplying the rental value for the taxable period by the fraction;[34]

$$\frac{\text{such part of the value of the land as can reasonably be attributed to the property originally disposed of by the individual (or, where the disposal was a non-exempt sale, the appropriate proportion of that value)}}{\text{value of the land}}$$

"Non-exempt" sale and "the appropriate proportion" have the same meanings as were discussed above.[35]

Tracing problems

It is not difficult to anticipate both theoretical and practical problems **3–19** in applying the "reasonably attributed test". What happens if, *e.g.* Albert gives his son Ben land worth £100,000, Ben retains the land for a few years after which it is compulsorily acquired for £1,000,000 with Ben using £200,000 of the proceeds to buy Albert the country cottage he always dreamt of? What part of the value of the cottage at the valuation date can reasonably be attributed to the land Albert gave to Ben? How is Albert to self-assess? Consider also what would happen if, *e.g.* when the land is worth £300,000 Ben develops it, subsequently selling it for £2,500,000 and using £200,000 of the proceeds to buy Albert the country cottage? These uncertainties in the scope of the charge in a case like this where a taxpayer must be able to self-assess with certainty demonstrate the difficulties of applying of this legislation. Presumably any taxpayer should ensure he makes detailed disclosure on his tax return as to how he has done his reasonable attribution calculation and the basis of the values reached.

In many cases funds will have become mixed to such an extent that it will be difficult, if not impossible, to determine with any precision how much the taxpayer contributed to the land. The rule, rather than the exception, will be that individuals will either be

---

[34] See Sch.15, para.4(2)(b).
[35] Sch.15, para.4(4).

unable to retrieve relevant information or will be able to do so only with considerable difficulty and often at no little cost.

Contribution condition

3–20 Where the contribution condition is satisfied, the appropriate rental value is found by multiplying the rental value for the taxable period by the fraction:[36]

$$\frac{\text{such part of the value of the land as can reasonably be}}{\text{attributed to the consideration provided}}{\text{value of the land}}$$

Tracing problems

3–21 Again, it is not difficult to anticipate both theoretical and practical problems in applying the "reasonably attributed test". What happens if, *e.g.* Charles gives his daughter Dorothy £50,000 "to invest wisely". Dorothy invests £25,000 in ICI shares and £25,000 in Biotech Ltd. The ICI shares languish but the Biotech Ltd shares have grown tenfold in value. Five years later Dorothy sells all the shares and uses the £25,000 from the ICI shares and £125,000 from the Biotech Ltd shares (the permutations are endless) to buy Charles a cottage in Wales. What part of the value of the cottage at the valuation date can reasonably be attributed to the consideration provided by Charles?

It is likely that individuals will often be unable to obtain relevant information or will be able to do so only with considerable difficulty and often at no little cost. Even if they can obtain the necessary information as to how the gifted cash was used, it is still not clear how the "reasonably attributed" test should be applied.

Note that non-exempt sales do not apply to the contribution condition.

Determining the chargeable amount—relevance of payments made

3–22 It is only **after** determining the appropriate rental value according to the above rules that any payments made in pursuance of a legal

[36] Sch.15, para.4(2)(c).

obligation by the individual concerned to the owner of the land are taken into account in determining the chargeable amount on which the individual pays income tax. This is important in relation to the annual £5,000 exemption.[37]

The fact that payments must be made pursuant to a legal obligation means that voluntary payments which may come within the IHT ameliorating provisions in the Finance Act 1986, Sch.20, para.6(1)(a) will not be taken into account for this purpose. This, however, should not matter because if the para.6(1)(a) full consideration let-out is available the para.3. charge will not apply. Bear in mind in this connection that "full consideration" for the purposes of para.6(1)(a) may be quite different from the annual value that is relevant under para.4.[38]

Example

Chris gave his house to his son Johnny in 2000. As part of the arrangements made then, Chris paid a capital sum upfront for the right to continue in occupation for seven years. This has been accepted as full consideration for IHT purposes and therefore there is no reservation of benefit FA 1986, Sch.20 para.6. Such a payment is not a payment that could ever reduce the chargeable amount for the purposes of the Regime but since Chris has the para.6 protection he is also given exemption from an income tax charge under para.11(5)(d). If Chris pays nothing for his continued occupation after 2007 or less than full consideration then he has reserved a benefit in the property and therefore there is no Regime income tax charge since he is protected by para.11(5)(a).[39]

---

[37] See 9–03.
[38] See 7–11.
[39] See Chapter 7 for exemptions under the Regime.

CHAPTER 4

THE PARA. 6 CHARGE ON CHATTELS

WHEN THE PROVISIONS APPLY

4–01 Paragraph 6 applies where an individual is in possession of, or has the use of, a chattel, whether alone or together with other persons and either one of two conditions is met.

The threshold test is that the individual must be in possession of, or have the use of, the chattel.[1] "Possession" and "use" are not defined and so bear their normal meaning. Compare, in the reservation of benefit legislation the requirement that the donee has not assumed "possession and enjoyment of the property."[2] It is considered that a mere legal right to have possession of the chattel is not enough: control of the chattel must be assumed by the individual (or, presumably, his agent). If goods are stored (*e.g.* at a warehouse) it is considered that they are in the possession of the person responsible for the storage.

The disposal condition

4–02 The first condition, called "the disposal condition", is that:

    (a) at any time after March 17, 1986, the individual, whether alone or jointly with others, owned

        (i) the chattel, or
        (ii) any other property the proceeds of the disposal of which were directly or indirectly applied by another person towards the acquisition of the chattel, and

---

[1] Compare the land charge under para.3 which depends upon "occupation".
[2] FA 1986, s.102(1)(a). See *Dymond's Capital Taxes* at 5.406.

(b) the individual disposed of all, or part of, his interest in the chattel or the other property, otherwise than by an excluded transaction.[3]

Limb (a)(i) and (b) cover direct acquisitions, *i.e.* cases where X previously owned and disposed[4] of the chattel which he now uses or enjoys. Limb (a)(ii) and (b), on the other hand, cover representative acquisitions, *i.e.* cases where the chattel in question was acquired by someone other than X using the proceeds from the disposal[5] (by whatever person) of property previously owned by X. So, if X gives Y a violin and Y sells the violin and buys a painting which X then possesses, the disposal condition in limb (a)(ii) and (b) is satisfied.

The contribution condition

The second condition is "the contribution condition". It is that at any **4–03** time after March 17, 1986 the individual has directly or indirectly provided, otherwise than by an excluded transaction, any of the consideration given by another person for the acquisition of:

(a) the chattel, or

(b) any other property the proceeds of the disposal of which were directly or indirectly applied by another person towards the acquisition of the chattel.[6]

Limb (a) of this condition covers directly funded acquisitions, *i.e.* where X provides Y with the cash to acquire a chattel, which X then, possesses or uses. It also covers exchanges where, *e.g.* A gives a violin to B who then exchanges it for a painting, which A possesses. Limb (b) covers indirectly funded acquisition, *i.e.* where X provides Y with the funds to acquire a piano, which Y acquires and subsequently sells, using the proceeds of sale to acquire a statue, which X then possesses.

For these purposes, a disposition which creates a new interest in a chattel out of an existing interest in a chattel is to be taken to be a disposal of part of the existing interest.[7] The draftsman has purposely introduced the term "disposition" for this purpose, in contra-distinction to "disposal", but it is difficult to see to what effect. In

---

[3] Sch.15, para.6(2).
[4] Otherwise than by an excluded transaction.
[5] *ibid.*
[6] Sch.15, para.6(3).
[7] Sch.15, para.6(4).

particular the extended IHT definition of "disposition" does not apply.

THE CHARGE

4–04 Where para.6 applies to the individual in respect of the whole or part of a year of assessment, an amount equal to "the chargeable amount" is treated as income of his chargeable to income tax.[8]

The chargeable amount

4–05 For any taxable period, *i.e.* the year of assessment or part thereof during which para.6 applies[9]—the chargeable amount is the "appropriate amount", less the amount of any payments made by the individual in pursuance of any legal obligation to the chattel's owner in respect of the individual's possession or use.[10] The relevance of such payments is discussed at 4–15. If possession and use is only for part of a tax year, the chargeable amount is reduced accordingly.

The appropriate amount varies according to whether it is the disposal condition or contribution condition which is in point. However, in all cases regard is had to three considerations. The first is "the valuation date" which, in relation to a taxable period, simply means such date as may be prescribed.[11] The second is the value of the chattel. For this purpose regulations may, in relation to any valuation date, provide for a valuation of the chattel or any interest in it by reference to an earlier valuation date subject to any prescribed adjustments.[12] The third is the amount of the interest that would be payable for the taxable period if interest were payable at the prescribed rate on an amount equal to the value of the chattel at the valuation date.[13] For convenience, this will be called "the prescribed interest" and will in the following examples be assumed to be at 5 per cent per annum.[14]

Assume X is, as the settlor of a discretionary trust, allowed by the trustees to use a chattel worth £400,000. The chargeable amount is £400,000 × 5 per cent = £20,000.

---

[8] Sch.15, para.6(5).
[9] Sch.15, para.7(4).
[10] Sch.15, para.7(1).
[11] Sch 15, para.7(4). See Chapter 12.
[12] Sch.15, para.7(3).
[13] Sch.15, para.7(2).
[14] This is currently the official rate of interest which the Revenue is proposing to adopt—see the August Consultation Document in Appendix II.

There is a significant contrast between the way in which the benefit to the individual is calculated under the chattel rules and under the provisions dealing with land. Under the latter, a market rent will be arrived at on the basis of empirical evidence (the letting of comparable properties). For chattels, however, such comparable evidence is largely lacking. Hence the taxpayer is treated as benefiting on the basis of a percentage of the market value of the chattels.[15] In effect the charge is a percentage of capital value.

Valuation

It is likely that chattels will throw up difficult valuation problems. **4–06** Values may fluctuate year on year as particular items come in and out of fashion.[16] For a consideration of the likely content of the Regulations that will deal with valuations and fixing the amount of the deemed benefit, see Chapter 12.

Position if a retained interest

Where the disposal condition is that the individual previously owned **4–07** the chattel so satisfying the disposal condition, the appropriate amount is found by multiplying the prescribed interest (N) for the taxable period by the fraction[17]:

$$\frac{\text{value of interest in the chattel disposed of (DV)}}{\text{value of the chattel (V)}}$$

Thus, if the person possessing or using the chattel retained an interest in it, the amount on which he is charged is reduced.[18] Assume X effected an "*Ingram*" scheme by giving away the freehold interest in a chattel subject to a lease over it which he has reserved to himself.[19]

---

[15] See the Consultation Document of December 11, 2003 reproduced in Appendix II.

[16] See 18–20 in the Responses to the Consultation Process (reproduced in Appendix II).

[17] FA 2004 Sch.15, para.7(2)(a). The figure is expressed in the legislation as N × DV/V.

[18] Compare the similar position under the para.3 charge on land: see 3–10.

[19] For *Ingram* chattel schemes, see 18–02. The use of the terms leasehold and freehold interests in the case of chattels is to be preferred to bailment and ownership.

At the valuation date the chattel is worth £400,000 and the encumbered freehold worth £300,000. The calculation is therefore:

$$£20,000 \times \frac{£300,000}{£400,000} = £15,000$$

Cash sales at an undervalue

4-08 The legislation also caters for sales at an undervalue so as to reflect the fact that the proceeds from the sale may be comprised in the value of the vendor's estate. It does so by providing that where the disposal of an interest in a chattel is a "non-exempt" sale, the annual rent is reduced to take account of the undervalue.

"Non-exempt sale" is then defined as a sale which, although not an excluded transaction, was a sale of his *whole* interest in the chattel for a consideration paid in money in any currency.[20] By referring to a sale that is not an excluded transaction the draftsman appears to be flagging up a sale at an undervalue.

In such a case the "appropriate amount" is reduced to take account of the undervalue by multiplying it by the following fraction[21]:

$$\frac{\text{the appropriate proportion of the value of the interest in the chattel disposed of}}{\text{value of the chattel}}$$

In relation to a such a sale, "the appropriate proportion" is[22]:

$$\frac{\text{value of the interest in the chattel at the time of the sale less the amount paid}}{\text{value of the interest in the chattel at the time of the sale[23]}}$$

This is expressed in the legislation as:

$$\frac{MV - P}{P}$$

---

[20] Sch.15, para.7(3). The wording is the same in relation to non exempt sales of land: see 3–11.

[21] Sch.15, para.7(2)(a).

[22] Sch.15, para.7(3).

[23] Sch.15, para.7(2)(a).

Example:

Assume X sold a painting worth £1,000,000 for £800,000. The appropriate proportion is:

$$\frac{£200,000 \ (£1,000,000 \ - \ £800,000)}{£1,000,000} = \tfrac{1}{5}\text{th}$$

The appropriate amount is then arrived at under para.7(2) by the formula:

$$N \times \frac{DV}{V}$$

Where **N** is the prescribed interest (5 per cent) applied to the value of the chattel at the valuation date. In this case 5 per cent × £1,000,000 = £50,000.

DV is the appropriate proportion of the value of the interest in the chattel disposed of at the valuation date. Taking the 1/5 proportion and the value as £1,000,000 DV is £200,000.

V is the value of the chattel at the valuation date (£1,000,000)

Notice that in the above example it has been assumed that the values at the time of disposal remain unaltered at the valuation date.

Cash limitation

The non-exempt sale relief is only available in respect of cash sales. **4–09** As with land, this limitation may result in some unfairness. For example, no relief will be available in respect of an exchange. Assume X transfers his Van Gogh worth £1,000,000 to Y in consideration of Y transferring to X a Rembrandt worth £800,000 and that, without any reduction, the chargeable amount of the Van Gogh is £50,000. In fairness this should be reduced to £10,000, but no such reduction will be available under the non-exempt sale relief.

It may be argued that the position is saved in this sort of case as result of the exemption from charge provided for in para.11(1)(b).[24] Can it be said that X's estate includes the Rembrandt whose value is derived from the Van Gogh which he had exchanged for it. As noted in 26–03 and 3–15, it is unlikely that this argument will succeed. The value of the Rembrandt is not as such derived from the Van Gogh.

---

[24] This is considered in detail at 7–07.

The position under the non-exempt sale relief is also not clear where there is a part exchange at an undervalue with cash adjustment, *i.e.* instead of Y transfers a Rembrandt worth £800,000 to X in exchange for jewellery worth £300,000 and £500,000. It is to be hoped that in such a case the appropriate amount would fall to be reduced to take account of the payment of the £500,000.

Property limitation

4–10 The relief is available only if the donor has disposed of his *whole* interest in the chattel. If X grants a lease to Y over a chattel at an undervalue no account will be taken of the consideration received by X. Again, this appears capable of producing unfairness.

Note that a non-exempt sale (*i.e.* a sale at an undervalue) will commonly involve a gift with reservation but the non-exempt sale protection will afford an exemption for the sale element.[25]

Funded acquisitions

4–11 Where the disposal condition is satisfied by the individual funding the acquisition as discussed in 4–02, above, the appropriate amount is found by multiplying the prescribed interest for the taxable period by the fraction[26]:

$$\frac{\text{such part of the value of the chattel as can reasonably be attributed to the property originally disposed of by the individual (or, where the disposal was a non-exempt sale, the appropriate proportion of that value)}}{\text{value of the chattel}}$$

"Non-exempt" sale and "the appropriate proportion" have the same meanings as were discussed above.[27] Values are taken at the "valuation date".

Tracing problems

4–12 It is not difficult to foresee both theoretical and practical problems in applying the "reasonably attributed test". What happens if, *e.g.*

[25] See 3–16 for a full discussion of this point.
[26] Sch.15, para.7(2)(b).
[27] Sch.15, para.7(3).

Ernest gives his son Frank shares worth £25,000 in E & F Ltd, the family company for which they both work. The company prospers and five years later is sold, Frank receiving £3,000,000 for his shares. He purchases an organ for £350,000 which is installed in Ernest's house. What part of the value of the chattel can reasonably be attributed to the shares Ernest gave to Frank?

Contribution condition

When the contribution condition is satisfied, the appropriate amount **4–13** is found by multiplying the prescribed interest for the taxable period by the fraction[28]:

$$\frac{\text{such part of the value of the chattel as can reasonably be attributed to the consideration provided by the individual}}{\text{value of the chattel at the valuation date}}$$

Values are, of course, to be taken at the valuation date.

Tracing problems in applying the contribution condition

Again, it is not difficult to anticipate both theoretical and practical **4–14** problems in applying the "reasonably attributed test". What happens if, *e.g.* George lends his daughter Henrietta £75,000 to start up an internet business. Henrietta's business takes off and six years later she sells it for £3,000,000. She repays George and purchases a yacht for £500,000 which George is free to use any time he wants. Without George's initial loan Henrietta could not have gone into business. What part (if any) of the value of the yacht at the valuation date can reasonably be attributed to the funding provided by George?[29]

Relevance of payments made

It is only after determining the appropriate amount according to the **4–15** above rules that any payments made in pursuance of a legal obligation by the individual concerned to the owner of the chattel are taken into account. This is important in relation to the annual £5,000 exemption.[30]

---

[28] See Sch.15, para.7(2)(c).
[29] Note the seven year defence: see 5–09. See also Chapter 13 for a full discussion of the problems of compliance under self-assessment.
[30] See Chapter 9.

51

The fact that payments must be made pursuant to a legal obligation means that voluntary payments made to satisfy the IHT ameliorating provisions in the Finance Act 1986, Sch.20, para.6(1)(a) will not be taken into account for this purpose. This, however, may not matter because if the para.6(1)(a) full consideration let-out is available the pre-owned assets charge will not apply.[31]

Note that the deduction allowed is only for payments made by the chargeable person to the owner of the chattel. It is common in sale and leaseback arrangement for the terms of the lease to impose a burden on the donor/tenant to insure the chattel. Such payments, not being made to the owner, would not be deductible under para.7(1). Accordingly, if the particular arrangement is caught[32] by the Pre-Owned Assets Charge it will be sensible to amend the terms of the lease so that the donee owner insures and is reimbursed under the lease by the donor/tenant.

---

[31] For this exemption, see 7–17. For a discussion of its application to chattel schemes (which is somewhat surprising given that one of the main purposes of the pre-owned assets charge was said to be to catch arrangements where there was no ready market), see 18–07.

[32] As discussed at 18–07 it seems that these arrangements will not generally be caught. Either the full consideration exemption will be available or they will fall foul of the reservation of benefit rules.

CHAPTER 5

EXCLUDED TRANSACTIONS

These are defined in para.10. Note carefully the following points: **5–01**

(i) Excluded transactions are relevant in preventing a charge arising under either para.3 (land) or para.6 (chattels). **They have no application to the charge on settled intangible property in para.8.**

(ii) Paragraph 10 deals separately with exclusions which prevent the **disposal** conditions[1] from being satisfied and exclusions preventing the **contribution conditions**[2] from being met. Paragraph 10(1) deals with the former: para.10(2) with the latter.

Dealing separately with disposal and contribution conditions means that there is a degree of repetition in the legislation: *i.e.* certain of the exclusions for the disposal condition are repeated almost word for work for the contribution condition. This may be summarised as follows:

Exclusion	Disposal condition	Contribution condition
Spouse	10(1)(b)	10(2)(a)
Iip trust for spouse	10(1)(c): requires a "gift"	10(2)(b) requires property to become settled on acquisition
Section 11 of the IHTA 1984	10(1)(d)	10(2)(d)
Section 19 or 20 of the IHTA 1984	10(1)(e)	10(2)(e)

[1] Paragraph 3(2)—being the disposal condition for land refers to the disposal of land being "otherwise than by an excluded transaction". See also para.6(2) which is in similar terms for disposals of chattels.

[2] See para.3(3)—the contribution condition for land—referring to a provision of consideration "otherwise than by an excluded transaction". Paragraph 6(3) is in similar terms in relation to the chattel condition.

These may be termed "general excluded transactions" and will be considered first in relation to both disposal and contribution conditions.

Paragraph 10(1)(a) deals with an excluded transaction only relevant to the disposal condition ("**an arms length sale**") and para.10(2)(c) with an excluded transaction relevant only to the contribution condition ("**the seven-year defence**"). These two "limited" excluded transactions will be looked at separately.

Excluded transactions prevent one of the pre-conditions for the land or chattels charge from being satisfied. By contrast, the exemptions from charge (which are relevant to charges under the settlement provisions of para.8 as well as to land and chattels)[3] provide for certain exemptions from charge when the pre-conditions of the charge have been satisfied. Hence the correct procedure (taking the charge on land as an illustration) is first to consider whether the pre-conditions to the charge applying have been met (which will involve a consideration of whether there is an excluded transaction under para.10) and, if the answer is yes, then consider whether an exemption from charge under para.11 applies.

GENERAL EXCLUDED TRANSACTIONS

5–02 As noted above the "general excluded transactions" are excluded transactions for the purpose of both the disposal and contribution conditions.[4]

Spouse exemption

5–03 A transfer of property by an individual is an excluded transaction (so that the disposal condition is not met)if the property was transferred to his spouse (or where the transfer has been ordered by a court, to his former spouse).[5] The transfer can be by any means, *i.e.* it need not be by way of gift, nor need it satisfy any conditions other than those stated. This relief is thus considerably wider than both the IHT spouse exemption and the CGT relief for disposals between spouses. Note that, unlike the IHT exemption, the spouses' domiciles are irrelevant.

---

[3] See Chapter 7.

[4] It is clear that what may initially have been an excluded transaction may subsequently cease to be excluded: see para.10(3) in the context of a spouse's interest in possession coming to an end. It is not clear if the converse is true: see n.13.

[5] See Sch.15, para.10(1)(b).

"Spouse" for this purpose means a person who is legally married.[6] A marriage ceases only on the grant of a decree absolute.[7] When enacted, the Civil Partnership Bill 2004 may have a profound impact in this area. Although the Bill does not amend s.18 of IHTA 1984 to include a civil partner, it seems clear from amendments to other legislation such as the family law legislation that this is likely to happen.

The provision by a person of consideration for another's acquisition of any property is an excluded transaction (so that the contribution condition is not met) if the other person was his spouse (or, where the transfer has been ordered by the court, his former spouse).[8] So, if X buys a house in his spouse's name the disposal condition will not be satisfied and the provision by X of the funds will be an excluded transaction in relation to the contribution condition.

Spouse entitled to an interest in possession

A disposal by an individual is an excluded transaction if it was a **5–04** disposal by way of gift[9] (or, where the transfer is for the benefit of his former spouse, in accordance with a court order) by virtue of which the property became settled property in which the individual's spouse or former spouse is beneficially entitled to an interest in possession.[10] But this condition ceases to be satisfied if the spouse/former spouse's interest comes to an end during her lifetime.[11] Note that if the spousal interest comes to an end on his/her death then there is no income tax charge on the donor.

This exemption is similar to the post-*Eversden* let-out for spouse exempt gifts in the reservation of benefit provisions.[12]

"Interest in possession" is not defined and so will have the same general meaning as for IIIT. Note that, unlike the IHT exemption, the spouses' domiciles are irrelevant. Unlike the para.10(1)(c) exclusion for outright "transfers" between spouses, where the transfer is to a trust it must be by way of gift.[13]

---

[6] *Holland v IRC* [2003] S.T.C. (SCD) 43.

[7] *Fender v St John Mildmay* [1938] A.C. 1.

[8] See Sch.15, para.10(2)(a).

[9] For the meaning of "gift", see 16–15 *et seq.*

[10] See also 16–19 for further comments.

[11] See Sch.15, paras 10(1)(c) and (3).

[12] See 16–19 though for an analysis of the differences: in particular the donor may be caught by the reservation rules even if the spouse's interest ends on death.

[13] Although presumably a sale at an undervalue would qualify as a gift—see Chapter 16. It is clear that the gift must result in the property becoming settled. It is not, however, certain that the spouse had to enjoy and interest in possession **at that time**. The authors incline to the view that if the spousal interest subsequently arises the disposal will thereupon become an excluded transaction.

5–05   In practice para.10(3) (which imposes a charge on termination of the spousal interest) is only likely to be relevant if the transaction was done pre-June 20, 2003. If it is done after that date, it will be caught under the reservation of benefit provisions anyway and therefore will fall outside the Regime.[14]

Similarly, the provision of consideration for the acquisition of any property is an excluded transaction if on its acquisition the property became settled property in which his spouse or former spouse is beneficially entitled to an interest in possession. There is therefore no objection to, *e.g.* X settling cash on the trustees of settlement under which his spouse has an interest in possession who then acquire a house in which X subsequently lives, so long as his spouse continues to have an interest in possession in the house.

Example:

In July 2003 John settles his family home on revocable interest in possession trusts for his spouse Emma who is UK domiciled. John and Emma both occupy the home. John is protected by para.10(1)(c) from any income tax charge under the Regime. There is also no reservation of benefit because of s.102(5) of the Finance Act 1986 (spouse exempt gift).

In July 2004, Emma dies. Her interest in possession ends and the home is now held on continuing trusts for her children (and inheritance tax may or may not be paid depending on values) but John still occupies the property. There is no income tax charge under the Regime because her interest ended on her death. Paragraph 10(1)(c) protection continues to apply. However, this does not protect John from a later IHT charge since he is treated as having made a reservation of benefit under s.102(5A)(c). The fact that Emma is dead does not matter. A reservation of benefit arises at her death and the home will be taxed on John's death unless he ceases to occupy it more than seven-years before his death.

Suppose Emma's interest ended while she was alive. In these circumstances there would be no protection under para.10(1)(c) from an income tax charge on John because of para.10(3) but since John will have reserved a benefit anyway (see ss.102(5A)(c) and 102(5B)) he is protected from an income tax charge by virtue of para.11(5)(a).[15]

If, however, John had made the gift into trust prior to June 20, 2003, even though Emma's interest was terminated after this date ss.102(5A) and (5B), FA 1986 do not apply so there is no reservation of benefit by John. Hence unless Emma's interest is

---

[14] See 16–19 and para.11(5) of Sch.15.
[15] See Chapter 7.

terminated on her death, John is subject to an income tax charge under the Regime once her interest ends.

Family maintenance dispositions

A disposal by an individual is an excluded transaction if the disposal **5–06** was a disposition within the relief afforded to family maintenance dispositions by s.11 of the IHTA 1984.[16]

Similarly the provision of consideration by a disposition falling within s.11 is an excluded transaction so that the contribution condition is not met.[17]

Annual and small gifts exemptions

A disposal by an individual is an excluded transaction if the disposal **5–07** is an outright gift to an individual and is for IHT purposes a transfer of value that is wholly exempt by virtue of the annual exemption or the small gifts exemption.[18] Gifts to trustees (other than bare trustees) will thus not qualify.

There is a similar exclusion from the contribution condition where the provision of the consideration is an outright gift within either s.19 or s.20 of IHTA 1984.[19]

Curiously whilst gifts within s.20 are outside the reservation of benefit rules,[20] there is no exemption for gifts falling within the annual exemption: *i.e.* the reservation of benefit rules are capable of applying in such cases.

ARM'S LENGTH SALES

This is one of the most important exclusions because the intention is **5–08** to exclude normal commercial sales from the income tax charge. It only applies in relation to the **disposal condition**, not the contribution condition. Under the land charge and the chattels charge, the disposal is an excluded transaction if it was of the individual's *whole* interest in the property, except for any right expressly reserved by him over the property, either:

[16] See Sch.15, para.10(1)(d).
[17] See Sch.15, para.10(2)(d).
[18] See Sch.15, para.10(1)(e).
[19] See Sch.15, para.10(2)(e).
[20] See FA 1986, s.102(5)(b).

(a) by a transaction made at arm's length with a person not connected with him, or

(b) by a transaction such as might be expected to be made at arm's length between persons not connected with each other.[21]

Subject to one qualification, the arm's length or equivalent transaction test is the same as that in s.10(1)(a) and (b) of the IHTA 1984. The qualification is that the definition of "connected persons" in s.839 of the Taxes Act 1988 is modified so that:

(a) "relative" is extended to include uncle, aunt, nephew and niece, and

(b) "settlement", "settlor" and "trustee" have the same meanings as for IHT.[22]

In the Standing Committee debates and at Report Stage the point was made by Opposition MPs that the requirement that the disposal had to be of the vendor's whole interest in the property was unfair. It would not, *e.g.* cover a sale of a half share in a property. This is particularly important in relation to equity release schemes; see Chapter 26. At Report Stage, the Paymaster General, having undertaken in Committee to reconsider this but not having had time to do so by Report Stage, stated:

"We accept that an owner could sell a part-interest as an element of an arm's length equity transaction while retaining the right to occupy the property. We are ready to explore that issue further with firms that undertake such transactions to determine whether action is needed."[23]

Paragraph 10(1) is a key provision which is considered further in Chapter 26 on equity release arrangements within the family and in Chapter 17 in the context of Home Loan Schemes. So far as the latter are concerned it is generally considered that the necessary arm's length element will be missing and that such arrangements do not therefore amount to excluded transactions. For instance, the fact that the loan is left outstanding indefinitely is not the sort of arm's length transaction one would "expect" to make with an unconnected party.

---

[21] See Sch.15, para.10(1)(a).
[22] See Sch.15, para.2.
[23] Hansard, July 7, 2004, col.898.

The provision by a person of consideration for another's acquisition **5–09** of land or chattels is an excluded transaction (so that the contribution condition is not met) if it constituted an outright gift of money in any currency by the individual to the other person and was made at least seven years before the earliest date on which:

(a) in the case of land, the individual occupies the land, whether alone or together with any person[24]; and

(b) in the case of a chattel, the individual is in possession of, or has the use of, the chattel, whether alone or together with other persons.[25]

So, if X gives Y £100,000 which Y uses to purchase a house and X occupies the house at least seven years after the cash gift, the contribution condition will not be satisfied. This provision incorporates into the land and chattels charging codes the equivalent of a PET.

The aim was to try and ease compliance. Thus where someone has made a gift of cash more than seven years ago and not yet occupied land or used chattels purchased by the donee the donor does not need to be concerned about the Regime. Note though that the exclusion does not apply unless there is an outright gift of money so that there are still potentially serious compliance problems.

Example:

Eric gives Ernie shares worth £100,000 in 1987. Ernie mixes the shares with his own portfolio and sells the whole lot for £200,000 in 1997. He uses the cash to buy a house which Eric then occupies. Eric is not within any of the para.10 exclusions even though the occupation takes place more than seven years after the gift. The gift was in shares not cash.

However, Eric may be caught by the reservation of benefit provisions (because the tracing provisions apply) in which case the Regime does not apply because of the exemption under para.11(5).[26]

---

[24] See Sch.15, para.10(2)(c) and para.3(1)(a). The actual wording refers to (*inter alia*) the gift being made "at least 7 years before the earliest date on which the chargeable person met the condition in para.3(1)(a)." It is thought that this means no more than occupies the land but it has been argued that the condition in para.3(1)(a) cannot be met (*e.g.* there cannot be a chargeable person) until April 6, 2005 (when the Schedule takes effect). If this argument were correct, cash gifts made before April 6, 1998 would not be caught by the Regime.

[25] See Sch.15, para.10(2)(c) and para.6(1)(a).

[26] See Chapter 7.

5–10   It appears that if the occupation has occurred within seven-years of the gift it will be caught even if the occupation arose prior to April 2005. It is also thought that if a person goes into occupation within seven years and then moves out but reoccupies later, even if seven years has long expired, he will be outside the protection of the exclusion.

The relatively long-term planning opportunities for cash gifts opened up by this excluded transaction are considered in Chapter 25. The exclusion is similar to the approach adopted in relation to *Ingram* schemes in 1999—where the lease is carved out more than seven years before the gift of the freehold then such transaction is not caught by the reservation of benefit rules (although such a transaction will now be caught by the Regime).[27]

---

[27] See further Chapter 14.

CHAPTER 6

INTANGIBLE PROPERTY COMPRISED IN A SETTLOR-INTERESTED SETTLEMENT: PARA.8

Introduction

Paragraph 8 can apply only to intangibles. It does not apply to land **6–01** or chattels whether or not caught under the para.3 or 6 charge. Moreover it applies only to intangibles held within a settlement. As noted previously, intangibles is defined to include cash, equities, insurance products and indeed all property other than land or chattels.

Three conditions must be satisfied in order for a para.8 charge to arise. First, the terms of a settlement, as they affect any property comprised in the settlement, are such that any income arising from that property would be treated as the income of the settlor by virtue of s.660A of the Income and Corporation Taxes Act 1988.

Secondly, the property in the settlement must at any time in the year comprise intangible property.

Thirdly, the intangible property in the trust is or represents property which the individual either settled or added to the settlement after March 17, 1986.[1]

Curiously, although para.8 is framed by reference to s.660A the term "settlement" is given the meaning it has for IHT purposes, not the meaning it has under s.660G for purposes of s.660A.[2] As will be seen below, this may be significant.

---

[1] See Sch.15, paras 8(1)(a) and (2).
[2] See Sch.15, para.1.

Spouse ignored

6–02 For this purpose s.660A is applied ignoring any benefit or possible benefit to the settlor's spouse from the settlement.[3] Thus a settlor cannot be caught simply because his spouse can benefit.

> *Example:*
> On May 18, 2003 John settles property on interest in possession trusts for his wife Emma. He is excluded from all benefit. The trust holds cash. John is not caught by para.8 even though his spouse can benefit. However, if John can potentially benefit under the settlement (*e.g.* under the terms of an overriding power of appointment) then even though this is not a reservation of benefit (since the transaction took place pre-June 20, 2003[4]) he would be subject to tax under para.8.

It is therefore necessary to review all trusts set up after March 17, 1986 where the settlor retains some interest in the trust. Although such trusts may not have been set up for inheritance tax reasons, if they hold any property other than land or chattels, the settlor will be within para.8. There is no let out or exclusion just because the spouse retains an interest in possession. The consequences of this can be severe as explained later.

6–03 Since land or chattels comprised in a settlement do not fall within para.8 nor, if the settlor did not occupy the land or use or enjoy the chattels, would the land be within para.3 or the chattels within para.6, trustees of a settlement otherwise within para.8 should consider selling their intangible investments and purchasing tangible assets, *e.g.* let land or chattels.

The property test and sub-funds

6–04 What matters is that the settlement is settlor-interested in relation to the property in question, not that the settlement is settlor-interested generally.

> *Example:*
> Assume X is the settlor of a settlement with two sub-funds. Sub-fund A, from which the settlor can benefit, contains land, while sub-fund B, from which the settlor cannot benefit, contains

---

[3] See Sch.15, para.8(1)(b).
[4] See Chapter 16 (*Eversden* schemes).

intangible property. The settlement as a whole is settlor-interested, but that does not matter. What matters is that the settlement is not settlor-interested in relation to sub-fund B and is not within para.8 in relation to sub-fund A while it holds only tangible property.

Absence of income

The fact that no actual income arises does not prevent an income tax **6–05** charge under the Regime.[5] It may be that income arises to the settlement which would be treated as the income of the settlor under s.660A otherwise than by reason of the terms of the settlement, *e.g.* where the settlor waives dividends on shares he owns personally with the result that the dividend paid on shares in a non-settlor interested settlement is increased. In this case the Regime does not apply because the income does not arise *from* the settled property.

An entirely different approach

It is vital to understand that para.8 adopts an entirely different **6–06** approach to that adopted under the para.3 land provisions and the para.6 chattels provisions, in a number of ways.

Psychic income and the comfort factor

First, under the para.3 and para.6 provisions the taxpayer must have **6–07** actually benefitted. For example, what matters under para.3 is actual occupation of land and not merely an unexercised right to occupy. Under para.8, on the other hand, what matters is the mere possibility of benefitting.

It is understood that in their discussions with the Association of British Insurers the Revenue justified this difference in approach on the basis that a settlor who might benefit from settled intangible property (or the income from it) is in receipt of "psychic income" in having the comfort of knowing that he had the possibility of benefitting from the settlement.

---

[5] See 6–17 for the practice if income tax is suffered on income which does arise in the settlement.

6–08 Secondly, none of the "excluded transaction" let-outs can operate to prevent para.8 from operating.[6] Accordingly, the favoured treatment available to transfers to spouses is unavailable: as noted earlier, if X settles intangible property on trusts under which his spouse has an interest in possession which is subject to the exercise by the trustees of a power of appointment which can be exercised in favour of a class of beneficiaries including X then para.8 will apply.

The "no bounty" rule

6–09 If the s.660G definition of "settlement" applied, the existence of an arm's length transaction would be relevant in relation to para.8, not because of any provision in the Regime but because of income tax case law in relation to s.660A. Under a string of cases, culminating in *IRC v Plummer*,[7] it is well established that what would otherwise be a settlement for purposes of s.660A will be prevented from being a settlement if it lacks any element of bounty. So, entirely commercial arrangements which involve intangible property being held in trust will be outside s.660A. A good example is where partners in a firm, in order to provide funding to purchase the shares of a deceased partner, take out insurance policies on their own lives and then settle them on trusts under which the policies are held for all the partners. The arrangement is entirely commercial and in no way intended to benefit any partner gratuitously. If the s.660G definition of "settlement" applied, such an arrangement would *prima facie* fall outside the terms of para.8 in relation to each of the partners. The relevant definition, however, is the IHT definition, which is not subject to any such "no bounty" limitation. It therefore appears that the "no bounty" defence is not available.

Practical scope: relevance of blanket exemptions

6–10 Although none of the "excluded transactions" provisions apply in relation to para.8, all of the blanket exemptions do apply, and this is likely to restrict the operation of para.8 in practice for two reasons.[8]

---

[6] Excluded transactions are considered in Chapter 5.
[7] [1980] A.C. 896; [1979] S.T.C. 793.
[8] See Chapter 7 for a consideration of these exemptions.

The settlor has an interest in possession

First, where the settlor has an interest in possession in intangible **6–11**
property, the exemption given to property already comprised within
the settlor's IHT estate will prevent para.8 from applying. Thus
where at present the settlor's spouse has an interest in possession in
such a trust but the settlor could be appointed such an interest, it is
worth considering terminating the spousal interest and appointing an
interest in possession to the settlor.

Trustees can benefit the settlor under non-*Eversden* trusts

Secondly, where the settlor does not have an interest in possession **6–12**
but is capable of benefitting under the trust because, *e.g.* he is a
member of a discretionary class of beneficiaries in whose favour the
trustees can exercise a power of appointment, the settlor is likely to
have reserved a benefit in respect of the settlement so that the
exemption given under para.11(5)(a) prevents para.8 from
applying.

Trustees can benefit the settlor under *Eversden* trusts

If the settlement is one under which the property is held under an **6–13**
Eversden arrangement (see Chapter 16) on discretionary trusts under
which the settlor can benefit, the property will not be caught by the
reservation of benefit rules and therefore para.8 will not be prevented
by the "reservation of benefit" blanket exemption from applying.
Indeed, *Eversden* arrangements are the primary target of para.8.[9]

Settlor has a reversionary interest

If the settlor has settled property on trusts such that he retains a **6–14**
reversionary interest, the carve-out principle will have prevented the
reservation of benefit provisions from applying.[10] The only relief
available which will reduce (although not eliminate) the para.8
charge is given by para.11(1)(b) as restricted by para.11(2).[11]

---

[9] See Chapter 16 for a fuller analysis.
[10] See, for instance, *Re Cochrane* [1906] 2 I.R. 200 and see 23–03.
[11] See 7–07.

6–15 Where para.8 applies in respect of the whole or part of a year of assessment an amount equal to "the chargeable amount" is treated as the individual's income chargeable to income tax.[12]

The chargeable amount

6–16 For any taxable period—*i.e.* the year of assessment or part thereof during which para.8 applies[13]—the chargeable amount is N minus T where N is what we will call "the prescribed interest" and T is what we will call "the tax allowance". For this purpose:

(a) **"the prescribed interest"** is the amount of interest that would be payable for the taxable period if interest were payable at the prescribed rate (likely to be 5 per cent)[14] on an amount equal to the value of the intangible property at the valuation date.[15] The "valuation date", in relation to a year of assessment, means such date as may be prescribed.[16]

(b) **"the tax allowance"** is the amount of any income tax or CGT payable by the individual in respect of the taxable period by virtue of s.547, s.660A and s.739 of the Taxes Act 1988 and s.77 and s.86 of the Taxation of Chargeable Gains Act 1992 so far as that tax is attributable to the intangible property.[17] The use of the word "payable" means that the "allowance" is available whether that tax is actually paid or not and even if it is reimbursed by the trustees.

No tax credits

6–17 The chargeable amount on which tax under the Regime is levied is reduced only by reference to amounts of tax that are payable under the other provisions (s.660A, s.77, etc). It would, arguably, be fairer for *the tax due* under the Regime to be reduced by a tax credit. This

---

[12] See Sch.15, para.8(3).

[13] See Sch.15, para.9(3).

[14] See the August Consultation Document in Appendix II.

[15] See Sch.15, para.9(1).

[16] See Sch.15, para.9(3). By para.9(2), regulations may in relation to any valuation date provide for a valuation of the land or any interest therein by reference to an earlier valuation date to apply subject to any prescribed adjustments.

[17] See Sch.15, para.9(1).

matter was raised in the Standing Committee debates where the Government made the point that both the charge under the existing rules in s.739, etc. and the charge under the Regime were free-standing charges imposed by reference to separate codes and were therefore justified in their own right. In the Government's view, any relief at all was generous!

> ***Example:***
> Waldo is the settlor of a non-resident settlor-interested settlement. Assume that the value of the intangible property in the settlement is £1,300,000. In tax year 2005–2006 the trustees receive UK source income of £50,000 which is attributed to Waldo by s.660A and realise capital gains of £100,000 which are deemed to be Waldo's gains by s.86 of the Taxation of Chargeable Gains Act 1992. Waldo's circumstances are such that £20,000 is payable in income tax on the £50,000 and £40,000 in CGT on the £100,000. The tax allowance is thus £60,000. If the chargeable amount is, *e.g.* £65,000 before any tax allowance this will be reduced by the tax allowance to £5,000 (with the result that the chargeable amount is within the £5,000 annual exemption; see Chapter 9).

Operation of relieving provisions

Assume that the settlor has retained a remainder interest under a **6–18** settlement which falls within para.8 (as in a classic reverter to settlor trust[18]). The IHT position is as follows:

(i) the settlor is not caught by reservation of benefit because the remainder interest is considered to be property which was never given away (it is a "carve out"); and

(ii) the remainder interest is taxed as part of the settlor's estate.[19]

So far as the para.8 charge is concerned the remainder interest (comprised in the settlor's estate) derives its value from the relevant property (the intangibles comprised in the settlement). An exemption from charge is therefore given under para.11(2) which provides that "the chargeable amount in para.9 is to be reduced by such proportion

---

[18] See Chapter 23.
[19] It is not excluded property for IHT purposes: see IHTA 1984, s.48(1)(b). In practice the value of the interest may be small: *e.g.* if it is subject to overriding powers of appointment vested in the trustees.

as is reasonable to take account of the inclusion of the (remainder interest) in his estate".

> ***Example:***
> In 1987 Julia settles property on interest in possession trusts for her mother. She retains a reversionary interest so that on her mother's death the property will revert to Julia. The trust property initially comprises a house occupied by mother. In 2006 mother moves out and the trust sells the house and then holds cash of £1 million. For the purposes of para.8 the chargeable amount is 5 per cent of £1 million = £50,000. It is this sum which falls to be reduced by reference to para.11(2). For instance if the remainder interest was worth £100,000 (*i.e.* one tenth of the value of the trust fund) then a 10 per cent reduction in the chargeable amount would leave a sum chargeable of £45,000.
>
> This small reduction may result in the settlor wishing to make the election in para.22 (*i.e.* to opt into the reservation of benefit rules).[20]

Anomaly

6–19 It is also somewhat surprising that where the settlor retains an interest in the settlement but his spouse still has a continuing interest in possession he is nevertheless subject to an income tax charge under para.8. Why not limit the charge so that it is only applicable if the spousal interest has terminated? After all, the property is within the spouse's estate for IHT purposes and the settlor already pays income tax on any actual income produced. In practice, arrangements where the spouse continues to retain an interest in possession are usually established for matrimonial or succession rather than for tax saving reasons.

---

[20] See further Chapter 11.

CHAPTER 7

MAIN EXEMPTIONS UNDER THE REGIME

INTRODUCTION

This Chapter considers three main exemptions which, if they apply, **7–01** operate to prevent any of the three charging codes under the Regime (for land, chattels and settled intangible property) from operating.
  These exemptions are as follows:

1. The ownership exemption. This is contained in para.11(1), Sch.15 and exempts property from the Regime if its value is in the donor's estate for IHT purposes. In the same way, when other property is in the donor's estate which derives its value from (say) the land or chattels, exemption is given. The principle is that if the donor pays IHT then he should not also pay income tax. In fact, as we will see, this exemption does not always work in the way intended and can catch innocent transactions as well as let schemes designed to avoid tax escape.

2. The reserved benefit exemption. This exemption is found in para.11(5) and exempts property which is subject to a reservation of benefit and therefore still within the IHT net. Further, there is an exemption where property which derives its value from the relevant property is subject to a reservation (see paras 3(b) and 5). Again the principle is clear—where the donor pays IHT he should not also have to pay income tax under the Regime. In addition, if the property would be subject to a reservation of benefit but for some statutory let out in the inheritance tax legislation, then the intention is that the same statutory let out should apply to exempt the donor from the Regime. In other words, as the Government has decided that certain transactions should qualify for favoured treatment under the reservation of benefit rules, the same should apply under the Regime.

3. The posthumous arrangements exemption. This is found in para.16 of Sch.15 and aims to ensure that persons effecting deeds of variation and similar transactions should not be regarded as the donor for the purposes of the Regime.

Each of these exemptions is discussed in turn.

THE OWNERSHIP EXEMPTION

7–02 This provides that, subject to the qualification considered at 7–06, below, none of the three charging codes applies to an individual at a time when for IHT purposes his estate includes the relevant property.[1]

The purpose of this exemption is straightforward enough—property already within a person's estate is already *prima facie* within the scope of IHT. Were the Regime also to apply to it, there would be an element of double taxation.

Meaning of "IHT estate"

7–03 For IHT purposes the estate of a person includes all the property to which he is beneficially entitled.[2] In this connection two points should be borne in mind.

Interests in possession

7–04 Property already comprised within an individual's free estate will not normally be subject to the Regime, so this provision is therefore likely to be most relevant where an individual has an interest in possession in settled property. For IHT purposes such an individual is treated as being beneficially entitled to the settled property in which his interest subsists, regardless of the term of his interest.[3]

---

[1] See Sch.15, para.11(1)(a). "**Relevant property**" means in relation to paras 3 and 6 where the disposal condition in para.3(2) or para.6(2) is met, the property disposed of; and where the contribution condition in para.3(3) or para.6(3) is met, the property representing the consideration directly or indirectly provided. In relation to para.8 it means intangible property which is or represents property which the chargeable person settled, or added to the settlement after March 17, 1986; Sch.15, para.8(2) and para.11(9).

[2] See IHTA 1984, s.5(1).

[3] See IHTA 1984, s.49(1).

For IHT purposes, a person's estate includes, except immediately **7–05** before he dies, any excluded property to which he is beneficially entitled, including any settled property in which he has an interest in possession.[4]

Inclusion of value covered by an "excluded liability"

The above mentioned qualification is that relevant property is **7–06** not—to the taxpayer's disadvantage—treated as comprised in his estate (and so outside the Regime) if its value is reduced by an "excluded liability", except to the extent that the value of the property exceeds the amount of the excluded liability.[5] For this purpose a liability is an excluded liability if:

(a) the creation of the liability, **and**

(b) any transaction by virtue of which the person's estate came to include the relevant property or any derivative property or by virtue of which the value of the property in his estate came to be derived from the relevant property were associated operations for IHT purposes.[6]

Taking a simple example, if the value of the property is £400,000 and there is an excluded liability of £100,000 the ownership exemption only applies to £300,000 and £100,000 is within the Regime.

The purpose of this provision is believed to be to nullify the effectiveness of "home loan" schemes; see the discussion of these schemes in Chapter 17.

The definition of an excluded liability is not free from difficulties. For instance:

(i) It is a liability "**affecting any property**". What is meant by "affecting" in this context? Presumably property is affected if there is a charge over it (certainly a fixed charge but what of a floating charge?).

(ii) Paragraph 11(7) requires that the creation of the liability and any transaction by which the property became comprised in the taxpayer's estate must be linked within the meaning of the

---

[4] See IHTA 1984, ss.51(1) and 49(1).
[5] See Sch.15, para.11(6).
[6] Sch.15, para.11(7). Associated operations are defined in IHTA 1984, s.268.

associated operations rules. Accordingly a liability which pre-dates the ownership of the taxpayer will not generally be within the definition. Some of these problems are further explored in Chapter 17 in the context of the home loan scheme.

Notice also that just because there is a fully commercial liability (*e.g.* a bank mortgage to purchase property) does not mean it cannot be an excluded liability. If the definition is met then the liability is excluded! This can have implications when unravelling home loan schemes.[7]

Example:
Assume that "Westwinds" is a property now owned and occupied by David who had, some years ago gifted the property to an old aunt. She had left the property to David on her death with a charge over it for an annuity payable to her housekeeper. The value of the property is £250,000 and the charge is for £120,000. The analysis is as follows:

(1) the Regime will *prima facie* apply since David occupies Westwinds; and

(2) the disposal condition is satisfied since he had given the property to the aunt after March 17, 1986.

However, the property is in his estate and so *prima facie* covered by the ownership exemption. However, the charge satisfies the definition of an excluded liability so that only £130,000 of the value of the property is within the ownership exemption.

DERIVED PROPERTY

7–07 Paragraph 11(1) does not just cover situations where the donor's estate directly includes the relevant property. Paragraph 11(1)(b) provides that the Regime does not apply to an individual in respect of relevant property if that individual's estate includes property which *derives* its value from that relevant property.[8]

This exemption is more subtle than the first. It means that although an individual does not own the relevant property or have an interest in possession in it, an exemption will apply if other property to which

---

[7] See Chapter 17.
[8] Sch 15, para.11(1)(b). For the meaning of "Relevant property" see n.1.

he is beneficially entitled derives its value from the relevant property.

Example:
Assume that X occupies land which is the only asset owned by a company of which he is the sole shareholder. The land is not in his estate and so is not covered by the ownership exemption. But the shares derive their value from the land and so are covered by the value exemption.

The "substantially less" rule

It may be that the value of the derivative property—in the example **7–08** just given, the shares—is less than the value of the relevant property (the land). If the value of the derivative property is "substantially less" than the value of the relevant property, then the amount on which tax is charged under the Regime[9] is reduced by such proportion as is reasonable to take account of the inclusion of the derivative property in his estate.[10] It is expected that the Revenue will produce guidance as to the meaning of "substantially less". It may be that the CGT taper relief rules will be followed so that "substantially less" means a reduction in value of more than 20 per cent but the position is currently unclear.

Assume that X owns 75 per cent of the ordinary shares of X Ltd, that his brother Y owns the remaining 25 per cent of the ordinary shares, and that X occupies land owned by X Ltd in circumstances such that X is within the charge on land, *e.g.* because he provided the funds with which X Ltd acquired the land. The value of X's shares will be "substantially less" than the value of the land, so X will not be wholly outside the charge. The amount on which tax is charged will be reduced by, the authors suggest, 75 per cent. Difficulties may arise when the company is funded by loans rather than by share capital (see 20–34).

Anomaly

What would the position be if Mrs X owned the remaining 25 per **7–09** cent of the ordinary share capital of X Ltd, albeit Mr X has

---

[9] Strictly, the appropriate rental value in para.4, the appropriate amount in para.7 and the chargeable amount in para.9 (as the case may be); FA 2004, Sch.15, para.11(2).
[10] Sch.15, paras 11(1)(b) and (2).

73

contributed the entire purchase price? There is no provision to take into account her shareholding in X Ltd in determining X's position. This is so notwithstanding that, as will be seen below, the legislation generally attempts to take arrangements involving spouses outside the Regime, at least in relation to land and chattels.[11]

Next, consider the position if Mrs X also occupies the land. The value of her shares in X Ltd will be substantially less than the value of the land so, if she has contributed to the purchase price of the land she will not be outside the charge. Is the amount on which she is charged reduced by less than 25 per cent, because her shareholding is a minority shareholding? If she has contributed to the purchase price of the land then she cannot give her 25 per cent to Mr X and escape the charge.

It is not difficult to envisage valuation problems arising in relation to the "not substantially less" test.

Excluded liabilities

7–10 The excluded liabilities restriction that operates in respect of the direct ownership exemption also operates in respect of the derived value exemption, regardless of whether or not the "substantially less" rule applies.[12] So, the procedure is **first** to apply the excluded liabilities rule and **then** to apply the substantially less rule.

> ***Example:***
> Assume Y sets up an interest in possession trust for himself which owns shares in X Ltd. The shares are worth £750,000, but are subject to a mortgage of £250,000 which is an excluded liability. The company owns quoted investments worth £250,000 and a house, in which Y lives, worth £500,000. Accordingly, the shares derive two-thirds of their value from the house.
>
> (i) Apply the **excluded liability** rule: £250,000 of the value of the shares is not treated as comprised in Y's estate for the purpose of the exemption. Y is chargeable under para.8 on £250,000. The rules in respect of land also have to be applied.
>
> (ii) Shares worth £500,000 comprised in the estate of Y of which two-thirds is attributable to the value of the house.

[11] Of course were she to gift him her 25 per cent shareholding, the full value exclusion would then apply assuming Mr X has contributed entirely to the purchase price.

[12] See FA 2004, Sch.15, para.11(6).

Hence the tax charge is on relevant property having a value of £133,333 (one-third of £500,000).

Since (i) produces a higher chargeable amount than (ii), para.18 requires (i) to be adopted.

RESERVED BENEFIT EXEMPTION

The second main exemption is contained in paras 11(3) and (5). **7–11**
None of the three charging codes applies to a person by reference to any relevant property[13] at a time when that property is either caught by the reservation of benefit legislation in respect of that person or would be so caught but for a statutory exemption in FA 1986 applying.[14]

Assume that X gives his son a house which X continues to occupy in circumstances where the house is property subject to a reservation. In such a case, the property will be within the IHT net when X dies and so there is no need for the Regime to apply.

Derivative reserved benefit

Similarly the Regime does not apply to relevant property[15] from **7–12** which reserved benefit property derives its value.[16] Assume X owns shares in a company which purchases a house in which he lives. If X gives the shares to his son and lives in the house rent free, he will reserve a benefit in respect of the shares, which will be property subject to a reservation and so within para.11(5)(a) (see 7–11, above).

Accordingly, any para.8 charge (on settled intangible property) will not apply. The house, which is the relevant property for the para.3 charge (occupation of land) will not be caught by the reservation of benefit rules. However, the shares derive their value from the house, and so the house will be exempt under the derivative reserved benefit exemption.

Property which qualifies for the reserved benefit exemption and the derived reserved benefit exemption falls into categories.

---

[13] For the meaning of "Relevant property" see n.1, above.
[14] See Sch.15, para.11(3) and (5). The IHT reservation of benefit rules have been outlined in Chapter 2.
[15] The meaning of "Relevant property" is set out in n.1, above.
[16] See Sch.15, paras 11(3)(b) and (5).

(A) Property subject to a reservation

7–13 The basic category is property that would fall to be treated as property which in relation to the individual is property subject to a reservation for IHT purposes.[17] Although the reason for using the phrase "would fall to be treated" is clear enough in relation to the three exemptions discussed, below, because they make certain assumptions, the authors assume its use in relation to the first condition is based on the fact that "property subject to a reservation" is defined for IHT purposes by reference to the "relevant period",[18] *e.g.* the period of seven years ending with the death of the individual concerned, and at the juncture when the Regime is being applied the "relevant period" will normally not have arisen.

This requirement is less straightforward than it seems for the simple reason that the Revenue and the taxpayer may not see eye-to-eye on the question of whether or not property is caught by the reservation of benefit rules. There is, for instance, a difference of opinion between the Revenue and many practitioners as to whether or not certain reversionary lease schemes are within the reservation of benefit rules; see the discussion in Chapter 15. Such differences of opinion may cause problems under self-assessment.

(B) Property subject to a reservation but for certain exemptions

7–14 This category is not particularly exciting. It is that the property would be caught by the reservation of benefit rules but for the exemptions given by FA 1986, s.102(5)(d)–(i).[19] These exemptions apply where[20] the disposal by way of gift is an IHT exempt transfer by reason of various provisions in the Inheritance Tax Act 1984, namely: s.23 (gift to charities); s.24 (gifts to political parties); s.24A (gifts to housing associations); s.25 (gifts for national purposes, etc); s.27 (maintenance funds for historic buildings)[21]; and s.28 (employee trusts). This simply preserves the favoured IHT treatment available

---

[17] See Sch.15, para.11(5)(a).

[18] See FA 1986, s.102(1).

[19] On the assumption that the limitation in the reservation of benefit provisions concerning outright cash gifts did not prevent the provisions from applying; see FA 2004, Sch.15, para.11(8), discussed at 7–20.

[20] See Sch.15, para.11(5)(b).

[21] This condition does not exclude the application of the Regime in relation to a maintenance fund for an historic building unless the property in question remains subject to trusts which comply with the requirements of IHTA 1984, Sch.4, para.3(1); Sch.15, para.11(10).

to such property. The draftsman has simply used the IHT legislation for ease of reference.[22]

(C) UNDIVIDED SHARES IN LAND

This category consists of property which would[23] fall within the **7–15** reservation of benefit rules but for the let-out in FA 1986, s.102B(4) in respect of the shared occupation of land by a donor and donee.[24] This ensures the Regime does not apply to land sharing arrangements blessed by the reservation of benefit provisions. This exemption is of limited scope but extremely important in practice. A typical case where it is in point would be where Mrs A gives a 50 per cent interest in her house to her daughter and both occupy the property sharing all outgoings. Not only does Mrs A not reserve a benefit in the gifted moiety but she is not caught by the pre-owned assets charge.[25]

The exemption also applies to such arrangements which came into being before March 9, 1999.[26] Such arrangements are not within s.102B, which has effect only in relation to disposals of an undivided share of an interest in land made on or after that date, but benefited from an earlier Ministerial statement exempting them from the reservation of benefit rules.[27]

(D) PARAGRAPH 6 LET-OUTS

The fourth category is that the property would be caught by the **7–16** reservation of benefit rules[28] but for the application of the exclusion of benefit provisions in FA 1986, s.102C(3) and Sch.20, para.6(1)(a)(b).[29] This category requires careful consideration and can be divided into two let-outs.

[22] It may be noted that the *de minimis* exemption ("or virtually to the entire exclusion of the donor") has not been replicated. However such minimal user of the property will presumably fall within the £5,000 annual exemption.

[23] On the assumption that the limitation in the reservation of benefit provisions concerning outright cash gifts did not prevent the provisions from applying; see FA 2004, Sch.15, para.11(8), discussed in 7–14.

[24] See, FA 2004, Sch.15, para.11(5)(c).

[25] For a detailed consideration of the planning opportunities and pitfalls, see Chapter 22.

[26] See, FA 2004, Sch.15, para.11(5)(c).

[27] This statement is set out in Chapter 22.

[28] See FA 2004, Sch.15, para.11(5)(d); on the assumption where the contribution condition in para.3(3) or 6(3) is satisfied that the limitation in the reservation of benefit provisions concerning outright cash gifts did not prevent the provisions from applying; see FA 2004, Sch.15, para.11(8), discussed below.

[29] See FA 2004, Sch.15, para.11(5)(d).

7–17 The first let out is that in determining whether any property is enjoyed to the entire or virtually to the entire exclusion of the donor:

> (a) retention or assumption by the donor of the actual occupation of land or actual enjoyment of an incorporeal right over the land, and

> (b) retention or assumption by the donor of actual possession of the chattel

are disregarded if the retention or assumption is for full consideration.

This is a most important exemption since the full consideration provision has been widely used in practice as a way of avoiding the reservation of benefit provisions.

> *Example:*
> A gives his house to his son B and continues to occupy the property under an agreement for full consideration: not only will he not fall foul of the reservation of benefit rules but the pre-owned assets charge will be equally inapplicable. Of course, it will be important for him to be able to show that he is furnishing full consideration and the evidence of experts in the market should be obtained. Further it will be important to show that the arrangement is reviewed and the consideration adjusted in accordance with market conditions (in effect there should be "rent review clauses").

Many taxpayers who would wish to give away their house with a view to saving IHT cannot afford to pay a full rent for continued occupation or fear that they may not, in the future, be able to afford to pay that rent. Hence for the average taxpayer these arrangements are unavailable. Of course, instead of paying a rent (with consequent risks of future upward increases at a time when the taxpayer may not have the finances available) a lease could be granted, say for the taxpayer's life, at a premium arrived at on an actuarial basis.[30] Provided that it can be shown that this is "full consideration", the exemption will apply. Bear in mind that any rent/premium paid will be subject to income tax in the hands of the recipient.

---

[30] Provided that full consideration is paid, this will not create an IHT settlement under the lease for life provisions in IHTA 1984, s.43(3).

Paragraph 6(1)(a) is also important in the context of chattels where schemes have been set up on the basis of gifts and lease back. These are considered in detail in Chapter 18.[31]

Change in donor's circumstances: para.6(1)(b)

The second let out, in para.6(1)(b), is that in certain cases occupation **7-18** by the donor of land is disregarded if certain conditions concerning *inter alia* changes in his circumstances are satisfied. This provision is severely restricted: *e.g.* the donor must have become unable to maintain himself through age, infirmity or otherwise and the occupation must represent reasonable provision by the donee (a relative) for the care and maintenance of the donor.

Ambiguity in wording

There has been some confusion as to whether the full consideration **7-19** exemption does in fact apply due to the use of the word "and" in para.11(5)(d). Paragraph 11(5)(d) gives exemption to property (or derived property) which would be subject to the reservation of benefit provisions "but for s.102C(3) of **and** para.6 of Sch.20, to the 1986 Act." Section 102C(3) deals only with post-March 1999 gifts of land and (broadly) provides that there is no reservation of benefit where the donor reoccupies due to hardship. Paragraph 6 on the other hand applies to gifts of any property made after March 17, 1986 and gives both the full consideration and the hardship exemption.

Is para.11(5)(d) limited just to gifts of land made on or after March 9, 1999 where the donor reoccupies due to hardship? If so, then the full consideration exemption referred to above does not apply. Further, if this were the case then the reference to para.6 in para.11(5)(d) would be meaningless. Indeed para.6(1)(b) does not itself apply anyway to post-March 8, 1999 disposals of land (which are by definition covered by s.102C(3)), and therefore arguably it would never be possible to satisfy both s.102C(3) and para.6 of Sch.20.

---

[31] The IHT legislation provides no guidance on how to arrive at "full consideration". However, it will depend upon the benefits enjoyed by the donor in the particular case. Contrast the provisions in the Regime dealing with "rental value" which provides fairly precise guidance as to the terms of the hypothetical lease. See 11–12 for a consideration of the effects of opting into the reservation rules and then paying full consideration.

It is accordingly thought that the "and" should be read disjunctively so that arrangements over any property where full consideration is paid or (in the case of land) the donor reoccupies due to hardship are covered. The slight concern against this reading is that para.11(5)(d) does not refer to s.102A(3) and s.102B(3) which give favoured inheritance tax treatment to full consideration arrangements in respect of disposals of land post-March 8, 1999. If the draftsman felt the need to specify s.102C(3) in para.11(5)(d) why did he not also cross-refer to these sections?

Although the problem was raised at Report Stage by Howard Flight (a Conservative M.P.) the Paymaster General did not clarify the point. Given the importance of the full consideration exemption it is to be hoped this point will be expressly clarified in the guidance notes. It is believed that the Revenue accept that the full consideration let-out is avoidable.

Cash gifts

7–20   The reservation of benefit property tracing provisions do not apply to property purchased with outright (*i.e.* non-settled) gifts of currency.[32] Accordingly, if X gives £100,000 to his son and his son of his own volition uses it to purchase property which X occupies the reservation of benefit provisions cannot apply in respect of the purchased property. The Revenue is understood to have accepted that this is the case and it is doubtless one of the reasons for the introduction of the pre-owned assets charge.

The Regime takes account of this by providing that if the para.3(3) or para.6(3) contribution condition is met (see Chapters 3 and 4) the fact that the reservation of benefit provisions would not apply to the cash contribution is ignored in deciding whether the three exemptions discussed above operate.[33] Thus, continuing with the example in 7–20, the contribution condition in para.3(3) will be met. In determining whether any of the three exemptions apply, it is **assumed** that the reservation of benefit provisions apply.

This means that cash gifts may be taken outside the Regime under those exemptions. Accordingly, if X provides full consideration for his occupation, the let out under para.11(5)(d) should be available (subject to the point raised above regarding the reading of the word "and").

---

[32] See FA 1986, Sch.20, para.2(2)(b) and see Chapter 25.

[33] See Sch.15, para.11(8): since the tracing limitation does not operate in respect of settled property, there is no need to disapply the limitation in relation to the para.8 charge on settled intangible property.

Excluded property

Assume X dies, having reserved a benefit in respect of excluded **7–21** property held on discretionary trusts. Revenue practice in such a case is not to impose a charge on the property on the basis that, as excluded property, it does not form part of X's estate immediately before he died.[34] But this does not prevent the property from being reserved benefit property for the purposes of this exemption. Similarly, if X reserves a benefit in company shares but occupies a house owned by the company then he can generally rely on para.11(3)(b) (reservation of benefit in derived property) to give him exemption under the Regime in respect of his occupation of the land.

The "substantially less" rule[35]

The substantially less rule does not apply where the person directly **7–22** reserves a benefit in the relevant property. It is applicable in relation to derivative reserved benefit property: for example, where someone reserves a benefit in, say, company shares but occupies land owned by the company which has been owned by him. In these circumstances if the person reserves a benefit in company shares whose value is "substantially less" than the relevant property the rule discussed above at 7–08 applies.

The "excluded liabilities" rule

The excluded liabilities rule does not apply either to any property or **7–23** any derived property in which the donor reserves a benefit.

Posthumous arrangements

Any disposition made by a person in relation to an interest in the **7–24** estate of a deceased person is disregarded if under s.17 of the IHTA 1984 that disposition is not treated as a transfer of value for IHT purposes.[36] Section 17 provides that none of the following is a transfer of value:

---

[34] See Chapter 20.
[35] Sch.15, para.11(4).
[36] See Sch.15, para.16. See Chapter 29 for a consideration of the use of instruments of variation.

(a) variations and disclaimers falling within s.142;

(b) dispositions made pursuant to precatory trusts within s.143;

(c) an election by a surviving spouse under s.47A of the Administration of Estates Act 1925; or

(d) the renunciation of a claim to legitimacy within the period mentioned in s.147(6).

The exemption does not extend to IHTA 1984, s.93 disclaimers, apparently on the basis that in order for a disclaimer to be legally effective it must be made before any benefit is taken from the entitlement and the person disclaiming is not as a matter of property law treated as having made a disposition. Hence it is assumed that any subsequent arrangements under which the person disclaiming occupies property that has been disclaimed would not be caught by the Regime anyway because the basic disposal condition is not satisfied.

Tax trap—the missing transfer of value?

7–25 Although the draftsman's intention was clearly to replicate the IHT favoured treatment, the position in one case is not entirely free from doubt. Assume X dies leaving his estate to his widow who within two years of X's death enters into a deed of variation under which, instead of taking X's estate absolutely, she decides to settle it on trusts under which she retains an interest in possession with remainders over to her children. This would be a perfectly valid deed of variation for IHT purposes, but will it qualify for favoured treatment under the Regime? Under s.49(1) of the 1984 Act the widow will, by virtue of her interest in possession under the new settlement, still be treated as owning X's estate with the result that she will not as such make a transfer of value. The question then arises as to whether s.17, which provides that a s.142 deed is not a transfer of value, will nevertheless be relevant for the purposes of obtaining protection under para.16.

On a narrow reading it is arguable that the deed is not a transfer of value because of s.49(1) not by virtue of s.17 of the 1984 Act. Therefore, para.16 does not apply to protect the gift.

However, it is not thought this view is correct. The variation is within s.142(1) if it is a variation made within two years of death and the other conditions are met. Section 17 then states that a variation or disclaimer to which s.142 applies is not a transfer of value. The fact that the variation may not be a transfer of value for some other reason as well would not appear to matter. Hence the better view is that the

Regime does not apply to such variations. If the Regime did apply, then although it would not matter while the widow retained an interest in possession, it could become a problem if that interest were terminated and she continued to be able to benefit from the settlement.

CHAPTER 8

TERRITORIAL SCOPE

8–01 This chapter sets out the territorial exemptions and limitations given under para.12 of Sch.15. In particular, the scope of the Regime is limited under para.12 by reference to a person's residence and domicile and to the *situs* of property.

BASIC RELIEFS

8–02 There are three basic reliefs:

1. the non-residence relief under para.12(1): the Regime does not apply to non-UK residents at all wherever they are domiciled;

2. the *situs* relief under para.12(2): the Regime does not apply to persons not domiciled or deemed domiciled in the UK in respect of property situated outside the UK; and

3. the settled excluded property relief under para.12(3): the Regime does not apply to settled property which is excluded property for IHT purposes even if the person is resident and deemed domiciled in the UK.

Further exemptions

8–03 Before looking at each of these reliefs in more detail it is important to appreciate that the para.12 rules, if read in isolation, would give a distorted picture of the way the Regime operates where foreign domiciliaries are concerned. The para.12 rules must be read in conjunction with the para.11 exemptions discussed in Chapter 7. The interaction of paras 11 and 12 of Sch.15 is discussed in Chapter 20.

Paragraph 12(1): non-residents

The Regime does not apply to a person for any year of assessment **8–04** during which he is not resident in the United Kingdom.[1]

FOREIGN DOMICILIARIES

There are two reliefs regulating the treatment of foreign dom- **8–05** iciliaries. These provisions are similar to, but by no means identical to, the IHT rules. The IHT deemed domicile rules apply for the purposes of both provisions and it will therefore be helpful to review the IHT deemed domicile rules before considering the Regime rules.[2]

Deemed domicile rules

By s.267 of the IHTA 1984 an individual is deemed to be domiciled **8–06** in the United Kingdom for most IHT purposes even though he is domiciled elsewhere under general law if either one of two tests are satisfied, as follows.

Three-year rule

The individual will be deemed to be domiciled in the United **8–07** Kingdom at any time if he was domiciled in the United Kingdom within the three *years* immediately preceding that time.[3]

Seventeen-year rule

The individual will be deemed to be domiciled in the United **8–08** Kingdom at any time ("the relevant time") if he was resident in the

---

[1] See Sch.15, para.12(1).
[2] See Sch.15, para.12(4).
[3] See IHTA 1984, s.267(1)(a).

United Kingdom in not less than 17 of the 20 *years of assessment* ending with the year of assessment in which the relevant time falls. Residence for this purpose is determined as for income tax, but without regard to any dwelling-house available for the use of the person in question.[4]

The calendar year trap

8–09 Note that there is a trap here. The three-year rule is normally thought of as applying to a person who emigrates from the United Kingdom, while the 17-year rule is normally thought of as applying to a foreign domiciliary who is a longstanding resident of the United Kingdom. While this may normally be correct, it is important to bear in mind that the 17-year rule can also apply to a United Kingdom domiciliary who emigrates from the United Kingdom, with potentially catastrophic results. Assume that Fred is a United Kingdom domiciliary who has lived in the United Kingdom all his life. On retiring, he emigrated to Spain, arriving there on January 1, 2002, at which time he became domiciled in Spain as a matter of general law. Under the three-year rule he ceased to be domiciled in the United Kingdom on January 1, 2005, but under the 17-year rule he will not cease to be domiciled in the United Kingdom until April 6, 2005.

The basic relief—para.12(2)

8–10 Where an individual is not domiciled in the United Kingdom for IHT purposes, the Regime does not apply to him unless the property by reference to which the Regime operates is situated in the United Kingdom.[5] Assume Tatiana, a foreign domiciliary, occupies foreign *situs* land owned by an offshore trust of which she is the settlor. Paragraph 12(2) prevents the Regime from applying to the land. But if Tatiana becomes domiciled in the United Kingdom the protection of para.12(2) will cease to be available.[6]

Comparison with IHT

8–11 The approach adopted under para.12(2) differs significantly from the IHT approach to foreign *situs* property. Under IHT a basic distinction

---

[4] See IHTA 1984, s.267(1)(b).

[5] See Sch.15, para.12(2).

[6] Whether she is then subject to a charge under the Regime will depend on whether any other reliefs or exemptions are available—see Chapter 20.

is drawn between settled and non-settled property. Under the Regime, on the other hand, the relief in para.12(2) simply looks at the domicile of the individual and the *situs* of the Regime property, regardless of whether such property is owned by an individual, comprised in a settlement, or, indeed, held by a company.

The settled property relief—para.12(3)

A more complex protection is given in para.12(3) which provides **8–12** that "in the application of this Schedule to a person who was at any time domiciled outside the United Kingdom for IHT purposes, no regard is to be had to any foreign *situs* property which is excluded property" by reason of being comprised in a settlement made by a settlor who was not domiciled in the United Kingdom when he made the settlement.[7] This confers protection in relation to individuals who though domiciled abroad when setting up the trust become domiciled in the United Kingdom and who are accordingly unable to shelter under the basic rule in para.12(2). As with para.12(2) it covers only foreign *situs* property (since UK property by definition cannot be excluded).

Returning to the example of Tatiana, although the basic relief will cease to be available if she becomes domiciled in the United Kingdom the settled property relief will be available so long as she was domiciled abroad when she made the settlement.

It is not clear whether the settled property relief applies only in respect of an individual who has become domiciled in the United Kingdom, but given the basic relief, nothing appears to turn on this. It is, however, arguably unclear whether the effect of para.12(3), given the instruction to ignore excluded property for all Sch.15 purposes, is that one then also ignores such excluded property for para.11 purposes. In that event, the para.11 exemptions might not be available (see Chapter 20). It is believed that the Revenue does not take this view.

Comparison with IHT

The settled property relief is similar but less generous than the IHT **8–13** rule that applies in determining whether property comprised in a settlement is excluded property, in two ways.

---

[7] For the definition of an excluded property settlement for IHT purposes, see IHTA 1984, s.48(3).

First, because so far as IHT is concerned, favoured treatment depends only on the domicile of the settlor. Where the Regime is concerned, on the other hand, both the domicile of the settlor and the domicile of the individual who is potentially chargeable are relevant, though it appears that so far as the individual is concerned, all that matters is that he was not domiciled in the United Kingdom at some time, whether or not that time occurred during the year of assessment in which he is potentially chargeable.

Secondly, it is vital to note that the settled excluded property relief affords relief only in respect of settled property. Assume Max, a foreign domiciliary occupies foreign *situs* land owned by an offshore company all the shares in which are owned by trustees of a discretionary settlement made by him. So far as IHT is concerned, the relevant asset is the shares in the company which will be excluded property (because non *situs*) even if Max becomes domiciled in the United Kingdom. Under the Regime, on the other hand, there are two relevant assets—the shares, and the land. If Max becomes domiciled in the United Kingdom the settled property relief will protect him in relation to the shares (being settled foreign *situs* property which is excluded property), but it will not protect him in relation to the foreign *situs* land, because that land is not settled property. It may be, however, that Max is protected in respect of the land by a para.11 exemption: see Chapter 20.

EXEMPT GILTS[8]

8–14 The Regime does not afford favoured treatment to settled exempt gilts, but this is unlikely to be important since both non-settled exempt gilts and settled exempt gilts will normally qualify for favoured IHT treatment only if owned beneficially or (in the case of settled gilts) held in trust by a person who is not ordinarily resident in the United Kingdom. Such a person will be non-resident and so outside the territorial scope of the Regime anyway.

[8] IHTA 1984, s.6(2).

CHAPTER 9

£5,000 ANNUAL EXEMPTION

An individual is not chargeable in a year of assessment if the *aggregate* of:

a) the appropriate rental value under para.4(2);

b) the appropriate amount under para.7(2); and

c) the chargeable amount under para.9

does not exceed £5,000.[1]

Not a nil band

Assuming a notional five per cent "benefit", the broad effect of this **9–02** exemption is to take out of the charge property worth up to £100,000. This figure does not, however, constitute an equivalent to the IHT nil rate band because if the £5,000 exemption (even by £1) is exceeded the exemption is lost altogether.[2]

Tax trap: the ungenerous exemption

The exemption is less generous than it looks. Assume A falls within **9–03** para.3 in respect of land worth £150,000, that the appropriate rental value is £7,500 and that A pays B £5,000 per year in rent. The amount on which A is actually chargeable is only £2,500 (£7,500 less £5,000) but the exemption operates by reference not to that amount

---

[1] See Sch.15, para.13(1)–(3). (The figure proposed in the original consultation document had been £2,500).

[2] A similar position applies to the Stamp Duty Land Tax rate bands.

but by reference to the appropriate rental value, *i.e.* £7,500. The exemption therefore does not apply at all. The exemption also operates in this way in relation to chattels.[3]

Note, by contrast, that where an individual pays income tax or CGT in respect of settled intangible property, the tax allowance he is given (see 6–17) reduces the para.8 chargeable amount.[4]

A married couple both of whom are with the POA charge (*e.g.* in respect of a property which they jointly occupy) will each have a £5000 annual exemption. In such a case, property worth in the region of £200,000 may not be caught by the Regime.

Motive and the annual exemption

9–04 Concerns have been expressed that individuals who enter into arrangements without any intention of avoiding IHT might find themselves caught by the Pre-Owned Assets charge. Certainly there is no motive requirement. However, in some cases the £5,000 annual exemption will help: in others the general exemptions will assist in preventing any charge.

Take the example of Mrs A who owns her flat worth £200,000 and is concerned to ensure that the property will pass to her daughter Maisie. As she has no other significant assets, IHT saving is not an issue: all she is concerned about is ensuring that Maisie benefits from the flat. With this in mind she might:

(a) gift the flat to Maisie and rely upon her to allow her to continue in occupation; or

(b) transfer the flat into an interest in possession settlement under which she retains the interest in possession with remainder to Maisie. As compared to (a) Mrs A now has a right (under the settlement) to occupy.

Is the regime capable of applying to Mrs A in these circumstances? It is irrelevant that she is not motivated by a wish to avoid IHT since, as noted, the Regime takes no account of motive. Nor will the *de minimis* exemption help given that value of occupation benefit is likely to exceed £5,000. As can be seen Mrs A is not therefore in

---

[3] The payment of consideration is irrelevant under para.8.
[4] Sch.15, para.9(1).

any sense a "special case" and the reason why the Regime will not apply follows from general principles. In the case of (a) because of Mr A's gift falls within the reservation of benefit rules, the Regime does not apply.[5] In the case of (b), the Regime does not apply because Mrs A's estate includes the relevant property.[6]

---

[5] See the para.11(5)(a) exemption from charge.
[6] See the para.11(1)(a) exemption from charge.

CHAPTER 10

AVOIDANCE OF DOUBLE CHARGES

10–01 The legislation makes provision to prevent the imposition of certain double charges to income tax.

Employment benefits charge

10–02 It may be that in a year of assessment a person is chargeable to income tax in respect of his occupation of any land or his possession or use of any chattel under both the benefits code in Pt 3 of the Income Tax (Earnings and Pensions) Act 2003 and the Regime. In that case the Pt 3 charge takes priority and displaces the Regime, except to the extent that the amount chargeable under the Regime exceeds the amount treated as earnings under Pt 3.[1]

Double charges under the Regime

10–03 It may be that a person is chargeable under either para.3 or para.6 by reason of his occupation of land or his possession or use of a chattel and under para.8 by reference to intangible property which derives its value, whether in whole or in part, from that land or chattel.

> ***Example:***
> Assume X effected an *Eversden* scheme[2] in respect of company shares. Mrs X's interest in possession has been terminated and the shares are held on interest in possession trusts for X's children. The company has now purchased land which is occupied by X. In these circumstances he is assessable under

[1] See Sch.15, para.19.
[2] See Chapter 16 for a detailed consideration of *Eversden* schemes.

para.3. in respect of the land and para.8 in respect of the shares (assuming he is not caught by Pt 3 of ITEPA 2003).

Accordingly, he is charged under whichever provision produces the higher chargeable amount, which is the amount that is taken into account in applying the annual exemption.[3]

If the shares were advanced to the children absolutely then the para.8 charge would cease to apply (the intangible property would not be settled) but the para.3 charge would still be applicable so long as X occupied the land.

---

[3] Sch.15, paras 18(1) and (2).

Chapter 11

OPT OUT ELECTIONS INTO RESERVATION OF BENEFIT

11–01 A taxpayer who is otherwise caught by the Pre-Owned Assets charge can avoid the payment of income tax by opting out of the Regime and into the IHT reservation of benefit provisions. The position differs slightly according to whether the individual is chargeable in respect of land/chattels or settled intangible property.

One vital point of general application is that the owner of the property, who will be the person primarily liable for any IHT resulting from the election having been made has no say in the matter.

Land and chattel opt outs

11–02 To opt out of the charge on land and chattels the individual:

    (a) must be chargeable[1] in any year of assessment (called "the initial year") under para.3 or para.6 by reference to his enjoyment of the property in question, and

    (b) must not have been chargeable under para.3 or para.6, as the case may be, in respect of any previous year of assessment by reference to his enjoyment of the relevant property, or of any other property for which the relevant property has been substituted.[2]

If these conditions are satisfied he can elect that the Regime shall not apply to him by reference to the relevant property in the initial year

---

[1] If he did not opt out of the charge. It is thought that a purported election is of no validity unless the charging provisions of Sch.15 would otherwise apply. In a case where the taxpayer is uncertain whether the Schedule applies or not, he may consider making a precautionary election: see 17–21.

[2] See Sch.15, para.21(1).

and subsequent years of assessment and that instead, so long as he continues to enjoy that property or any substituted property the chargeable proportion of the property is to be treated for IHT purposes as property subject to a reservation to which ss.102(3) and (4) of the Finance Act 1986 shall apply.[3] For these purposes, a person "enjoys" property where land is concerned if he occupies the land and where a chattel is concerned if he has possession or the use of the chattel.[4]

The chargeable proportion

The meaning of "the chargeable proportion" in relation to any **11–03** property is determined by reference to the formulae that apply for determining:

a) in a case involving land, the appropriate rental value; and

b) in a case involving chattels the appropriate amount.

These formulae are discussed in Chapters 3 and 4 respectively. For the purposes of the election, they are subject to two qualifications.[5] First, that the transactions to be taken into account in determining the numerator of the fractions involved included transactions after the time when the election takes effect as well as transactions before that time.[6] Secondly, that any reference in para.4(2) or para.7(2) to the valuation date were a reference:

a) in the case of property falling within s.102(3), to the date of the death of the person; and

b) in the case of property falling within s.102(4), to the date on which the property ceases to be treated as property subject to a reservation.[7]

The reason for adopting the "chargeable proportion" test is to reflect **11–04** the fact that, in appropriate cases, some of the value of the property in question will already be included in the individual's IHT estate. Assume X effected an "*Ingram*" scheme by giving away the freehold interest in a chattel subject to a lease over it which he has reserved to himself. At his death the chattel is worth £400,000 and the

[3] See Sch.15, para.21(2).
[4] See Sch.15, para.21(4).
[5] See Sch.15, para.21(3).
[6] See Sch.15, para.21(3)(b).
[7] See Sch.15, para.21(3)(a).

encumbered freehold £300,000. The chargeable proportion of the chattel would be:

$$\frac{£300,000}{£400,000}$$

so that only 75 per cent of the property would be treated as property subject to a reservation. This would broadly reflect the fact that the value of the lease was already included in the individual's estate. (It is not clear how the loss of marriage value would be treated).

Intangible settled property opt out

11–05 To opt out of the charge on intangible settled property the individual:

    (a) must be chargeable[8] in any year of assessment (called the "initial year") under para.8 by reference to the property in question ("the relevant property"), and

    (b) must not have been chargeable under para.8 in respect of any previous year of assessment by reference to the relevant property or any property which the relevant property represents or is derived from.[9]

Where an individual is subject to the para.8 charge on settled intangible property he can elect that the Regime shall not apply to him in the initial year by reference to the relevant property or any property which represents or is derived from the relevant property and subsequently, instead the relevant property (and any representative or derivative property) shall be treated for IHT purposes as property subject to a reservation and ss.102(3) and (4) of the Finance Act 1986 shall apply so long as two conditions are satisfied, *i.e.* so long as:

    (a) the relevant property (or the representative or derivative property) remains comprised in the settlement, and

    (b) any income arising under the settlement would be treated by virtue of s.660A as his income.[10]

---

[8] If he did not opt out of the charge.
[9] Sch.15, para.22(1).
[10] Sch.15, paras 22(2) and (3).

Double trouble

It is to be noted that the entirety of the property in respect of which **11–06** the election is made will be subject to the reservation of benefit regime, because the opt out provisions for settled intangible property contain nothing equivalent to "the chargeable proportion" rule that operates in respect of land and chattels. In other words, there is no reduction for the value of the interest retained. So, if X settled property on trusts under which he retained a reversionary interest and he opts out of the Regime there will be an element of double taxation. First, the reversionary interest will not be excluded property for IHT purposes and so on his death will be comprised in his estate. Subject, for example, to the spouse exemption, it will then attract a charge to IHT. Secondly, the whole of the settled property will be subject to the reservation of benefit rules with the result that the value of the property *prima facie* subject to the IHT will exceed the value of the settled property. This contrasts with the position where a Regime charge is imposed on the settled property when an allowance is made for the reversionary interest; see 6–18.

It might be thought that the reversionary interest should be excluded from the election on the basis that because para.11(1) provides exemption for this property in relation to the income tax charge, it is not necessary nor even possible to elect over the reversionary interest. However, para.11(2) (the "substantially less" rule) does not mean the person is not actually chargeable under para.9 on the relevant property only that the charge is reduced. Paragraph 22(1)(a) refers to a person being chargeable "by reference to any property" ("the relevant property") which *would* include the reversionary interest. It is not, under the legislation, a separate piece of property which is excluded from the election.

> ### Example:
> George has a remainder interest in a trust which holds cash. The interest will vest on the death of his mother who has an interest in possession. George does not elect. The cash is worth £1 million, the remainder interest is worth £50,000. He pays income tax on 5 per cent of £950,000.
>
> If he elects, he pays IHT on his death on £1 million (the property subject to the reservation) and on £50,000 (the remainder interest already in his estate).

The election

The election must be made in the prescribed manner on or before the **11–07** relevant filing date which is January 31 in the year of assessment that immediately follows the initial year[11] unless the individual in question can show a reasonable excuse for the failure to make the election before that date.[12] Where he can do so, the election must be made on or before such later date as may be prescribed.[13] Once made, any election may be withdrawn or amended at any time during the individual's life before the relevant filing date.[14]

Subject to its being withdrawn or amended, the election takes effect for IHT purposes from the beginning of the initial year or, if later, the date on which the person would[15] have first become chargeable under the Regime by reference to the property to which the election relates.[16]

> ***Example:***
> A gives cash to his son in 2003. In January 2007 he moves into a house bought by the son with the cash. He has occupied within seven years of the gift so is caught under para.3(3). A needs to make an election at the latest by January 31, 2008. He can revoke that election before January 31, 2009.

Factors to be taken into account in deciding whether to elect

11–08 Regard needs to be had to a number of factors in deciding whether or not to make the election.

Opting into reservation of benefit

11–09 It may be that opting into reservation of benefit has no adverse IHT implications for one or more of the following reasons:

1. *Business/agricultural relief*: the property in question may qualify for 100 per cent business property relief or agricultural property relief by virtue of para.8 of Sch.20 to the 1986 Act.[17]

2. *Nil rate band*: the property when cumulated with his remaining estate may fall within the taxpayer's unused IHT nil rate band.

[11] Sch.15, para.23(2).
[12] Sch.15, para.23(3).
[13] Sch.15, para.23(4).
[14] Sch.15, para.23(5). Note that the election cannot therefore be withdrawn by the executors of a deceased taxpayer.
[15] But for the election.
[16] See Sch.15, para.23(6).
[17] See 27–05.

Even if there are adverse IHT implications, the taxpayer may still wish to elect out of the Regime in order to avoid the income tax charge.

Reasons for not opting for reservation of benefit

On the other hand, the taxpayer may prefer to be taxed under the **11–10** Regime.

1. *Elderly/unwell taxpayer*: the taxpayer's life expectancy may be such that it is likely to be less expensive to pay the annual charge under the Regime than it is to bear IHT on the property.

2. *Tax burden on donee*: the taxpayer may not wish to burden the donee with the IHT on the property.

3. *Annual exemption*: the taxpayer may find that the taxable benefit falls within the annual exemption (see Chapter 9).

What is the effect of s.102(3) applying?

Section 102(3) provides for reservation of benefit property to be **11–11** subject to IHT on the death of the donor "to the extent that the property would not, apart from this section, form part of the donor's estate immediately before death". Is the effect of the election that this condition has to be met before a charge can arise? This question is considered in the context of Home Loan Schemes at 17–18.

The impact of s.102(4)

It is clear that if the election is exercised, the reservation of benefit **11–12** provisions may subsequently cease to apply:[18] *e.g.* if the taxpayer ceases to occupy land. At that time FA 1986, s.102(4) will apply and there will be a deemed PET by the taxpayer.

There are, of course, other events which bring the reservation of benefit to an end: crucially if the taxpayer pays full consideration for his use or enjoyment of land and chattels so that FA 1984, Sch.20, para.6(1)(a) applies. This may have apparently bizarre results:

---

[18] Sch.15, para.21(2)(b); para.22(2)(b).

(i) In the case of land the rental value under the Regime may well be different from the full consideration required under FA 1986 (in particular it may be more!).

(ii) In the case of chattels the proposed charge under the Regime is **intended** to be greater than the full consideration calculation. *Ingram* chattels schemes may be unscrambled with an election followed by the payment of full consideration which may be cheaper than suffering the para.6 charge (see further, Chapter 18).

(iii) If it is likely that the taxpayer will, *e.g.* cease to occupy land within para.3 it is important that he does not make the election and then shortly afterwards cease to occupy since that will result in a deemed PET arising.

CHAPTER 12

REGULATIONS

The power to make regulations

Schedule 15 gives extensive powers for secondary legislation to be **12–01** made in a number of areas:

(i) Paragraphs 4(5), 7(4) and 9(2) provide for regulations in relation to valuation issues.

(ii) Paragraph 14 gives power for regulations to be issued conferring further exemptions from the charge to income tax imposed by paras 3, 6 and 8. (It is not clear whether this power would be wide enough to extend the number of excluded transactions.)

(iii) Most importantly, para.20 gives the broadest possible powers to "make different provision for different cases and include transitional provisions and savings".

There is power also to prescribe different rates of charge in relation to property of different descriptions. Thus the regulations can change the scope of the charging provisions if it is felt necessary. Given the extensive amendments at Committee and Report Stage in the Commons and the controversy these produced, the Revenue may prefer to deal with any anomalies on the charging provisions by secondary legislation, which is subject to less intense Parliamentary scrutiny.

For example, the Government is currently considering whether to allow sales of part of an asset at full market value to be excluded transactions. (See Commons Debates Report Stage, July 7, col.897). If it were eventually decided to give the taxpayer such an exclusion, while this probably cannot be dealt with by regulation under para.14, para.20 would seem to contain sufficient powers to enable a regulation to be issued covering this point.[1]

Consultation

12–02 At the time of writing the Regulations have not yet been issued. However, on August 16, 2004 the Revenue issued a further consultation paper[2] setting out the valuation issues that it believes the Regulations should cover and this consultation period will run until November 18, 2004.

The consultation paper also invites comments on the sort of guidance which will need to be given to taxpayers and their advisers about the practical operation of the Regime.[3] The intention is to publish draft regulations and guidance in late November with final versions in early 2005.

Whilst the rules for establishing the benefit which is chargeable are set out in Sch.15, the precise machinery and therefore the matters to be covered in the Regulations will depend upon the nature of the asset in question.

12–03 In the case of land, the "cash equivalent" of enjoyment in a particular tax year is derived from *market rent* that would be paid for use of the land over the taxable period (that is a tax year or any shorter period during which the taxpayer occupies the property).[4]

In the case of chattels the "cash equivalent" of enjoyment in a particular tax year is found by applying a specified rate of return over the "taxable period" to the *capital* value of the asset as at the valuation date.[5]

In the case of intangible assets the "cash equivalent" is calculated, as with chattels, by applying a specified rate of return over the taxable period to the *capital* value of the intangibles in the settlement as at the valuation date.[6]

In each case there is provision for scaling down where the occupation, use or benefit only continues for part of the year.

12–04 The key matters that the regulations need to address therefore are:

---

[1] Given the valuation difficulties the Government may in the end only allow an exclusion for sales of part if the sale is to an unconnected third party. In connection with valuation issues see 3–13 and 16–38.

[2] See Appendix II.

[3] As those dealing with the new disclosure rules have found, the difficulty about such guidance is that it often deals with deficiencies in the legislation and ends up having the status of law.

[4] See Chapter 3.

[5] See Chapter 4.

[6] See Chapter 6.

(a) what valuation date should be taken;

(b) how is it to be adjusted; and

(c) what rate of return should be specified for chattels and intangible assets.

Guidance will surely also be needed as to how a taxpayer will be able to self-assess with certainty.

For example, how will he know that his valuations are accepted by the Revenue? Suppose the Revenue disagrees with the reasonable attribution that a taxpayer makes when he occupies land which has been purchased by the donee using proceeds of sale which are derived from property formerly gifted to the donee and from property which has always been the donee's own? (see Sch.15, paras 4(2)(b) and 4(2)(c).)[7]

Valuation date

The Consultation Document proposes that the Valuation Date should **12–05** be fixed at the earliest time in the tax year when Sch.15 applies to the asset in question.

> *Example:*
> Ben gave cash to his son in 1999. His son invests the cash in shares which he mixes with his own share portfolio. He sells all the investments in 2001; buys a house with the proceeds and lets it out, keeping the rent. In 2002, Ben moves into the house, paying no rent. He is not caught by the reservation of benefit rules[8] but is caught by the Regime. The valuation date will be fixed at April 6, 2005. Ben will have to make a reasonable attribution to work out how much of the property was purchased using his funds and how much using his son's property.

If, however, Ben did not move into the house until January 2006, the valuation date will be January 2006.

If Ben only moves into the house in 2008, more than seven years has elapsed since the original cash gift and therefore he is not subject to the Regime.[9] If Ben moves out of the house in 2006 and then back into the house in 2008 he is still caught by the pre-owned asset charge.

---

[7] These issues are discussed further in Chapter 13.
[8] On cash gifts, see Chapter 25.
[9] See 5–09.

12–06   If taxpayers find it more convenient to do a valuation at a later date in the tax year the Revenue will not challenge it unless "there is some indication that the date was chosen for tax-saving reasons". This statement is puzzling. Suppose a trust holds a share portfolio and the settlor is within the para.8 charge. The settlor forgets to do a valuation at April 6, when the shares are worth £1 million. He does his tax return in September by which time the value has fallen to £0.8. Can he take the lower value?

One of the particular difficulties with chattels is that values are often subject to wide margins of uncertainty. An insurance valuation or even an estimate by a reputable firm is often quite different for what a picture sells for at auction. In these circumstances, how can the taxpayer self-assess in order to avoid a discovery enquiry later?[10]

In relation to intangibles it will often be easier to fix on a precise value at a definite date (although private company shares will inevitably pose problems) but what happens if the value fluctuates radically over the year which could well happen given the vagaries of the stock market. Someone could be paying tax on capital values which have disappeared over the year! These issues are not going to be easy to resolve.

Revaluing

12–07   The second question is how the taxable benefit will be computed each year. Is the taxpayer to obtain repeated annual valuations which could involve substantial compliance costs or will he be allowed to adjust the value by reference to an index each year? If so, what index will be used?

The consultation document suggests that obtaining annual valuations for intangibles is not problematic and therefore it is likely that the taxpayer will have to obtain a fresh valuation each year in cases where a para.8 charge is being levied. This may not be easy where private company shares are involved.

For land and chattels the suggestion in the consultation paper is that the taxpayer could be given a choice as to whether to index each year from a base valuation or to have a new valuation. However, the choice once made would be binding over a cycle of (say) five years.

---

[10] See further Chapter 13. It is to be hoped that this will be considered during the consultation process.

The rate of return

The fact that the legislation imputes a yield on chattels and intangible **12–08** assets by reference to capital values rather than actual income that is produced raises other difficulties. The starting point in the consultation document is that the rate of return shall be the official rate of interest multiplied by the capital value of the asset. At present, the Revenue is unwilling to envisage a lower rate of interest than the official rate—currently 5 per cent—on the basis that such an approach is used in relation to employee benefits such as occupation of company houses. (Of course, there the charge is based on *cost* rather than current values.)

CHAPTER 13

ADMINISTRATION

Introduction

13–01 It appears from the consultation document published in August 2004 that Capital Taxes, Nottingham Office, will have overall responsibility for implementing the legislation and carrying out appropriate compliance checks. That is helpful because determining whether someone is subject to the Regime will often depend on a detailed understanding of the IHT legislation.

Under Code of Practice 10 on Information and Advice, since this is new legislation the taxpayer will be entitled to ask for guidance as to the application of the legislation and an interpretation on any particular point even if the transaction has not yet been completed.

This is likely to be particularly relevant in the area of elections. For example, suppose the taxpayer asks the Revenue for advice as to whether he is caught by the Regime at all? He is told that he is not caught by the Regime, *e.g.* because he can rely on a particular exemption and therefore does nothing. Subsequently it emerges that he was caught by the Regime and should have been paying income tax. He faces interest (even if not penalties) and he has now missed the time limit for the election which is January 31, in the tax year immediately following the year in which he first became chargeable under the regime.[1] In these circumstances the taxpayer would be able to demonstrate reasonable excuse for failing to make the election in time and would presumably be permitted a late election.[2]

---

[1] On the election, see Chapter 11.
[2] See Sch.15, para.23(3).

Difficulties of self-assessment

The Regime is part of the income tax system and taxpayers are **13–02** required to self assess in the usual way. One of the objections raised during the first consultation period was that taxpayers will not always be aware that they are chargeable. If they do not file tax returns there will be nothing to jog their memory and unless they are in the habit of receiving regular advice from professionals they are likely to be unaware that a transaction that they carried out in, say, 1987 is now caught by the Regime.

> *Example 1:*
> Dan gave £400,000 cash to his son Michael in March 1987. Michael invested the cash in property which he let out but in 1990 Dan moved into the property. There is no reservation of benefit[3] but since Dan has occupied the property within seven years of making the gift he is now within the Regime. Dan has forgotten all about the gift made 17 years ago.
>
> It is possible that Dan submits a tax return each year and will notice on the tax return and presumably in the explanatory notes, that he could be subject to a charge under Sch.15. However, it will be difficult in the explanatory notes to cover all the possible scenarios under which somebody could be caught.
>
> In the Standing Committee Debates, the Paymaster General, Dawn Primarolo observed that "record keeping is required to start at 1986 anyway under current inheritance tax rules"[4] but, of course, as far as Dan is concerned there is no reason why he should have kept a record any longer of the cash gift made 17 years ago! The position becomes more complex still where Dan gives property which is then mixed by the donee with other assets. The Paymaster General's statement is misleading as to the very practical difficulties of self-assessment that taxpayers will face.

> *Example 2:*
> Dan gives £300,000 in cash to his son James to help him start his business. James works hard and does spectacularly well. He sells out within five years for £4 million and buys his father a house for £300,000 out of the sale proceeds. In these circumstances how is the charge to be calculated? Has Dan's cash gift been applied for the acquisition of the house or could one argue

---

[3] A gift of cash: see Chapter 25.
[4] Hansard, May 18, 2004, Standing Committee A, col.257.

that none of it has, since James had enough surplus cash from the sale of the business?

In these circumstances what sort of disclosure should a taxpayer make to ensure that he is protected from a Taxes Management Act 1970, s.29 discovery enquiry after the one-year period has expired?

13–03 Under the 1970 Act a taxpayer must self-assess and deliver his tax return by January 31 of the year following the year of assessment. Thus for tax year 2005/06 he will need to deliver the tax return by January 31, 2007. The requirement is for the return to disclose all the relevant information and for the taxpayer correctly to assess the tax due. The Revenue may enquire into the return by issuing a formal notice within 12 months after the filing date: in the above example by January 31, 2008. If the Revenue makes no enquiry and the taxpayer has not amended his return, a self assessment return becomes final on the expiry of that 12 months enquiry period subject only to the possibility of a discovery assessment under s.29.

A discovery assessment can be made if there was fraud or negligence on the part of the taxpayer or the Revenue officer "could not have been reasonably expected on the basis of the information made available to him before that time, to be aware of such failure or excessive claim for relief."

13–04   The difficulty is that the Court of Appeal decision in *Langham (Inspector of Taxes) v Veltema*[5] has increased the possibility of the Revenue making a successful discovery assessment under the Regime, at least in relation to valuation issues. The case related to a disputed valuation and the ultimate income tax liability under Sch.15 similarly depends on the valuation of particular assets.

The taxpayer had received property from a company and had disclosed the value of the benefit as £100,000 and paid tax on this basis. He did not send in the actual valuation. The Inspector raised no enquiry. In the event the company accounts were queried and a value was eventually agreed at £145,000 but after the enquiry period for the taxpayer had expired. The Court of Appeal overturned the High Court decision and held that the Inspector was entitled to make a discovery enquiry and therefore collect tax from the taxpayer on the additional benefit.

How then is a taxpayer to know that he has self-assessed correctly? Even if he sends in a copy of the valuation it is not clear from the decision in *Langham* whether doing this and expressly asking the Revenue to look at it will be sufficient to protect him from a discovery assessment. This is a point that needs to be dealt with in the consultation process.

[5] [2004] EWCA Civ. 193; [2004] S.T.C. 544.

The taxpayer may base his subsequent income tax liabilities under Sch.15 on that valuation, indexing it up each year.[6] Yet he will not have finality until after the time limits for making discovery have elapsed.

The valuation issues are particularly difficult. Other points are slightly easier. Where a taxpayer is doubtful as to whether he is caught by the Regime in the first place he can put full details of his arguments on the additional information pages of the return and presumably would then be treated as having made full disclosure and be protected from a discovery assessment. In any event he could under Code of Practice 10 obtain a ruling from the Revenue and rely on this.

Of course, even if a taxpayer does obtain finality in one tax year, **13–05** this will not prevent the Revenue raising an enquiry in later years if the taxpayer continued to self assess on the basis that the Regime does not apply to him. Suppose the Revenue does not enquire into the taxpayer's return for 2005/6. In 2006/7 he continues to self assess on the basis that he is outside the Regime; the Revenue makes an enquiry and it is established that the taxpayer was wrong to self assess on the basis that no income tax was due under the Regime. Possibly a court case clarifies the position or there is a change in legislation which is deemed to have always had effect.

In these circumstances the taxpayer will have missed the deadline for making the election (he first became chargeable under the Regime in 2005 and therefore needed to elect by January 31, 2007)[7] and will have to continue paying the income tax charge or else try to unravel the arrangement. It is for this reason it may be worthwhile making a protective election, *i.e.* an election that is valid only in the event that income tax is due.[8]

The position of personal representatives

The Regime is likely to be a particular headache for personal **13–06** representatives. For example, Ben dies not having paid income tax under Sch.15 because he believed that he was not within the Regime. The Revenue investigates the matter after his death and considers that the Regime did apply. Income tax should have been paid. Obviously no election can now be made. Perhaps the IHT savings from the arrangement are secure but the income tax will be a liability of the estate (doubtless borne by residue).

[6] See Chapter 12.
[7] For the election, see Chapter 11.
[8] See further 11–02, n.1.

In these circumstances the personal representatives may find that they have a substantial income tax charge. Indeed, the matter may not come to light immediately after Ben's death. Suppose Ben is within the Regime because he made a gift of cash to his son in 1997 and then occupies a house purchased with that cash. He may not have been made aware of any problem. He dies in 2012. The Revenue may not pick up the problem for some time. One anticipates that the IHT 200 form will be amended to ask whether the deceased made *any* gifts since March 17, 1986 and if so how the proceeds were used.

Unless such a question is put on the IHT200 form it may never come to light that Ben was in fact within the Regime until professional advisers start looking into the son's affairs and investigate how and why he received the house and who occupied it (for example on a later disposal by the son).

Fortunately, a back duty assessment on a deceased's personal representatives can only be made within three tax years of January 31 following the year of his death and only for fraudulent or negligent conduct by the deceased in any of the six years up to and including the year of his death.[9]

13–07 In effect, therefore, if Ben dies in 2006/7, the Revenue has until January 30, 2011 in which to assess his personal representatives for loss of tax because of Ben's fraudulent or negligent conduct. Personal representatives are likely to want to retain assets for that minimum period in case there are unexpected income tax liabilities under the Regime.

Personal representatives will be under a duty to make additional enquires to establish whether the taxpayer made gifts of cash or other assets after March 17, 1986 and if so what happened to the proceeds and how they were used.

There is another issue to consider on the death of the taxpayer. Suppose that he has made an election under para.21 or 22. There is no necessity to notify the donee (who is, of course, the owner of the property!) of such election but if the taxpayer has elected to be within the Regime he has elected that the reservation of benefit provisions should apply to him.

In that event, the question of who pays the inheritance tax liability will be decided in accordance with the normal reservation of benefit rules. The result is that it is the donee (the person in whom the property is vested) who is primarily liable to pay any tax arising out of the election; the donor's personal representatives only have a secondary liability up to the value of the property under their control which arises to the extent that nobody else is liable for the tax or to

---

[9] TMA 1970, s.40.

the extent that it is unpaid 12 months after the end of the month in which the taxpayer died.[10]

The donor's personal representatives will need to check whether **13–08** an election has been made. It is unclear whether the election will be made on the income tax return or to Capital Taxes in Nottingham who will then keep a record of the election which will be picked up on the taxpayer's death.

Suppose the taxpayer pays income tax on the basis that he is within the Regime and then finds that he is not, *e.g.* because the scheme that he carried out has failed for IHT purposes and he has reserved a benefit? There is no provision in the legislation for reimbursement of income tax paid already or for setting such income tax liability off against the IHT now due on death. An error or mistake claim may be possible.

---

[10] See IHTA 1984, s.204(1)(a) as limited by *ibid.* s.204(a) and note the PR's right of recovery if they do pay the tax in *ibid.* s.211(3).

PART III: PLANNING IN PRACTICE: REACTIVE PLANNING

This Part looks at the impact of the new charge on arrangements which have already been implemented. It discusses whether the charge applies to the particular transactions and, if it does, what options are now open to the taxpayer.

CHAPTER 14

INGRAM SCHEMES

BACKGROUND

If an individual gives away his house (*e.g.* to his daughter) and **14–01** continues to live there, he is within the reservation of benefit rules. It is, however, possible to carve land up into different interests and the individual might, for instance, retain an interest which gave him a continued right of occupation and then give away the remaining interest in the land. What then will be the IHT consequences?

A key point to bear in mind is that the reservation of benefit rules apply to gifts of property in which the donor has reserved a benefit. If the taxpayer has effected the division of his land into different interests (a process usually referred to as a "shearing operation") then the question which arises is what property has he given away. Specifically has he merely given the remainder interest in the land subject to the retained interest?

Divisions of land may be horizontal (as in the above example, when a single property is being carved into different slices) or vertical. In respect of the latter Lord Simmonds commented as follows:

> "[By retaining] something which he has never given, a donor does not bring himself within the mischief [of the reservation of benefit rules]—In the simplest analysis if A gives to B all his estates in Wiltshire except Blackacre, he does not except Blackacre out of what he has given: he just does not give Blackacre."[1]

Horizontal severances remained more problematic but the general consensus amongst advisers was that they could operate in such a way that the reservation of benefit rules were not infringed. Hence

---

[1] *St Aubyn v AG* [1952] A.C. 15: the case was concerned with the application of the reservation of benefit provisions in the estate duty legislation. These provisions were, of course, very largely incorporated into the IHT legislation by FA 1986.

many such schemes were implemented after 1986, mainly in respect of landed estates and substantial properties.

The main attraction for taxpayers was that:

(i) the interest retained, which gave a continuing right to occupy, would be a wasting asset whose value would be relatively small at the date of death; and

(ii) the interest given away (typically the encumbered freehold) would be a PET and so the gift would be free of IHT provided that the donor survived by seven years. Further, it would be an appreciating asset: as the value of the retained interest fell so that of the gifted interest would increase. But that increase in value would, in any event, fall outside the IHT net.

THE *INGRAM* DECISION[2]

The facts

14–02 Lady Jane Ingram transferred landed property to a nominee in 1987; the following day (on her directions) he granted her a 20-year rent-free lease in the property and on the next day transferred the property (subject to the lease) to trustees who executed declarations of trust whereby the property was held for the benefit of certain individuals, excluding Lady Jane. The arrangements, all part of a pre-planned scheme, amounted to a classic shearing operation. Lady Jane died in 1989 and the Revenue issued a determination that, because of the reservation of benefit rules, the gifted property still formed part of her estate at her death.

The Revenue's claim

14–03 The Revenue argued that the grant of a lease by a nominee in favour of his principal was a nullity with the result that although it was accepted that the trustees took the property subject to the interest of Lady Jane (as *per* the abortive lease), that interest took effect by way of a leaseback. Hence Lady Jane's interest could only arise contemporaneously with the gift made to the trustees, thereby resulting in a reservation of benefit. Alternatively, and even if the nominee

---

[2] *Ingram v IRC* [1995] 4 All E.R. 334; on appeal [1997] 4 All E.R. 395 (CA) revs'd; [1999] S.T.C. 37, HL.

lease was effective, the same result would follow as a result of applying the *Ramsay* principle.

The approach of the House of Lords

Lord Hoffmann referred to the long history of the legislation in this **14–04** area and noted that the decided cases showed that although its provisions prevent a donor from "having his cake and eating it", there is nothing to stop him from "carefully dividing up the cake, eating part and having the rest". He decided the appeal on the assumption that the lease granted by the nominee was a nullity, *i.e.* on the basis that the leasehold interest came into existence only at the time when the freehold was acquired by the trustees.

The consequences of such a "contemporaneous carve-out" involved a consideration of the estate duty case of *Nichols v IRC*[3] which had concerned a gift by Sir Philip Nichols of his country house and estate to his son, Francis, subject to Francis granting him an immediate leaseback. Goff J., giving the judgment of the Court of Appeal, concluded that such an arrangement involved a reservation of benefit by Sir Philip:

> " . . . we think that a grant of the fee simple, subject to and with the benefit of a lease-back, where such a grant is made by a person who owns the whole of the freehold free from any lease, is a grant of the whole fee simple with something reserved out of it, and not a gift of a partial interest leaving something in the hands of the grantor which he has not given. It is not like a reservation or remainder expectant on a prior interest. It gives an immediate right to the rent, together with a right to distrain for it, and, if there be a proviso for re-entry, a right to forfeit the lease. Of course, where as in *Munro v Commissioner of Stamp Division (NSW)*[4] the lease, or, as it then may have been, a licence coupled with an interest, arises under a prior independent transaction, no question can arise because the donor then gives all that he has, but where it is a condition of the gift that a lease-back shall be created, we think that must, on a true analysis, be a reservation of benefit out of the gift and not something not given at all."

In the event the *Nichols* case fell to be decided on the basis of the covenants given by the son in the lease in which he assumed the burden of repairs and the payment of tithe redemption duty, and which amounted to a reservation. The wider statement of Goff J. quoted above to the effect that a leaseback must *by itself* involve a reservation constituted the main authority relied upon by the Revenue (and the comment that the *Munro* case involved a "prior independent transaction" had subsequently been widely debated).

Lord Hoffmann unequivocally rejected this approach:

---

[3] *Nichols v IRC* [1975] 2 All E.R. 120, CA.
[4] [1934] A.C. 61, PC.

"It is a curious feature of the debate in this case that both sides claim that their views reflect the reality, not the mere form of the transaction, but the Revenue's version of reality seems entirely dependent upon the *scintilla temporis* which must elapse between the conveyance of the freehold to the donee and the creation of the leasehold in favour of the donor. For my part I do not think that a theory based on the notion of a *scintilla temporis* can have a very powerful grasp on reality . . . If one looks at the real nature of the transaction, there seems to me no doubt that Ferris J. was right in saying that the trustees and beneficiaries never at any time acquired the land free of Lady Ingram's leasehold interest."

The nominee lease

14–05 Given that no reservation was involved, even if the nominee lease was a nullity it was not strictly necessary for their Lordships to express any view on the validity of such an arrangement. Lord Hoffmann, however, indicated that he was of the opinion that such a lease was valid as a matter of English law for reasons given by Millet L.J. in the Court of Appeal. (Nominee leases are, in fact, widely used in practice.) It should, however, be appreciated that nothing in the speeches affects the proposition that a man cannot grant a lease to himself[5] nor the position under Scots law.[6]

Ramsay[7]

14–06 Given the conclusion that a leaseback did not involve any reservation of benefit the question of the *Ramsay* principle being used to nullify the nominee lease did not arise, and neither Lord Hoffmann nor Lord Hutton expressed any views on this matter.

The meaning of "property" in FA 1986, s.102

14–07 Lord Hoffmann pointed out that s.102 is concerned with a gift of "property" and that term does not necessarily refer to something which has a physical existence such as a house, but is used in a technical sense and requires a careful analysis of the nature of what has been gifted. A landowner may, for instance, gift an unencumbered freehold interest in his house, in which case were he to

[5] *Rye v Rye* [1962] A.C. 496, HL.
[6] *Kildrummy (Jersey) Ltd v IRC* [1990] S.T.C. 657.
[7] The so-called "*Ramsay* principle" is derived from a line of cases starting with *Ramsay (WT) Ltd v IRC* [1982] A.C. 300. It enables the courts to excise artificial steps in a pre-planned tax saving scheme.

continue to occupy that property (in the absence of a payment of full consideration and assuming that such occupation was more than on a *de minimis* level) then he would reserve a benefit. By contrast, he might retain a leasehold interest and only give away the encumbered freehold interest gifted. As Lord Hoffmann concluded, s.102 "requires people to define precisely the interest which they are giving away and the interest, if any, which they are retaining".

The use of shearing arrangements

The speeches demolished the argument that the creation of the lease **14–08** and the gift of the encumbered freehold had to be independent transactions. The lease could be carved out contemporaneously with the gift. Accordingly, a prior nominee arrangement is not necessary; the arrangement could be structured as a gift and leaseback. However, it was essential that all the relevant terms of the lease were agreed before the freehold gift was made so that it is clear that the proprietary interest retained was defined with the necessary precision.

FA 1999: THE ANTI-*INGRAM* LEGISLATION[8]

It was no great surprise that amending legislation followed in FA **14–09** 1999 which:

(i) reversed the *Ingram* decision in respect of gifts of interests in land made after March 8, 1999,

(ii) but otherwise did not change the existing legislation.

It was a classic example of narrowly-targeted anti-avoidance legislation.

The legislation extended the reservation of benefit provisions so that they apply if the following two conditions are met:

Condition 1: There must be a gift of an interest in land. In respect of this condition, note that the trigger for the application of this new legislation is a "gift"[9] and that these rules are only concerned with gifts affecting land.[10]

---

[8] See FA 1999, s.104 inserting new s.102A–C into FA 1986: see Appendix I.

[9] A gift is of course required if the reservation of benefit rules generally are to apply and this leads to problems in relation to the main body of the IHT legislation which is based on a transfer of value: see 16–14.

[10] *Ingram* schemes have been developed for chattels: see Chapter 18.

Condition 2: The donor must retain "a significant right or interest in relation to the land" or be party to a significant arrangement in relation to the land.

Looking back at the facts in *Ingram* it can be seen that both conditions are satisfied: the gift of the encumbered freehold satisfies Condition 1 whilst the retention of a lease satisfies Condition 2. Hence, from March 9, 1999 new *Ingram* arrangements in respect of land are ineffective so that on the death of the donor the gifted freehold interest will be taxed as part of his estate under the reservation rules.

Limitations on the ambit of the new legislation

14–10 Condition 2 is not met if:

  (a) the donor pays full consideration for the retained right or interest; or

  (b) the right or interest was obtained at least seven years before the gift. Hence in a very limited way *Ingram* schemes falling outside the reservation of benefit rules remain possible but only if the lease is carved out and the taxpayer then waits at least seven years before gifting the freehold. In practice such long term planning has not, so far as the authors are aware, been undertaken.

It is also considered that the new legislation does not apply:

  (a) if a property is divided so that A retains (say) the granny annex and gives away the main house; and

  (b) if the retained interest is not significant, *e.g.* if A gives away land which surrounds his house whilst retaining a right of way to that house.

OTHER ISSUES

14–11 As has been noted, a large number of *Ingram* schemes were carried out before March 9, 1999 and professional advisers need to be aware that as and when the donor dies the following problems may arise:

  (i) what value is to be attributed to the retained lease? Specifically did it give security of tenure/a right to enfranchise; and

(ii) if, after death, the family wish to sell the property, bear in mind that the deceased donor merely owned a lease at death so that the CGT uplift will be limited to this asset. The freehold acquired by the family is likely to have a low base cost and will not benefit from the CGT main residence relief.

Other problems may arise during the life of the donor: for instance if he wishes to sell the property and move (*e.g.* to a retirement bungalow) he will find that all he owns is a lease which may have a relatively low value. If the family are prepared to co-operate in selling the freehold, this may give rise to a CGT charge as noted above whilst an application of the proceeds of sale for the benefit of the donor may lead to the reservation of benefit rules applying.

In some cases the lease retained may expire before the death of the donor.[11] If he wishes to continue in occupation of the property he must pay a commercial rent to avoid being caught by the reservation of benefit rules.[12]

In many cases the scheme will have been implemented more than seven years ago so that the PET of the freehold interest will have now become an exempt transfer.

IMPACT OF THE PRE-OWNED ASSET REGIME

The December Consultation Paper[13] suggested that the Regime **14–12** would not apply to *Ingram* schemes since it referred to the charge being subject to "an exclusion for cases where the donor has expressly reserved a right to continued occupation when making the gift." Any celebrations were, however, premature and the Revenue made it clear during the consultation exercise that whatever this proposed exclusion meant it was not intended to apply to *Ingram* schemes. The final legislation accordingly confers no special treatment on these schemes.

The **para.3** charge will therefore apply given that:

(i) the donor is in occupation of land; and

(ii) the disposal condition is met in respect of that land.

---

[11] The most convenient arrangement would have been to reserve a lease limited to the life of the donor but that was made impossible by IHTA 1984, s.43(3) which treats the arrangement as a settlement with the donor/tenant as having an interest in possession.

[12] See FA 1986, Sch.20, para.6(1)(a).

[13] See Appendix II.

It is irrelevant that he is in occupation under a reserved lease.

All that remains is to calculate the chargeable amount in relation to the land. In applying the **para.4** rules the appropriate rental value will need to be apportioned using the formula:

$$R \times \frac{DV}{V}$$

given that the donor has not disposed of his entire interest in the land. This can best be understood by taking an example.

In 1998, A retained a 20-year, rent free lease in Blackacre and gave the encumbered freehold to his daughter. Assume that on the "**valuation date**" the value of the interest disposed of (the freehold) is £750,000 and the value of the "**relevant land**" (on the basis of a freehold with vacant possession) is £1.5. Assume further that the rental value (calculated in accordance with the provisions of para.5) is £15,000 p.a.

<u>Applying the formula</u>

$$R = £15,000$$

$$DV = £750,000$$

$$V = £1,500,000$$

So that the appropriate rental value is —

$$15,000 \times \frac{750,000}{1,500,000} = £7,500$$

A's chargeable amount is therefore £7,500 so
that if he is a higher rate taxpayer he will suffer
income tax of <u>£3,000.</u>

The benefit is taxed each year whilst A continues to occupy the land. "The valuation date" in relation to a taxable period means such date as will be prescribed by Regulations. The August Consultation Document[14] indicated a preference for the earliest time in the tax year when the Regime applies. Hence, if this proposal is adopted, the first valuation will be required on April 6, 2005.

Does a revaluation have to be carried out on each April 6? The basic valuation rule in the legislation requires the taxable benefit to be computed afresh for each tax year by reference to the valuation date for that year. The Regulations may amend this by, *e.g.* allowing a value to be used for more than one year with or without an adjustment. Of course, in the case of *Ingram* schemes it is likely that the value of the gifted freehold (DV) will increase as the retained

---

[14] See Appendix II.

lease wastes away. Hence the chargeable amount will increase year on year.

Chattels

As discussed in Chapter 18, *Ingram* schemes have been employed for **14–13** chattels and these were not affected by the anti-avoidance legislation in FA 1999 which was limited to land. The Regime, however, will apply to such schemes and the calculation of the chargeable amount under **para.7** will be arrived at in a similar fashion, in this case by applying the formula:

$$N \times \frac{DV}{V}$$

where N is the amount of the interest that would be payable for the taxable period if interest were payable at the prescribed rate on an amount equal to the value of the chattel at the valuation date. The prescribed rate of interest is to be laid down in the regulations but is expected to be the same as the "official rate" which applies on beneficial loans to employees.

PRACTICAL ADVICE

There are limited options open to the taxpayer who has effected an **14–14** *Ingram* scheme, namely:

(1) **pay the income tax charge**: this will in effect be 40 per cent (for most individuals) of a full rent for the property[15] but with a discount which reflects the value of the retained lease. In those cases where seven years have elapsed so that the PET of the freehold is outside the IHT net and the taxpayer can afford to pay the tax this may be the most attractive option;

(ii) if the taxpayer is in poor health and may not live more than (say) five years, again paying the tax will be attractive; or

[15] It is generally thought unlikely that the payment of a market rent will be attractive. However, if the freehold interest is held in trust then opportunities for sheltering the income tax charge on such a rent may arise (*e.g.* if the beneficiaries include non-taxpayers). It will be important to ensure that the rent paid will be deducted from the appropriate rental value and this requires the payment to be made under a legal obligation (see 3–22). Given that in *Ingram* arrangements the donor will be in occupation of the property under a lease which provides for only a nominal rent, the answer may be for him to execute a deed of covenant in favour of the donee.

(iii) **cease to occupy the property**: if it is desired to retain the IHT advantage but not pay any income tax then this affords the only way out. Of course alternative accommodation will need to be found. Before surrendering the lease consider carefully any tax implications: *e.g.* if the freehold gift is accelerated will this amount to an associated operation? The authors do not consider this to be the case and nor do they consider that it would give rise to *Ramsay* type arguments.

14–15 Opt into the reservation of benefit rules: for the individual wishing to remain in occupation of the property and unable/unwilling to pay the income tax charge this is the only option left. There are two points to note:

(a) The person who will eventually end up suffering the IHT will be the donee.[16] Curiously enough there is no provision which requires that person to be notified of the making of the election: accordingly the eventual tax bill may come as something of a shock!

(b) It will potentially be a complete own goal if, having made the election, the donor then ceases to occupy the property. At that point he will make a deemed PET under s.102(4) and so will start the seven-year clock running all over again.

In considering the equity of the pre-owned assets charge the plight of taxpayers who have effected successful *Ingram* schemes is striking. Arrangements concluded perhaps 19 years before are being subjected to an income tax charge unless the invidious decision is take to accept a future IHT charge or to leave one's home. In considering Human Rights arguments the position of the donee in these arrangements merits close consideration. The owner of the freehold interest in the land will, if the donor makes the election, suffer an IHT charge on that property. Surely this is an undue interference with an individual's property rights.

14–16 The use of reverter to settlor trusts as a way of unscrambling arrangements is considered in Chapter 23. In the case of *Ingram* arrangements it is unlikely that this will be appropriate since the freehold interest is likely to have a low CGT base cost so that a disposal will produce an unacceptably large CGT liability.

---

[16] See 13–07.

CHAPTER 15

REVERSIONARY LEASES

BACKGROUND

The development of reversionary lease arrangements is closely **15–01** linked to *Ingram* schemes which were considered in the last chapter. In particular:

  (i) The attraction for taxpayers in entering into these arrangements was the same: see 14–01.

 (ii) Like *Ingram* schemes reversionary leases involved a shearing operation: see 14–01 *et seq.*

(iii) Similar CGT problems would arise in the event of a sale of the property: see 14–11. Hence they were ideal in cases where it was envisaged that the property would never be sold but would be retained within the family.

Once it was clear that the Revenue were going to challenge *Ingram* shearing arrangements, taxpayers and their advisers turned to the reversionary lease as an alternative. Specifically it appeared to offer an advantage over an *Ingram* shearing arrangement in that it was a single transaction. Whereas in *Ingram* arrangements it was necessary **first** to carve out a lease and **then** to gift an encumbered freehold reversion, reversionary leases were a single stage transaction involving merely the grant of a lease.

HOW THE REVERSIONARY LEASE WORKS

Assume that Jasper owns Biddecombe Manor which he wishes to **15–02** pass on to his eldest son, Rufus. He wishes to occupy the Manor for the rest of his life. It is inconceivable that the property will be sold outside the family. The "scheme" operates as follows:

(i) Jasper grants Rufus a long lease over the property (say 125 years) to take effect in 20 years time. Because the lease does not give Rufus occupation rights immediately it is known as a deferred or reversionary lease. The terms of the lease do not involve the payment of any rent nor do they impose onerous conditions on Rufus.

(ii) Jasper can continue to occupy the property for the next 20 years because he remains the freeholder and the lease has not given Rufus an immediate right to occupy.

(iii) The gift of the lease is a PET by Jasper and so free from IHT provided that he survives by seven years.

(iv) The freehold interest (of diminishing value) remains in Jasper's estate and will be taxed accordingly on his death.

(v) Of course if Jasper is still alive at the end of 20 years and wishes to continue to occupy the property he will need to pay Rufus a market rent: otherwise he will have reserved a benefit in the lease gifted to Rufus.[1]

RESERVATION OF BENEFIT ANALYSIS

15–03 Jasper continues to occupy by virtue of his retained freehold property: he does not retain a benefit in the gifted property which is the reversionary lease. Like *Ingram* the arrangement is a horizontal carve-out: see 14–01. This analysis has been accepted by the Revenue in respect of reversionary lease arrangements set up before March 9, 1999.

The Revenue considers, however, that the legislation introduced in 1999 to stop *Ingram* arrangements also catches reversionary lease schemes. This view is not shared by most practitioners and, on its face, the legislation appears to be carefully targeted at *Ingram* schemes (and there was no mention in the accompanying Press Release of other similar arrangements being caught).

The argument that reversionary leases are not caught is as follows[2]:

(i) the basic conditions in the legislation that have to be satisfied are first that the taxpayer disposes of an interest in land by way of gift (this Jasper undoubtedly does when he grants Rufus the deferred lease). Secondly, he must retain "a significant right or interest or (be) party to a significant

---

[1] For the full consideration let out, see FA 1986, Sch.20, para.6(1)(a).
[2] The legislation is in Appendix I.

arrangement in relation to the land." Of course Japer retains his freehold interest—does that satisfy the second requirement?

(ii) the short answer is that it all depends on the facts! By s.102A(5), "a right or interest is not significant [for the purposes of the second condition noted above] if it was granted or acquired before the period of seven years ending with the date of the gift." In the vast majority of cases persons wishing to enter into reversionary lease arrangements will do so in relation to property which they have owned for at least seven years. In such cases it is considered that the s.102A(5) let out applies and the gifted lease is not property subject to a reservation.[3]

(iii) An alternative argument would be based on s.102A(3) which excludes a right interest or arrangement which enables the donor to occupy the land "for full consideration in money or money's worth." If Jasper had originally purchased his freehold interest (whether or not within seven years of the date of the gift) for full consideration then this let out should apply so that again the arrangement remains outside the amended reservation of benefit legislation.

That, of course, means that a reversionary lease granted within seven years of Jasper inheriting the property would be caught because neither of the let-outs would then be available.

MISCELLANEOUS TECHNICAL POINTS

The precise arrangements involved in reversionary lease schemes **15–04** gave rise to a number of uncertainties:

(i) Could the period of deferral exceed 21 years? This might be desirable if Jasper were (say) in his mid 60's so that he could easily live for another 25 years. This involves the construction of s.149(3) of the Law of Property Act 1925 which provides "a term [*i.e.* lease] at a rent or granted in consideration of a fine, limited to take effect more than 21 years from the date of the instrument purporting to create it, shall be void." It has been suggested that a lease which does not

---

[3] It may be noted that s.102A(5) provides for the right or interest not to be significant. Can it be said that Jasper is party to a significant arrangement (which is not protected). The authors do not consider that he is.

involve the payment of any rent (or fine) is outside these provisions.

(ii) If the lease is granted for a term in excess of 300 years then when it vests in interest the tenant is entitled to call for the freehold interest: see s.153 of the Law of Property Act 1925.

(iii) Could the lease be made to vest on the **earlier** of 21 years from the date of grant and the death of Jasper (the free-holder)? If so, this would have an obvious attraction in reducing the value of the freehold interest in Jasper's estate. Some concern has been felt that this could convert the reversionary lease into a lease for life under IHTA 1984, s.43(3).

Advisers also gave some thought to alleviating the capital gains tax position on the leasehold interest if the property were ever sold. A few arrangements had been structured so that both the freehold and the lease were held within a single settlement (albeit in different funds) with the intention of taking advantage of the principal private residence relief available to trustees.[4]

IMPACT OF THE PRE-OWNED ASSET REGIME

15–05 It is considered that taxpayers such as Jasper who have entered into reversionary lease arrangements will be subject to an income tax charge under the Regime from April 6, 2005. The analysis is much the same as for *Ingram* schemes: see 14–12 *et seq.*

As with those schemes an apportionment will be necessary under Sch.15, para.4 of the appropriate rental value. The property gifted (the leasehold interest: DV in the formula) is likely to show a year-on-year increase in much the same way as the freehold reversion in *Ingram* schemes.

PRACTICAL ADVICE

15–06 In essence, the practical advice to taxpayers such as Jasper will be much the same as for persons who have effected *Ingram* schemes and hence the comments at 14–14 —14–16 will be relevant.

There is, of course, the curious point that the Revenue considers that post-March 8, 1999 reversionary lease arrangements are caught by the reservation of benefit rules. Of course, if this is correct the pre-owned assets charge is inapplicable!

[4] See TCGA 1992, s.225.

CHAPTER 16

EVERSDEN SCHEMES

Background

Eversden arrangements were a prime target of the Regime with the **16–01** Government intending that such schemes, in relation to both insurance bonds and the family home, should be caught. Indeed, the Paymaster General, Dawn Primarolo, may have had such planning specifically in mind when she talked about inheritance tax schemes over the home being a "one-way bet" and having "no lasting effect", see 1–06.

It is certainly true that *Eversden* arrangements were often marketed on the basis that there was no real downside for the taxpayer. Unlike many of the other schemes involving the family home, the scheme did not create "new" chargeable assets; there were generally no capital gains tax problems and there were few complications if the client wanted to move house. Moreover it was a scheme that most clients could understand, at least in principle, and it could be unscrambled relatively easily.

The facts of *Eversden*, the decision of the Court of Appeal and the amending legislation preventing future *Eversden* planning are discussed at 2–09 onwards.

Eversden arrangements were first used mainly in relation to insurance schemes (see also Chapter 19) but became popular in relation to the family home after the decision in favour of the taxpayer in the High Court.[1] As with the home loan scheme discussed at Chapter 17, demand was fuelled by the rise in house prices in recent years.

---

[1] [2002] S.T.C. 1109.

Who used these schemes?

16–02 The typical clients would be married with combined assets in excess of two IHT nil rate bands. They would generally both be domiciled in the UK.[2] The house would usually be their most valuable asset but they may also have had some cash which they were prepared to put into trust provided they had some possibility of retaining access to the funds in the future.

Types of *Eversden* arrangement

16–03 Suppose John and Emma are married and in their early 60s. They have equities worth about £300,000, an unmortgaged house in joint names worth around £800,000 and cash of about £200,000, in John's sole name. Their three children are all adult.

Eversden and insurance bonds

16–04 John was advised to transfer his cash (usually of an amount equal to his IHT nil rate band) into an interest in possession trust for Emma. The trustees invested the cash in an insurance bond, usually on the lives of both spouses and children in the hope of avoiding an unexpected chargeable event on the death of a spouse. The trustees were John's solicitors.

After six months, Emma's interest in possession over the bond was terminated (without her consent being required) and discretionary trusts arose. Such a transfer was chargeable but fell within Emma's nil rate band so no inheritance tax was payable.

John and his issue would be members of the discretionary class of beneficiaries. The spouse Emma was sometimes excluded from benefiting from the insurance bond after termination of her interest in possession in case she had made a gift with reservation (see 16–17).

The trustees could cash in up to 5 per cent of the bond each year without any income tax liability and could exercise their discretion to appoint the proceeds to John if he required funds.

---

[2] In order for the spouse exemption under IHTA, s.18 to be fully available and therefore for FA 1986, s.102(5) to afford protection it was necessary for: (a) at least the recipient spouse to be UK domiciled, (b) for both spouses to be domiciled here, or (c) for both spouses not to be domiciled here.

By holding the assets in the bond structure, no income arose to be **16–05** taxed on the settlor under s.660A of the TA 1988 and administration of the trust was easy. The settlor had the satisfaction of knowing that he had access to the cash at the trustees' discretion, yet the capital value of the bond would fall outside his and his wife's estates for IHT purposes. If Emma survived seven years she would have a new nil rate band available. If the bond was worth an amount in excess of her nil rate band then terminable interest in possession trusts for the children were often appointed after her interest had been ended.

The main disadvantage of such structures related to the inflexibility of the investment. Clients needed to have liquid assets to settle. The bond could be expensive to take out and generally could not be surrendered without a penalty. It was usually taken out with one company and problems could arise if the trustees later wanted to diversify.

Nevertheless, the scheme represented a relatively straightforward means of effecting IHT planning without the client feeling that he had lost control of the asset—precisely the sort of "have your cake and eat it" arrangements that the gifts with reservation rules were designed to stop.

EVERSDEN AND THE FAMILY HOME

Arrangements involving the family home were structured a little **16–06** differently. Suppose that Emma transferred her half share in the family home on flexible interest in possession trusts for John. On termination of his interest in possession, one would want to avoid discretionary trusts arising since John would be making a chargeable transfer in excess of his nil rate band.

In addition, the comments of Lightman J. in *Eversden* at the High Court suggested that there could be difficulties if discretionary trustees own a share in a house, because of the implication that, at least in the case of any replacement property, the trustees had allowed the settlor into exclusive occupation and therefore conferred an interest in possession on her.[3]

Matters would generally therefore be arranged so that John's interest in possession would be terminated only[4] in part—say as to 95 per cent—with his children then taking revocable interests in possession with rights of occupation (albeit they might choose not to exercise such rights).

---

[3] See further 16–10 where Lightman J.'s comments are set out and discussed.

[4] Such termination might occur automatically after a fixed initial period or be at the discretion of the trustees—there were pros and cons of each option.

Capital gains tax issues

16–07 For CGT purposes, principal private residence relief would generally have been available under s.222 of the TCGA 1992 on the disposal of the house into trust.[5] The termination of the spousal life interest by the trustees was not a disposal for capital gains tax purposes since the property remained settled property within the same trust.

Similarly the beneficial interests could be rearranged within the trust at any time without triggering a CGT charge. On a sale of the house during the parents' lifetimes, there would be a disposal by the trustees for capital gains tax purposes, but any gain arising on that sale would qualify for principal private residence relief under s.225 of the TCGA 1992.

In the above example, it was not necessary for John to have an interest in possession in the entirety of the property he occupied for the trustees to benefit from principal private residence relief.[6] That relief is available provided that he occupied the house under the terms of the settlement (in this case by virtue of his 5 per cent interest).

On the death of John, there would be a capital gains tax free market value disposal and reacquisition by the trustees in respect of the portion of the house in which his interest in possession subsisted.[7] There would be no CGT base cost uplift on the balance but main residence relief would continue to be available if the house was sold within 36 months of John's death.[8] (In practice his 5 per cent share was often left to Emma so that relief would continue to be available until her death).

Income tax issues

16–08 If the house was sold in John and Emma's lifetimes and cash or other investments were acquired with part of the proceeds, John would be subject to income tax on any trust income under s.660A of the TA 1988[9] and to CGT under s.77 of the TCGA 1992.

After the death of the settlor, gains and income are taxable in the normal way, *i.e.* income is taxed on the life tenants in their

---

[5] This assumed the donor had occupied the property as his main residence for the entire period of his ownership bar the last three years and that the total plot did not exceed half an hectare.

[6] See TCGA 1992, s.225.

[7] *ibid.*, s.72.

[8] See TCGA 1992, s.223(2)(a).

[9] For the pre-owned asset charge that may now arise in this situation, see 16–28.

percentage shares and gains are taxed on the trustees at the rate of 40 per cent.[10]

PET on the clock

Once John's interest in possession has been terminated he makes a **16–09** transfer of value under s.52 of the IHTA 1984 and therefore needs to survive seven years for the full IHT savings to be secured. If it is decided to unravel the scheme because of the Regime, the fact that the PET may still be on the John's clock should be emphasised to clients. **They cannot be placed in exactly the same position as they were in before any planning was done.**

If John dies within seven years of the termination of his interest in possession, the PET of (say) £380,000 (95 per cent × 400,000) would become chargeable and IHT payable. The tax has been triggered earlier than if no planning had been done (assuming that the spouse exemption would have been used on the first death). Usually this potential downside was covered by taking out seven year term assurance on John's life to cover the possible failure of the PET.

Trusts of Land and Appointment of Trustees Act 1996

By retaining a 5 per cent interest in possession and, in practice, being **16–10** in sole occupation with Emma, has John retained an interest in possession in the whole of the house? If so, that would make any arguments regarding reservation of benefit irrelevant.

This is an argument that the Revenue have begun to raise in the context of both discretionary and interest in possession trusts, citing comments of Lightman J. in *Eversden*[11] and s.12 of the Trusts of

---

[10] Since April 6, 2004.

[11] Lightman J. commented as follows (see [2002] S.T.C. at para.27):

> "On the sale of Beechwood (the property originally settled) the trustees held 5% of the net proceeds as bare trustees for the settlor and 95% on the trusts of the settlement. On receipt of the net proceeds of sale the trustees were legally obliged to pay over the 5% to the settlor. The trustees could not unilaterally decide to invest the 5% in any other property (whether alone or together with the remaining 95%) without the agreement of the settlor as beneficially entitled to the 5%. The trustees invested the full net proceeds of sale in the purchase of Meadows. In the absence of any evidence to the contrary, it is common ground that the trustees must be presumed to have acted lawfully and in accordance with their fiduciary duties (see eg *Billingham (Inspector of Taxes) v Cooper* [2001] EWCA Civ. 1041 at [32], [2001] S.T.C. 1177 at [32]). Accordingly it must be presumed that the trustees and the settlor agreed that the trustees should invest both the settlement's 95% of the net proceeds of sale and the settlor's 5% in the purchase of Meadows and the bond; and it must likewise be presumed (in the light of the law as it stood prior to the coming into force of the 1996 Act) that the trustees and the settlor

Land and Appointment of Trustees Act 1996 ("the 1996 Act") although the arguments are slightly different in each case.

Discretionary trusts

16–11 In relation to discretionary trusts, the Revenue's argument seems to be that the trustees must have taken the positive decision to allow a beneficiary to enjoy sole occupation of the property.

Interest in possession trusts

16–12 In relation to interest in possession trusts, the Revenue argue that given the provisions of ss.12 and 13 of the 1996 Act, a beneficiary who is excluded from occupation can have no interest in possession and that where a beneficiary occupies alone or jointly he has (respectively) either the entire beneficial interest or an equal beneficial share.

Analysis of s.12

16–13 However, there is nothing in ss.12 or 13 to suggest that where part of the land is held on discretionary trusts and part is beneficially owned, the beneficial owner who does not pay a rent has an interest in possession in the entirety of the land even if he is one of the beneficiaries of the discretionary trust. Nor does s.12 suggest that beneficial shares must be equal if beneficiaries have rights of occupation. That Act expressly states that persons who are beneficially entitled to an interest in possession are not always entitled to joint occupation and enjoyment of the property so the converse must presumably apply.

Section 12 merely confers rights of occupation on an interest in possession beneficiary but it does not then say that someone in occupation has an interest in possession in the whole. In our example, as John's children's rights of occupation are preserved, it

---

agreed and intended that by virtue of her contribution of 5% of the purchase price the settlor should become entitled to a like right of occupation of Meadows as she had previously enjoyed in respect of Beechwood and that the purchase was made on this basis. This scenario entirely accords with the skeletal evidence before the commissioner, and most particularly the application of the settlor's money as 5% of the purchase price of Meadows (and the bond) and the subsequent occupation by the settlor of Meadows."

would appear that John does not retain an interest in possession in the whole property. It is the right to occupy rather than the fact of occupation which is determinative of whether there is an interest in possession.[12]

Is a transfer of value necessarily a gift?

There has been continuing concern about the Court of Appeal **16–14** *Eversden* judgment in that Carnwath L.J. seemed to equate transfers of value with gifts. That would mean the termination of the spousal interest (which is undoubtedly a transfer of value within s.52 of the IHTA 1984) would be regarded as a "gift" for reservation of benefit purposes.

If that is the case, then in typical *Eversden* schemes the spouse, not the settlor, would reserve a benefit and nothing would be achieved. (The point did not need to be decided in *Eversden* itself because the donee spouse had died before the donor spouse. Therefore, it was only the reservation of benefit by the donor spouse that fell to be considered.)[13]

Neither s.102 nor Sch.20 contains any definition of the word "gift" and the Revenue notes in its Manual that in the context of reservation of benefit "the word must be given its ordinary meaning."[14]

Comments of Carnwath L.J.

Does "gift" have an extended meaning for the purposes of the gifts **16–15** with reservation rules (s.102 of the FA 1986)? Worryingly Carnwath L.J. in *Eversden* suggested that this might be the case:

> "Rightly or wrongly the draftsmen clearly did find it possible to equate a disposal by way of gift with a transfer of value . . . ."[15]

These words might be taken to imply that any gift will be a transfer of value rather than that all transfers of value are necessarily gifts. His further comments refer to the extended definition of gift in s.3A of the IHTA 1984 and suggest that the same extended meaning

[12] See *Woodhall (personal representatives of Woodhall deceased) v IRC* 2000 S.T.C. (SCD) 558.
[13] The distinction between a transfer of value and a gift is critical in trust reorganisations (see Chapter 24) and flexible will drafting (see 28–07 *et seq*).
[14] See D29 CTO Advanced Instruction Manual.
[15] [2003] S.T.C. 822 at para.[22].

applies in the reservation of benefit context. On that analysis, a gift is not just confined to voluntary dispositions but applies to transfers deemed to be gifts under s.3A(2) which can then be treated as PETs under s.3A(1)(c).

Section 3A(1)(c) provides that "to the extent that it constitutes either a gift to another individual or a gift into an accumulation and maintenance or a disabled trust" the transfer of value is a PET.

Section 3A(2) then defines what such a gift is in the context of PETS:

> "a transfer of value falls within subsection 1(c) above as a gift to another individual [but is not necessarily a gift in the ordinary sense of the word] to the extent that the value transferred is attributable to property which becomes comprised in the estate of that other individual or the estate of that other individual is increased."

Does the same extended definition of gifts apply in the reservation of benefit context? Carnwath L.J. added:

> "Although the relationship is not spelt out in s.102(5) in the same detail it would be surprising if the draftsman was intending to use the term gift in a radically different sense in two places in the same Act."

Conclusions on the dichotomy

16–16 These remarks should be read in the context of the case. Counsel for the Revenue was arguing that the transfer of value had to be broken down into a number of distinct gifts (the life interest, the remainder interest, the interest of the discretionary class, etc.) and that the spouse exemption (and therefore protection from reservation of benefit) only applied to one of them, namely the gift of the life interest to the spouse. The Court of Appeal felt this distinction was artificial and held that there was just one gift of the settled property which became comprised in the spouse's estate by virtue of IHTA 1984, s.49(1), rather than a series of gifts comprising the equitable interests under the trust.

The main part of the judgment was accordingly based on applying a fundamental principle of inheritance tax (namely that under s.49(1) a person with an interest in possession is treated as beneficially entitled to the settled property). Therefore, the legislation does not permit the conclusion that the subject matter of a gift into an interest in possession trust is anything other than the asset which becomes settled property so that the sole donee of such a gift is the individual who enjoys an interest in possession.

The fact that a transfer of value into an interest in possession trust was treated as a gift of the entire settled property to the settlor's spouse is not the same as arguing that the termination of a spousal interest by the trustees must necessarily be a gift because it is a transfer of value. The voluntary transfer by the settlor of property into a trust for his spouse is clearly a gift by him—it is just a question of whether the gift is in the same property as the transfer of value and the combined effect of s.49 and 3A led the Court of Appeal to think it was.

By contrast, the termination of John's interest in possession by the **16–17** trustees through the exercise of an overriding power of appointment or the effluxion of time is not a gift at all in the natural sense of the word, albeit that IHTA 1984, s.52 deems it to be a transfer of value made by the life tenant. Even if the life tenant consents to such a termination the better view is that this is still not a "gift" by that beneficiary, although he might consider releasing the need for his consent if a termination was not in immediate contemplation.[16] By contrast an assignment or surrender of the life interest is clearly a positive act which could be a gift with reservation.

The settlor/life tenant conundrum

If the transfer of property to an interest in possession trust is a gift of **16–18** the whole of the property being settled to the person entitled to an interest in possession (rather than a gift of separate equitable interests), *Eversden* leaves open to question the IHT position where A (the settlor) retains the interest in possession. He is treated by IHTA 1984, s.49(1) as having continued to be the beneficial owner of the property and therefore does not make a transfer of value for IHT purposes.

But has he made a disposal by way of gift for the purposes of the reservation of benefit rules? The Revenue argues[17] that there can be a gift without a transfer of value, and therefore that a settlor who transfers property into an interest in possession trust has made a gift of the interest in remainder expectant on the determination of his interest in possession. However, this approach is hard to justify in the light of the *Eversden* decision on the scope of s.49(1).[18] In that event has he made a gift if nothing has passed out of his estate?

What is the position when the trustees exercise a power of appointment to terminate the settlor's interest in possession while nevertheless allowing the settlor to continue to be able to benefit from the trust? The settlor has not acted or omitted to act in relation

---

[16] If the release is done immediately before the termination by the trustees the concern is that one would have a gift by associated operations if the consent is indeed a gift. Query, however, whether for these purposes there can be a gift by associated operations: see 25–05.

[17] See D29 of the Advanced Instruction Manual.

[18] The settlor is treated as beneficially entitled to the settled property "for all the purposes of the Act" which includes FA 1986, s.102.

to the termination of his interest; he has made no voluntary disposition, and therefore it is considered that there is no gift with reservation.

The fact that such a fundamental point, namely whether someone who settles property on interest in possession trusts for himself has made a gift with reservation, demonstrates the difficulty that professionals will have in advising their clients on the applicability of the Regime. Unless they can determine whether or not there is a reservation of benefit, they cannot assess whether or not the Regime applies.[19]

THE ANTI-*EVERSDEN* LEGISLATION

16–19 As discussed at 2–10, as from June 20, 2003 it is no longer possible to avoid the gifts with reservation rules by granting an interest in possession to a spouse and then terminating that interest. The effect of the legislation[20] is that on termination of the spousal interest in possession, the donor's disposal by way of gift is treated for the purposes of s.102 as having been made immediately after the spouse's interest came to an end.

Suppose that on August 21, 2003 Ben settles his house on interest in possession trusts for his wife Janet. Janet dies with the property passing to her children but Ben continues to live in the house. At the termination of Janet's interest in possession, Ben is treated as having disposed of the house by way of gift. Since he continues to occupy the property the gift infringes the reservation of benefit rules so that on his death (if he is still in occupation) the house will be taxed as part of his estate. If he moves out before his death his reservation of benefit has ceased and he makes a deemed PET.[21]

It does not matter that Janet's interest in possession ended on her death rather than by exercise of trustees' powers. The settlor is still alive, and therefore s.102(5A) applies. This is in contrast to the Regime where the death of the spouse does not take away the protection of the spouse exemption.[22] Of course, if Ben dies before Janet's interest is terminated, s.102(5A) (and indeed the Regime) will have no application.

The sort of arrangements made by Ben in the example above may not be done in the context of IHT planning: Ben may, for instance,

---

[19] Indeed, where property subject to a reservation is an interest in possession in settled property the precise inheritance tax effects where there is a lifetime termination of such interest in possession is debatable since the scope of s.102(4) is unclear.

[20] IHTA 1984, s.102(5A)—(5C) inserted by FA 2003.

[21] Under FA 1986, s.102(4).

[22] A gift on interest in possession trusts for the settlor's spouse is an excluded transaction unless that interest terminates *inter vivos*: see FA 2004, Sch.15, para.10(2)(c); 10(2)(b); and 10(3).

settle property on interest in possession trusts for Janet for asset protection reasons. If he does so, he needs to take care because if her interest is terminated the reservation of benefit rules will catch him if he then occupies the property.

Note that under the legislation the gift by Ben is only treated as being made on the termination of Janet's interest for the purposes of the gifts with reservation rules. Thus he will not make an actual transfer of value when Janet's interest ends, just a deemed transfer of value.

The transfer of value by Ben was made on the initial gift into trust for his wife and this was spouse exempt. IHT is charged on the death of the wife as if she had made a transfer of value equal to the value of the house in the normal way. Accordingly, if Ben ceases to benefit from the settled property before termination of Janet's interest in possession he has not made a deemed PET under FA 1986, s.102(4).

POST-*EVERSDEN* PLANNING

As noted in Chapter 2, tax planners were not slow in responding to **16–21** the anti-avoidance provisions and by November 2003 had begun to market new "*Eversden* II" schemes. It was apparently rumours of these new schemes that finally prompted the Revenue to take a new approach to avoidance of the reservation of benefit provisions and to introduce the Regime.

It is not felt by the authors that many of the post-*Eversden* schemes had merit but they are outlined briefly here. They tended to rely either on not terminating the spousal interest in possession (and thus avoiding the effect of s.105(5A)) or avoiding an initial gift of settled property to the spouse altogether. Some thought that the legislation was defectively drafted in relation to successive spousal interests in possession and gifts of undivided shares in property.

A difficulty for any clients who implemented such schemes will be **16–22** to determine their position under the Regime:

(i) If the schemes do not work for IHT purposes because there is a reservation of benefit then the Regime does not apply.

(ii) If the schemes work for IHT purposes then the income tax charge applies and the taxpayer needs to self-assess and pay the tax.

The taxpayer may elect for the property to be in his estate for reservation of benefit purposes.[23] If, however, the taxpayer decides

---

[23] The election is discussed in Chapter 11.

that he would rather pay income tax and preserve the IHT benefits, what happens if it is later decided that the scheme did not work so that he did reserve a benefit? In these circumstances can he reclaim the income tax paid under a mistake of law? The case of *Kleinwort Benson v Lincoln City Council*[24] may prove helpful to a restitutionary claim but there is no express provision in the legislation. It may be that the Revenue will give some relief if an error or mistake claim is made.

Property not initially settled in favour of spouse by virtue of the gift

16–23 Under this scheme, H settles property on trust for himself for life, remainder to children. H is excluded from the default trusts. There is no transfer of value at this point since H is treated under IHTA, s.49 as beneficially entitled to the settled property.

The trustees have overriding powers to end his interest. H assigns his interest to his wife (this is an exempt transfer). The trustees then exercise their overriding powers and trusts for the children take effect. The wife makes a deemed PET but the property does not **become** settled property by virtue of the gift to the spouse; it is already settled property. Reading subss.102(5A)(a) and (b) together it seems reasonably clear that the property must become settled property by virtue of the **initial** gift into the trust being for the spouse and therefore exempt.

However, the Revenue could argue that reservation of benefit applies on the basis that the initial transfer on interest in possession trusts for H is a gift albeit not a transfer of value. Of course, the Revenue's argument that the settlor has made a number of gifts into trust involving distinct interests was rejected in *Eversden* so that a gift of property into an interest in possession settlement cannot any longer be so divided (see 16–18). The assignment by him to the spouse is a gift but an exempt gift and not within s.105(5A) for the reasons outlined above.

However, if this is correct why use the spousal interest at all? Why not simply terminate the settlor's interest in possession directly in favour of the children?

Sale at an undervalue

16–24 This scheme involves a sale at an undervalue to avoid a disposal by way of gift. The authors think this unlikely to succeed because a sale

[24] [1997] 2 A.C. 349. See 13–08.

at an undervalue is a gift with the property disposed of being in effect the undervalue.[25] The better view is probably that the property being disposed of by gift is the entire land but the same problem, *i.e.* that there has been a disposal by way of gift and therefore that the reservation of benefit rules apply, still arises.

Avoiding a disposal of property by way of gift: unexercised option

A further scheme was that the taxpayer granted an option over **16–25** the relevant asset to either a nominee or, say, a trust for his benefit ("the First Trust"), on terms that the holder of the option was, within the next (say) 90 days, entitled to acquire the asset for a nominal sum. The asset would then be sold at its reduced market value into a trust ("the Second Trust"), under which the taxpayer's wife had an interest in possession, with remainders over on interest in possession trusts for the taxpayer's children. The wife's interest in possession would then be terminated and the option in due course allowed to lapse.

Alternatively, the option might be allowed to lapse before the wife's interest terminated. The idea was that there had been no gift as such to the Second Trust but a sale for full consideration taking into account the reduced value of the property.

The authors consider that the *bona fides* of the option, which was not intended to be exercised, would not stand up.

Successive spousal interests in possession

A fourth scheme involved taking advantage of a perceived lacuna in **16–26** the wording of ss.102(5A)(c) and (d). The thinking was that:

(a) section 102(5A)(c), in referring to the "relevant beneficiary's interest in possession" appears to mean the spouse's initial interest in possession referred to in s.102(5A)(b); and

(b) section 102(5A)(d) provides that the conditions for the operation of ss.102(5A) are not satisfied if, on the "occasion on which that interest comes to an end" the spouse becomes entitled to another interest in possession in the same settled property.

Does "that interest" mean only the initial interest in possession of the spouse or does it include any successive interest in possession

[25] See *CTO Advanced Instruction Manual* at D30.

that the spouse takes? If the former interpretation is correct and the spouse was given two successive interests in possession such that s.102(5A)(d) applied then the condition in s.102(5A)(c) would not be satisfied when the first interest came to an end. The second interest in possession would not be caught by s.102(5A)(c) and therefore the gifts with reservation rules would remain disapplied by the spouse exemption in s.102(5)(a).

The authors do not have a great deal of confidence in this approach. First, they consider that any court would be reluctant to uphold the schemes and would conclude that in s.102(5A)(c) "the relevant beneficiary's interest in possession" is not limited to the relevant beneficiary's initial interest but extends to any successive interest coming within s.102(5A)(d), with the result that the conditions in s.102(5A) are satisfied when the spouse's second interest in possession comes to an end, in which case s.102(5)(a) will not apply.

Even if the court accepted the existence of the *lacuna*, it would not be difficult for it to conclude that the arrangement in question failed to take advantage of it. Although it may be possible in theory to arrange for successive interests (it is not entirely clear what the closing words of s.102(5A)(d) contemplate: they effectively replicate and appear to be modelled on the closing words in IHTA 1984, s.53(2)), the Court would be mindful of the fact that the sole purpose for inserting successive interests was to oust s.102(5A) and the authors would not be surprised if, in those circumstances, it was not prepared to accept the interests were genuinely successive.

Gift of an undivided share in land

16–27 This scheme may have the most merit. The argument is that a gift of an undivided share in land (to which FA 1986, s.102B applies) may not be caught by the anti-avoidance provisions in s.102(5A)–(5C). This is on the basis that s.102C(2) states that "an interest or share disposed of is not subject to a reservation under . . . s.102B(2) above if . . . the disposal is an exempt transfer by virtue of any of the provisions listed in s.102(5) above."

It is not clear that s.102C(2) requires that the availability of the spouse exemption under s.102(5)(a) is to be read as subject to the exception in s.102(5A).[26] On that basis, a person could settle a share of his home upon trust for his wife for life with remainder to his

---

[26] Although the same point arguably applies in relation to gifts of interests in land under s.102A, given the fact that s.102B takes priority over s.102 but s.102 takes priority over s.102A (see s.102C(6)(7) it might be thought that in relation to *Eversden* schemes this route will only work on gifts into trust for the spouse of undivided shares.

children and occupy the house without reservation of benefit problems on the basis that s.102C(2) does not incorporate s.102(5A). The courts might well argue that the opening words of s.102(5A) "subsection 5(a) does not prevent this section from applying" nevertheless mean that s.102(5A) is incorporated into s.102C and there is little doubt that the Revenue would change the legislation "retroactively" if it was felt this was a serious problem.

While the new schemes may not have been adopted on any major scale, it is clear that a large number of old-style *Eversden* schemes were effected in relation to both houses and bonds. How are such schemes affected by the Regime?

THE EFFECT OF THE REGIME

The purpose of the Regime is to ensure that "unacceptable" **16–28** inheritance tax schemes now have a downside—an income tax charge must be paid in exchange for preserving the IHT savings. *Eversden* schemes were certainly the sort of "have your cake and eat it arrangements" that the Government had in mind and in the authors' view are caught by the legislation. It is the very simplicity of *Eversden* schemes that has made them more vulnerable to attack under the Regime.

The irony is that while *Eversden* schemes were for all practical purposes stopped from June 20, 2003, any arrangements already completed before that date are caught by the Regime. By contrast, the home loan scheme has not been stopped by specific IHT legislation, and therefore can in theory still be used to save IHT in the context of let property.[27] And Sch.15 appears altogether less successful in imposing an income tax charge on such arrangements.

The effect of the Regime on *Eversden* schemes involving the family home

In our first example,[28] Emma gave her interest in the house to John. **16–29** She and John continued to occupy the house. John's interest in possession was terminated as to 95 per cent. The trust was set up prior to June 20, 2003.

---

[27] See Chapter 17 for a consideration of Home Loan Arrangements. It remains possible that such schemes will be challenged by the Revenue and will be found to involve a reservation of benefit.

[28] See 16–06.

The requirements of para.3 of the Regime are *prima facie* met since:

(i) Emma continues in occupation of the house, **and**

(ii) **the disposal condition** is met since she owned an interest in the house after March 17, 1986 and has disposed of the property.

Is there an exclusion?

16–30 Can Emma successfully contend that she made a disposal by way of an excluded transaction and is therefore out of the Regime?

Paragraph 10(1)(c) provides that in relation to the disposal condition the disposal of any property is an excluded transaction if it was a disposal by way of gift "by virtue of which the property became settled property in which his spouse ... is beneficially entitled to an interest in possession." Note that this let out does not cover sales,[29] although presumably a sale at an undervalue would still be treated as a gift for the purposes of the exclusion to the extent of the undervalue with the balance being covered by the non-exempt sale provisions (see 3–14).

When Emma made the disposal it was therefore an excluded transaction. However, para.10(1)(c) is more in the nature of a "safe harbour" rather than a total exclusion. Thus the disposal ceases to be an excluded transaction if the interest in possession of the spouse has come to an end otherwise than on death. In the above example, John's interest in possession was terminated while he is alive, and therefore Emma (not John) is subject to the para.3 income tax charge.

16–31 Note that if John now died, Emma would continue to be subject to the income tax charge because the interest did not terminate on his death. Contrast the position if John's interest in possession came to an end only on his death—in these circumstances the disposal remains an excluded transaction and there is no income tax charge.

This, of course, differs from the position under s.102(5A) of the FA 1986: if Emma had made the disposal into trust after June 20, 2003, she is not protected from the reservation of benefit charge if John's interest terminates on his death.[30]

It is not clear whether the para.10(1)(c) protection is only available if the initial gift is into a trust where the spouse has an interest in

---

[29] See 5–04.
[30] See 16–19.

possession or whether it is possible to obtain excluded status later if the spouse subsequently takes an interest in possession in settled property. The better view is that the spouse needs to take the interest in possession from the start.

None of the other exceptions or indeed the para.11 exemptions would be applicable in the case under consideration.

Options in relation to the family home

Should taxpayers who have entered into *Eversden* schemes involving **16–32** the family home elect into the reservation of benefit provisions? There are a number of options.

Avoid termination of the spousal interest in possession

If the spouse interest (in the example John's interest) has not yet been **16–33** terminated it may be sensible to leave the structure in place and do nothing to end John's interest.

If Emma dies then John's interest can be terminated (in part) by the trustees. The Regime will not apply to John because he has not made a disposal of land and it cannot apply to Emma because she is dead.

However, what happens if John dies with an interest in possession? The Regime can then never apply to Emma because the exclusion protects her permanently once John has died. John might want his share to pass back to Emma on revocable interest in possession trusts to avoid an IHT charge on his death. Can the trustees then carry out IHT planning at that point, terminating Emma's interest without a reservation of benefit if she continues in occupation?

In principle, if the original gift into trust was made prior to June 20, 2003, it would appear that they can do this. The fact that John's interest terminated after June 20 would not appear to have lost Emma the protection of s.102(5)(a). Of course, this is long term planning and depends on Emma surviving John by seven years.

Appointing back the house

Suppose John's interest in possession has been terminated in 95 per **16–34** cent of the trust fund. The trustees should appoint the house back to either Emma or John; in effect the inheritance tax planning is nullified but the couple are back in the same position as before **apart**

from the fact that John has made a PET (see below). In these circumstances, should the house be appointed back to John (the spouse who took the interest in possession) or Emma (the settlor)? On balance the house should be appointed back to Emma for the reasons indicated below.

16–35   If the trustees revoke the children's interests and appoint back 95 per cent to Emma and advance the whole property out (95 per cent to Emma and 5 per cent to John), then the reverter to settlor exemption should be available so that the children are not treated as making PETs.[31] The trust has ended but there should not be any CGT payable because main residence relief is available under TCGA 1992, s.225.

However it must be remembered that John has already made a PET on the termination of his interest in possession. If the property is appointed back to Emma outright and first John and then Emma die within seven years of the PET made by John, there is a double inheritance tax charge: once on the failed PET by John and again because the property is part of Emma's estate on her death. No relief is available under the Double Charges Regulations[32] because the charge arises in relation to different transferors.

If Emma dies before John she may leave the house back to John with the benefit of the spouse exemption and then if John dies within seven years of the PET, relief against a double inheritance tax charge **would** be available: see Regulation 4.

The position is not necessarily improved if the property is appointed back to John rather than Emma. Reverter to settlor exception is still available under IHTA 1984, s.53(4) to avoid a PET by the children. If Emma dies before John there is no inheritance tax payable anyway. If John dies before Emma his PET becomes chargeable but there is no inheritance tax if he transfers his share back to Emma which will be spouse exempt. On Emma's death, inheritance tax will be payable with no allowance for the inheritance tax on the PET made by John. On the other hand, if John leaves his share in the house to his children, double charges relief would be available on his death. In effect, there is one lot of inheritance tax and the property remains outside Emma's estate for inheritance tax purposes.

16–36   Assuming the house does not increase in value significantly during the seven-year period after the PET, the most IHT efficient course would therefore be to appoint the house back to John and ensure that in his Will for the next seven years he leaves it to his children (or on trust for them with his wife as a discretionary beneficiary under an overriding power of appointment). However, does such an approach

---

[31] See ss.53(3) & (4) of the IHTA 1984 and Chapter 23.
[32] See SI 1987/1130.

stop the Regime applying to Emma? One would expect it to do so because the house is now owned by John outright and thus within the IHT net. Paragraph 10(1)(b) provides an exclusion where property is transferred outright to a spouse. However, it is unlikely that such an exclusion can apply where the property is transferred back to the spouse outright but the original disposal was not within para.10(1)(b). There appear to be no other relevant exemptions to prevent an income tax charge on Emma.

Conclusion

In these circumstances the safest course is to transfer the property **16–37** back to Emma.

Pay the income tax charge

Suppose Emma is ill and therefore it will be worth preserving the **16–38** IHT advantages and, if necessary, paying the income tax charge. In these circumstances what tax will Emma pay? In the example, the value of the house is £800,000. Suppose the rental value of the house is £25,000. Emma is charged on:

$$\frac{£25,000 \times (DV)}{V \ (£800,000)}$$

The unknown figure above is DV—what is the value of the interest disposed of by Emma? Following the decision in *Arkwright*,[33] it appears that the Revenue has conceded the principle that IHTA 1984, s.161(4) has no application and that the value of a half share in a house owned by spouses is not necessarily a **mathematical one half of the vacant possession value of the property**. In any event, there is nothing comparable to s.161 in Sch.15 and so the general principles of valuing a share (giving a discount) will apply.

If, say, the value of Emma's interest (DV) is discounted to £340,000 the chargeable amount on which she would pay income tax is £10,625, giving rise to a tax liability (for a 40 per cent tax payer) of £4250 pa. In the circumstances this might be thought an acceptable price to pay. However, Emma cannot change her mind after January 31, 2007 and opt into the Regime.

---

[33] [2004] EWHC 1720 (CH); [2004] S.T.C. 1323.

16–39 Should Emma make an election under para.21? (It is Emma not John who needs to make the election because she is the one liable to the charge.) Generally no. *Eversden* schemes are relatively easy to unravel. Making an election poses the same potential problems on double charges as mentioned above if the property is appointed back to Emma, John has made a PET and yet the property is in Emma's estate for IHT purposes.

16–40 However, the effect of the election is that Emma has reserved a benefit in the property: it is not back in her estate for any other purposes. In these circumstances will the spouse exemption be available on Emma's death? The property is deemed to be comprised in her estate on her death by virtue of s.102(3) of the FA 1986. But it is not actually comprised in her estate so does not pass under her Will. Hence if the children's interest in possession continues there is no spouse exemption. But suppose by the time Emma dies the trustees have appointed the property on interest in possession trusts to John? Can it then be said that the value transferred on Emma's death is attributable to property which "becomes" comprised in the estate of her spouse John or, so far as the value transferred is not so attributable to the extent that his estate is increased? Arguably not because John's estate already has the property in it. The property does not at that time become comprised in his estate.

For the spouse exemption to apply, one would have to treat s.102(3) as deeming two things:

(a) that Emma has the property in her estate for IHT purposes, and

(b) that John does not have the property in his estate.

The safest course in these circumstances is to appoint the property outright to Emma so that the spouse exemption is available in the future rather than relying on the election route.

EVERSDEN ARRANGEMENTS AND INSURANCE BONDS

16–41 In the example,[34] John settled £200,000 cash on interest in possession trusts for Emma. The trustees invested the cash in a bond and

---

[34] See para.16–04, *et seq.*

Emma's interest was terminated with discretionary trusts arising from which John could benefit.

Suppose the bond is now worth around £220,000. No encashments have been made but John is saving the bond for a "rainy day" when his pension ceases. He does not think he needs to worry about the bond—it is not land, he receives no benefit at the moment and it produces no income.

The difficulty is that para.8[35] will catch these arrangements. It provides that:

(a) where the terms of a settlement are such that any income rising from the property would be treated by virtue of s.660A of the TA 1988 as the settlor's income, **and**

(b) the trust holds intangible property (defined to include anything other than chattels and/or land) settled after March 17, 1986

then there is an income tax charge on the "chargeable amount". Paragraph 8 does contain an exclusion if the only reason why the trust is treated as settlor interested for income tax purposes is because the spouse has an interest.[36] However, any interest retained by the settlor, however remote, is sufficient to bring the trust within the scope of para.8. It does not matter that John has received no benefit from the trust and indeed that the settled property produces no income.

Paragraph 10 (excluded transactions) does not apply so even if the spousal interest has not been terminated, if the settlor can benefit from the settlement there is an income tax charge. So even those half way through *Eversden* schemes where the spousal interest has not yet been terminated will be caught by para.8.

Paragraph 9 imposes a severe charge because it is calculated on the **16–42** basis of capital values rather than any actual income.[37] In the example the bond is worth £220,000. This will probably be treated as producing deemed or hypothetical income at the official rate of 5 per cent.[38] That produces £11,000 deemed income (probably taxed at 40 per cent in John's hands).

The trustees might encash the bond. That is a chargeable event which would trigger an income tax liability under TA 1988, s.547 on John. In those circumstances he can deduct (but not credit) that income tax against the £11,000 deemed income and he will then pay income tax on the lesser figure. It is not clear how the chargeable

[35] See generally Chapter 6.
[36] See FA 2004, Sch.15, para.8(1)(b).
[37] See further, Chapter 6.
[38] This depends on the Regulations: see Chapter 12.

amount will be quantified. Will the £220,000 figure be the value of the bond at the start of the year or as an average throughout the year? This point is currently subject to consultation and is discussed further in Chapter 12.

For most settlors an income tax charge based on a fixed percentage of capital value is likely to be unacceptable. Fortunately, there are greater opportunities to avoid the para.9 charge in relation to *Eversden* arrangements over bonds than there are over the home: some of these are as follows:

Exclude settlor from benefit

16–43 If John, as settlor, is excluded from any benefit then there is no para.8 charge even if the Emma still benefits. This is obviously not possible in all cases: for example, if the spouse has been excluded or has died. In the example, John is the member of a discretionary class of beneficiaries and he may also have a remainder interest in the settlement. If the trustees have an express power of exclusion they can exclude John and he can assign his remainder interest, *e.g.* to Emma. If the trustees do not have an express power of exclusion, then they will need to exercise their powers of appointment and exclude him under the terms of the appointment.

Appoint John an interest in possession

16–44 Alternatively, the trustees might decide to appoint John an interest in possession. In that event, the IHT savings have been lost since the property is back in his estate (albeit that Emma has made a PET). Given the sums involved, if John feels that he needs the money in the future this might be the easiest course. Since the settled property is back in John's estate for IHT purposes, John then has the benefit of the para.11(1) exemption.

Move out of intangibles

16–45 Another option is for the trustees to move out of intangible property. There is no great magic about using the *Eversden* scheme with bonds—bonds were popular simply because such products did not generally produce an income tax liability for the settlor. However, if the trustees sell the bond and move into (say) let property, the trust is outside para.8 and the charge cannot apply. The settlor is not in occupation of the land so there is no para.3 charge. There may, of course, be tax payable on encashment by the bond.

Under this route both settlor and spouse can continue to benefit. Obviously the income produced by the letting will be taxable on the settlor under TA 1988, s.660A but at least he is being taxed on actual rather than deemed income, and the amounts are likely to be significantly lower.

CONCLUSIONS

Eversden schemes involving bonds and family homes are caught by **16–46** the Regime. Unscrambling the scheme may ultimately be the best course in relation to the home. For the insurance bond there are other options but they will often depend on the settlor being prepared to give up any possible benefit.

CHAPTER 17

HOME LOAN ARRANGEMENTS

SETTING THE SCENE

17–01 The home loan (or as it is sometimes called the "double trust") scheme was a prime target of the Regime. Although a "guesstimate", it has been suggested that as many as 30,000 of these schemes have been implemented. It is therefore the undoubted expectation of the Government that the introduction of the Regime will lead to taxpayers opting into the reservation of benefit provisions[1] and thus bringing scheme purchasers safely back into the IHT net. This chapter will consider how likely it is that the Government's hopes will be realised.

As a matter of terminology it is proposed to call these arrangements "home loan schemes" rather than "double trust" schemes for the simple reason that whilst one trust has to be employed, the use of the second trust (to receive the benefit of the debt) was a matter of choice. If preferred the debt could have been held directly by (say) the taxpayer's daughter.

HOW THE SCHEMES WORKED

17–02 There was no "single" home loan scheme: rather there were a number of variants. Also whilst many were sold as a package, others were bespoke.

WHO USED THE SCHEME?

17–03 The demand for the scheme was generated by the significant rise in house prices in the 1990s which was not accompanied by a

---

[1] These are considered in detail in Chapter 11.

corresponding increase in the IHT nil rate band. The result was that many individuals found that simply by virtue of owning a house, IHT would be payable on their death. Accordingly, the deeply felt wish of many taxpayers to avoid paying IHT on their main capital asset—the house—was jeopardised. It is such individuals who were particularly receptive to the home loan scheme salesman who would offer the possibility of the individual giving away the value of his house whilst having a right to continue in occupation. Further, it would be possible to sell the current house and downsize if that in due course was what the taxpayer wanted.

It is possible to present the following "profile" of a typical home loan client:

  (i) his house will be worth at least £400,000 so that even if he has no other assets IHT of over £50,000 will be payable on his death;

 (ii) he will be in his 60s or early 70s and likely to survive for at least seven years since the scheme involved the making of a PET and hence, for its success, required seven year survival; and

(iii) it did not matter whether the property was freehold or leasehold but it was important that a disposal of the property would benefit from CGT main residence relief.[2] The existence of a mortgage on the property was a complicating factor.

Of course, other individuals used the scheme: persons in their early 40s (rather young to be engaged in heavy IHT planning) and persons who owned other substantial assets (and who thereby neglected the cardinal rule that using the main residence in any tax planning arrangement should always be the option of last resort).

The structure of a typical home loan scheme

Take for our typical taxpayer, Mischa, a widower aged 67 who owns **17–04** a substantial property (worth £450,000 with no outstanding mortgage) in Rotting Hill. He wishes to leave all his assets in due course to his daughter, Sasha, who is married with young children. The house will benefit from full principal private residence relief for capital gains tax purposes and Mischa thinks that in a few years he might wish to relocate to Brighton and see out his days in the seedy glamour associated with that town.

---

[2] As to the conditions for this relief, see TCGA 1992, ss.222–225.

17–05 **Step 1:** Mischa set up a life interest trust ("Trust 1") under the terms of which he is a life tenant with the right to enjoy the income of the trust or to enjoy the use of trust property. Normally the trustees will be given the usual modern flexible powers: *e.g.* to advance capital to Mischa or to terminate his life interest. The remainder beneficiaries of this trust are Sasha and her family.

17–06 **Step 2:** Mischa will set up a second trust ("Trust 2") for the benefit of Sasha and her family. As this trust will receive a gift from Mischa with a value in the region of £450,000 (the current value of his house) it is important—

(a) that Mischa is wholly excluded from all benefit under this trust; and

(b) that the gift made by Mischa qualifies as a PET for IHT purposes—hence whilst the trust could be interest in possession or accumulation and maintenance in form it should not be discretionary.

17–07 **Step 3:** Mischa will sell his house to the trustees of Trust 1 but as they will not have the resources to purchase the property Mischa will make them a loan to enable the transaction to proceed. In effect, the purchase price is left outstanding as a debt owned by Trust 1 to Mischa.

17–08 **Step 4:** the debt (*i.e.* the right to repayment in due course) is gifted by Mischa into Trust 2. Diagrammatically the position is as follows:

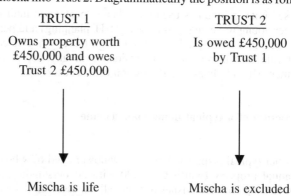

TRUST 1	TRUST 2
Owns property worth £450,000 and owes Trust 2 £450,000	Is owed £450,000 by Trust 1
Mischa is life tenant and hence can continue to live in the property. PPR relief will be available to the Trustees under TCGA 1992, s.225	Mischa is excluded from all benefit— the beneficiaries are Sasha and her family

Miscellaneous technical points

17–09

1. The sale to the Trustees of Trust 1 will attract SDLT: prior to
   December 1, 2003 (*i.e.* in the (good old) days of Stamp Duty)
   duty could be avoided by resting in contract. This was not
   possible after November 30, 2003 so given that rates of duty
   rise to 4 per cent it is likely that SDLT would have killed off
   the home loan scheme for most taxpayers.

2. On Mischa's death the position is as follows:

   (a) he enjoys a life interest in Trust 1 and so is subject to IHT
       on the house (see IHTA 1984, s.49(1)). On these facts and
       if we assume no movement in the value of the property,
       because the debt will reduce the value of the house to nil,
       the result is that the net value of the property subject to
       IHT is nil (value of house exactly offset by debt
       owing)[3];

   (b) provided he has survived by seven years, the PET of the
       debt will be left out of account (*i.e.* it will be an exempt
       transfer); and

   (c) if Sasha was given a life interest in Trust 2 then her estate
       will include the value of that debt. Normally, therefore,
       her husband will be given a subsequent revocable life
       interest (with a view to taking advantage of the IHT
       spouse exemption). Alternatively, life insurance would be
       taken out.

3. The precise terms of the loan varied from scheme to
   scheme:

   (a) in some it was an interest free demand loan;

   (b) in others it was interest free but repayable on the death of
       Mischa;

   (c) sometimes interest was payable and rolled up with the
       principal; in other cases the debt was indexed (*e.g.* by
       reference to a property index); and

   (d) one arrangement involved the use of a tripartite loan
       agreement between Mischa and the two sets of trustees,
       thereby avoiding the necessity for a separate assignment
       of the debt by Mischa. This might avoid certain capital
       gains tax problems on repayment of the debt to Trust 2
       (given that the trustees of Trust 2 would not otherwise be
       the original creditor).

---

[3] Generally the debt was not charged on the house in order to avoid problems with
s.103 of the FA 1986.

Revenue approach to Home Loan Schemes

17–10 The Revenue has been aware of the existence of such schemes for a number of years and for some time indicated that it would challenge their effectiveness. In the event no such challenge has materialised and with the introduction of the Regime it is thought that it the Revenue has now accepted, in general terms, that the arrangements are capable of working.[4]

DOES THE REGIME APPLY TO A HOME LOAN SCHEME OR IS IT AN EXCLUDED TRANSACTION?

17–11 At first blush it would appear that the requirements of para.3 are met since:

(i) the individual (Mischa) occupies land, *and*

(ii) the disposal condition is met given that he owned an interest in that land after March 17, 1986 and he disposed of the property otherwise than by an excluded transaction.

It might be thought that the sale to Trust 1 would be protected as an excluded transaction[5] on the basis that it was a sale of Mischa's whole interest in the property and, although to a connected person, was "a transaction such as might be expected to be made at arm's length between persons not connected with each other." The authors are not, however, persuaded of this, since the sale has a number of features not present in a commercial sale (notably the deferment in the payment of the price/financing the arrangement by a vendor loan).[6]

The para.11(1) exemption

17–12 As has been discussed elsewhere,[7] the Regime will generally not apply if the property is comprised in the individual's estate so that

---

[4] Of course, there will be cases where the paper work is defective so that the particular arrangement will remain caught. It is surprising that the Revenue did not act earlier in this area: taxpayers were, in some cases, lulled into believing that inertia amounted to approval.

[5] See Sch.15, para.10(1).

[6] An alternative way of viewing the Home Loan arrangement would be to see it as satisfying the contribution condition given that the loan is used to discharge the trustees' obligation to pay the purchase price.

[7] See Chapter 7.

IHT will be payable on it. Given that Mischa in our example is the life tenant of Trust 1 (which owns the property), it will form part of his estate for IHT purposes.[8] Doubtless realising that this would exclude the Home Loan Scheme from the Regime, the draftsman introduced the concept of an "excluded liability".[9] It is defined in para.11(7) as follows:

" . . . a liability is an excluded liability if

(a) the creation of the liability, and
(b) any transaction by virtue of which the person's estate came to include the relevant property or property which derives its value from the relevant property or by virtue of which the value of property in his estate came to be derived from the relevant property were associated operations, as defined by s268 IHTA 1984."

This provision is intended to operate in the following way. Assume that the value of the house is now £500,000 and the debt remains £450,000.

(a) To the extent that the value of the property exceeds the amount of the excluded liability (£500,000 – £450,000) the exemption from the Regime in para.11(1) operates. This is consistent with the general scheme of the legislation since £50,000 will be included in Mischa's estate for IHT purposes; and

(b) as to the amount of the excluded liability (£450,000), the Regime applies (in percentage terms to 90 per cent of the value of the house).

Problems with the definition—the relevant transaction

The definition in para.11(7) limits an excluded liability to one the **17–13** creation of which is associated with a transaction whereby the property becomes comprised in the individual's estate. Arguably this occurred at the moment when the property was sold to Trust 1, since it then became comprised in his estate under IHTA 1984, s.49(1). But is this the correct analysis? Given that Mischa had owned the house for a number of years, it may be said that selling the property to the trust did not affect the position (there was certainly no transfer of value at that time). On this argument, the liability was a subsequent

---

[8] See IHTA 1984, s.49.
[9] See 7–06 for a discussion of the meaning of an excluded liability.

event wholly unconnected with Mischa's original acquisition of the property. It was not an associated operation.[10]

It may, however, be argued that para.11(7) is to be read on the basis that the transaction in question is the most recent: *i.e.* the one which **now** is the reason why the property is in the taxpayer's estate. The sale, on this view, broke the chain of ownership and the only reason for the property now being in Mischa's estate is because of his interest in possession in Trust 1.

A side exit out of the excluded liability provisions?

17–14 If that is the case, the temporal link between the creation of the liability and the transaction may be exploited as follows. The trustees of Trust 1 could exercise their powers to apply the property for Mischa's benefit by declaring that they are holding it for him

---

[10] Does it matter that the creation of the debt was not in contemplation when the house was originally purchased? Can the operations still be associated? Operations are associated under IHTA 1984, s.268 if one of two heads is satisfied. Head (b) provides that where any two operations are effected with reference to the other they are associated. Clearly in this case the purchase of the house by Mischa (the transaction by which it became comprised in his estate) was not done with reference to the creation of the debt because the purchase occurred many years previously.

However, Head (a) provides that operations are associated if they affect the same property or one of which affects some property and the other of which affects property which represents directly or indirectly that property. The question here is whether these operations are over the same property: does the debt affect the house or represent the house? It is not charged on the house and it is not clear that it represents indirectly the house. The house is still there. On the other hand the debt would not have arisen if the house had not been sold. Does it represent in some way the sale proceeds of the house?

For IHT purposes the operations need to form *part of a disposition* by associated operations and in the light of *Macpherson v IRC* [1988] S.T.C. 362 and *Reynaud v IRC* [1999] S.T.C. (SCD) 185, it is thought that a series of associated operations which are not connected in terms of intention cannot be part of a single disposition for inheritance tax purposes even under Head (a). One might also argue that the purchase of the house might be an associated operation but is not a *relevant* associated operation because it was not at that point intended to confer a gratuitous benefit—see *Reynaud* where the Special Commissioner said that an associated operation is relevant only if it is part of the scheme contributing to the reduction of the estate. However in that case the point was that it was the **second** associated operation which contributed nothing to the diminution of the estate which had *already* occurred.

In fact, one could argue in the context of the home loan arrangement that neither the creation of the debt nor the purchase of the house as such diminish the settlor's estate. What diminishes his esate is the gift of the debt. So maybe neither of the operations listed in para.11(7) are in fact relevant even if associated!

The main difficulty is that para.11(7) merely refers to associated operations under IHTA 1984, s.268—and an operation can be associated without being relevant for IHT purposes. If an operation is associated but not relevant and not part of a single disposition for IHT purposes can one argue that it is outside the POA charge as well? The legislation is unclear on this point.

absolutely.[11] The trust has, in effect, become a bare trust and the property remains available to the trustees to discharge the liability. If it is accepted that we have to look at the last transaction resulting in the property becoming comprised in Mischa's estate, then it will be the deed of application in his favour (which makes him the absolute owner rather than merely the life tenant). Given that the liability already exists at that time (it is unaffected by the application) it cannot be an excluded liability. It is not thought that the creation of the liability and the advancement out of the house are associated operations. Such an advancement back to the settlor should not cause capital gains tax problems, assuming principal private residence relief is available on the whole property. Nor should the advancement to the settlor subject to the trustees' lien in itself result in an SDLT charge (even following the FA 2004 changes), provided some care is used in the drafting.

Non exempt sale—can it provide relief?

How the concept of a non-exempt sale relates to the Home Loan **17–15** Scheme is far from clear. An arm's length sale is an excluded transaction[12] and so a non exempt sale is defined (in para.4(4)) as a sale of the individual's "whole interest in the property for a consideration paid in money in sterling or any other currency." Mischa is certainly selling his whole interest to Trust 1 but has consideration been paid? The answer may depend upon the particular scheme used: in cases where the consideration for the sale is satisfied by a sterling loan it is certainly arguable that because nothing remains payable under the land contract the requirement is satisfied.

What is the result if the non exempt sale rules do apply? Given that the sale price will be equal to the then value of the house "the appropriate proportion" will be nil (see the formula in para.4(4)).

---

[11] It is assumed that the terms of Trust 1 contain such a power (or at least an overriding power of appointment exercisable in Mischa's favour). It is envisaged that the trustees will not transfer their interest in the property to Mischa. Instead they will hold it on bare trusts for his benefit. Bear in mind that if the arrangement was structured so as to "rest in contract" in order to avoid the Stamp Duty charge on sales (see 17–09) Mischa will have remained the legal owner. There may be attractions in the trustees securing the debt over the property (see further, 17–20). Whilst this should not have been done when the scheme was established because of the risk that the debt would then be an interest in land which was being gifted by Mischa (thereby producing reservation of benefit problems under FA 1986, s.102A) that will not be a problem at this stage when nothing is being gifted to Trust 2. Nor is it considered that securing the debt will lead to problems under FA 1986, s.103.

[12] See Sch.15, para.10(1) and 3–14, *ante.*

Using Mischa again as an example:

$$MV = £450,000$$
$$P = £450,000$$

Hence $\dfrac{MV - P}{MV} = \dfrac{0}{450,000} = 0$

If that appropriate proportion is then applied to find the appropriate rental value (under para.4(2)) DV will be nil and so the rental value will be nil. There are, however, arguments against the non-exempt sale route providing relief in this way depending on whether the home loan scheme breaches the contribution as well as the disposal condition.

Conclusion on the applicability of the Regime

17–16 What might have seemed obvious—that the Regime will catch Home Loan Schemes—turns out on consideration to be much less certain. Of course, it will be surprising if the Regime does not apply (given that such schemes were a principal target), and it is likely that the legislation will be amended in the future if it proves to be defective. Nevertheless, there is sufficient doubt to mean that it is not enough simply to advise clients that a charge will arise under the Regime from April 6, 2005 unless the election is made.

MAKING THE ELECTION

17–17 The mechanics involved in the making of an election have been considered in Chapter 11. In the case of home loan schemes a key matter to bear in mind is the time limit: for a scheme in existence on April 6, 2005 where the settlor occupies the home, the deadline is January 31, 2007. After that date it will not be possible—in the case of existing schemes—to elect.[13]

The effects of making the election are considered below but the intention behind the legislation is clear: by electing the taxpayer brings himself within the IHT reservation of benefit rules so that on his death the property occupied will be taxed as part of his estate. A taxpayer who therefore entered into a home loan scheme in (say) March 1998 will need to consider carefully the following matters:

---

[13] A late election is only permitted if a chargeable person can show "a reasonable excuse" for failure to make the election by that date.

(i) The PET of the debt, having been made more than seven years before April 2005 will, by the time the Regime becomes operative, be an exempt transfer. Electing will therefore involve **bringing the asset back into the IHT net**.

(ii) Can he afford to pay the income tax charge on the appropriate rental value? Bear in mind that this does not involve a taxpayer in paying a market rent: the rental value is used to measure the benefit on which he is subject to income tax. In a general sense therefore it may be said that **he has to pay 40 per cent of a full rent each year** in the form of income tax.

(iii) The taxpayer may decide that paying the income tax is a price worth paying to preserve the already accrued IHT advantage. But what if in a few years time he can no longer afford to pay that tax? In that event he is too late to make the election!

(iv) For a taxpayer who is in poor health and who may soon go into a nursing home (and so cease to occupy the property) the election should not be made. It will be worth the family clubbing together (if need be) to pay the income tax.

Does the s.102(3) condition apply?

The above discussion has assumed that the election provisions are **17–18** adequately drafted to achieve their intended purpose. However, as is the position with other parts of Sch.15, it is far from certain that this is the case!

The legislation[14] provides as follows:

(i) if an election is made the Regime shall not apply;

(ii) s.102(3) and (4) of FA 1986 shall apply;

(iii) s.102(3) deals with the situation where on the death of the taxpayer there is property subject to a reservation and provides that, for the purposes of the IHT charge, he is to be treated as beneficially entitled to that property immediately before his death; and

(iv) however, s.102(3) only applies to the extent that the property "would not, apart from this section, form part of the donor's estate immediately before his death."[15]

---

[14] Sch.15, para.21(2)(b).

[15] Curiously this limitation on the operation of s.102(3) is not included in s.102(4) which imposes a deemed PET when a reservation ceases *inter vivos*.

When s.102(3) is invoked does the restriction continue to apply: *i.e.* can the taxpayer make the election and then successfully argue that because he is the life tenant of Trust 1 the property forms part of his estate at death so that a charge to IHT will not arise under the reservation of benefit rules? Notice in particular that the wording in s.102(3) does not have any restriction for excluded liabilities.

The first argument is as follows:

The draftsman has throughout the Regime expressly adopted the IHT legislation to give effect to the Regime. Where an election is made, the legislation simply provides, without stating anything more, that the property in question is to be treated as property subject to a reservation and ss.102(3) and 102(4) are to apply. Had it been intended that s.102(3) were to be read as though important words had been excised from it, one would have expected the draftsman to provide as much. In the absence of express provision, it is hard to justify applying s.102(3) one way under the normal rules and another way when the taxpayer elects for it to apply under the Regime.

The counter-argument is as follows:

(i) para.21(2)(a) provides that, if the election is made, the chargeable proportion of the property **is to be treated** as property subject to a reservation, and

(ii) s.102(3) **shall apply**.

The intention is that what is being incorporated is the deeming effect of s.102(3): it is not envisaged that a further condition is incorporated and which must be satisfied. Further, it would surely be illogical to make express provision so that the debt, as an excluded liability, remains within the Regime whilst enabling that restriction to be side-stepped if an election is made.

Whatever the correct interpretation, there is no doubt that the consequences of making the election in para.21(2)(b) could have been more happily expressed.

What value is included in the taxpayer's estate if s.102(3) applies?

17–19 A further problem in considering the effects of the election is as follows: s.102(3) provides that the taxpayer is to be treated as beneficially entitled to the property in which he has reserved a benefit immediately before his death. Nothing is said about how that property is to be valued but presumably normal IHT principles apply.[16] It is therefore thought that liabilities affecting the property (*e.g.* the debt owed by the trustees of Trust 1) fall to be deducted and it is only the net value which falls into the IHT net. In practice this may result in a relatively small value being clawed into the IHT net.[17] This argument would be strengthened if the property were to be made subject to an express charge for the amount owed (see IHTA 1984, s.162(4): "a liability which is an incumbrance on property shall, so far as possible, be taken to reduce the value of that property").

PRACTICAL ADVICE

As has been discussed above: **17–20**

   (i) There are arguments that the Regime does not apply to the Home Loan Scheme due to the defective definition of excluded liability see 17–14) or that matters can be arranged so that the liability is not an excluded liability (see side exit strategy 17–15);

  (ii) Even if the election is made it is unclear whether the full value of the property will in fact be taxed on the taxpayer's death (see 17–18 and 17–19).

These certainties complicate the position for any adviser. It is likely that the advice will be heavily dependent on the precise circumstances of each case and on the type of Home Loan Scheme used.

In cases where the taxpayer wishes to preserve the IHT advantage and is willing to pay the income tax there is no downside in raising the arguments in 17–14 and 17–15. This should be done in the tax return.

When the taxpayer indicates that he cannot afford to discharge any income tax liability and would prefer to elect, the points raised in 17–18 and 17–19 concerning the effect of such an election may be

---

[16] The wording used is similar to that in IHTA 1984, s.49 which treats an interest in possession beneficiary as being "beneficially entitled to the property in which the interest subsists". Again nothing is said expressly about liabilities but in practice they have always been allowed so that the net value of the trust fund is taxed.

[17] The Revenue consider that personal liabilities of the taxpayer cannot be offset against the value of reservation of benefit property. The point discussed in the text is quite different and goes to the question of how to value the reservation property.

raised at the relevant time—which will be on the death of the tax-payer.[18]

Double charge

17–21 Bear in mind that making the election will not undo the transaction: *i.e.* **it does not unscramble the scheme**. The taxpayer—Mischa in the example used—will have made a PET equal to the value of the debt gifted to Trust 2 so that were he to die within seven years it would become a chargeable transfer. Further, if he had elected then (unless any of the arguments discussed above are valid) the property will be taxed as part of his estate. The Double Charges Regulations[19] provide relief in the situation where: (a) there is a failed PET of property, and (b) the taxpayer reserves a benefit in respect of that property. The difficulty in the case of Home Loan Schemes is that the gift is of different property (the debt) from that in which he elects to reserve a benefit (the house). It is to be hoped that, on being made aware of this anomaly, the Revenue will agree to amend the Regulations to extend the relief to cover this case.

Radical unscrambling

17–22 There has been talk of a more radical unscrambling along the following lines. First, the trustees of Trust 2 appoint the benefit of the debt to (say) the settlor's daughter; secondly, she then releases the debt,[20] and thirdly the trustees of Trust 1 appoint the benefit of the now unencumbered house to the settlor. Were this to occur then the unencumbered property is now part of the taxpayer's estate so that the Regime will not apply (he will, of course, have made a PET of the debt which will not be covered by the Double Charges Regulations). The daughter will, of course, make a PET and, more critically the trustees of Trust 2 may have committed a fraud on their powers in exercising the power to transfer the debt to the daughter. It is

[18] Of course the taxpayer might wish to have the possibility of utilising all the arguments whilst at the same time not running the risk of suffering an income tax charge. In that case he should consider making a "precautionary election": *viz.* opting into the reservation of benefit regime **in case** he is caught by the POA charge. Because the election is only valid if the POA regime does apply, that question will need to be resolved first after his death before consideration is given to the effect of the election and the size of any IHT charge (see further, 11–02, n.1).

[19] SI 1987/1130: see Regulation 5.

[20] Will this have CGT consequences? If the trustees are original creditors it may be better for them to release the debt (see TCGA 1992, s.251).

difficult to see that this reorganisation achieves anything: better to leave the arrangement alone and for the election to be made. A better option would be for the daughter (having been appointed the benefit of the debt as before) to assign it the settlor. The consequences would then be:

(i) the house remains in Trust 1 and hence in the settlor's estate but with a deduction for the debt;

(ii) the benefit of the debt is now part of the settlor's estate so that there is no Regime charge (see para.11(6)); and

(iii) the advantage of this rearrangement is that double charges relief will be available if the settlor dies within seven years of making the PET of the debt.[21]

Continued application

New home loan schemes in respect of the taxpayer's dwelling house **17–24** will not be entered into today: first, because of the very real risk of a pre-owned assets charge and, secondly, because of the SDLT charge (rates up to 4 per cent and no more resting in contract). However, for other assets possibilities remain. Consider the following:

1. Jason establishes an interest in possession trust along the lines of Trust 1 in the Home Loan Scheme: *i.e.* he is the initial life tenant.

2. Jason lends the trustees (say) £1m which they use to buy let commercial property. The benefit of the debt is gifted by Jason into Trust 2 (the children's trust).

3. The Regime does not apply because the requirement in para.3(1)(a) that Jason "occupies" land is not met.[21] It is irrelevant that the contribution condition is met. The para.8 charge does not apply because land is **not an intangible**.

---

[21] Restructuring by taking advantage of the reverter to settlor exemption might be considered (see generally Chapter 23). Consider the following: Trust 1 is divided into two funds. Fund A retains the house whilst Fund B is established with (say) £10. Mischa is the life tenant of both funds. The trustees of Trust 2 advance the benefit of the debt to (say) Mischa's daughter who puts it into Fund B. The trustees of Trust 1 then transfer the house into Fund B in satisfaction of the debt. The house is now held on a reverter to settlor trust for Mischa for life remainder to his daughter. By structuring the arrangement through two funds it is hoped that SDLT is avoided on the satisfaction of the debt.

4. Were the trustees to purchase stocks and shares, however, the Regime would then apply because Jason would be chargeable under para.8 on the basis:

(a) that the trust is settlor interested, and
(b) that it owns intangible property.

CHAPTER 18

CHATTEL ARRANGEMENTS

Background

For some taxpayers, chattel collections (or even the ownership of **18–01** individual items) raise the spectre of a substantial IHT liability on death. Hence there has been a demand for an arrangement under which the chattels can be given away (whether outright or into trust for children and issue) whilst at the same time leaving the taxpayer able to continue to use and enjoy them. In recent years two main "schemes" have been employed to meet these requirements.

Ingram schemes

In simple terms the arrangement blessed by the House of Lords[1] is **18–02** applied to the chattels: *viz.* the taxpayer retains a lease which enables him to continue to possess the chattels and gifts the "freehold" interest. Doubt had been expressed in some quarters as to whether a land shearing operation was capable of applying to chattels but it is understood that the Revenue have recently accepted that such arrangements are possible.[2] Of course the *"Ingram* scheme" was

---

[1] See 14–02.

[2] See *Taxation*, October 16, 2003 (Nicholas Brown). In the particular case the chattels in question were individually valued at under £6,000 but collectively had a value of £750,000. A lease for 17 years was retained and on the death of the taxpayers there was seven years left to run on the lease: the PET of the assets (subject to that lease) occurred more than seven years before the deaths and so was an exempt transfer. The value of the remainder of the lease was then worth £13,000 and the collection of chattels £1,380,000. The Revenue initially argued that unlike land it was not possible to create different interests in chattels with the result that there had been a gift of the entire interest in the chattels with a contractual arrangement (not involving the payment of full consideration) permitting their use and which amounted to a reserved benefit.

reversed by legislation in FA 1999 but that legislation was expressly limited to land and interests in land.[3]

Gifts and commercial leaseback

18–03 This alternative arrangement has been widely used for a number of years. The chattels are gifted and leased back by the donor who pays a commercial rent: hence the reservation of benefit rules are inapplicable.[4] In the case of land (to which a similar exemption applies), the amount of the required commercial rent will frequently be beyond the means of the taxpayer. In the case of chattels, however, there is no ready market in rentals and no standard type of agreement. In practice, experts are engaged by both donor and donee to negotiate a full value for the enjoyment of the chattels. It is thought that this will normally involve the payment of a relatively small rent (perhaps 0.75 per cent of the value of the chattels each year) provided that the donor/lessee is responsible for insuring and maintaining the item in question (which will often include the provision of a suitable security system). Similar negotiations will be necessary to agree the level of any rent reviews.[5]

The CGT dimension

18–04 In both arrangements it was important to bear in mind the CGT consequences of disposing of the chattel (or an interest in it). There is a general exemption for chattels which are individually worth £6,000 or less,[6] whilst if the item is a wasting asset then gains are exempt without limit. A wasting asset is one with a predictable useful life of 50 years or less and includes yachts, caravans, washing

---

[3] In the Press Release of March 1999 announcing the blocking of *Ingram* arrangements, it was stated that "if no action were taken, the [*Ingram*] decision would jeopardise a large part of the tax base. As the decision affects only gifts involving land, the changes to the gifts with reservation rules are limited to such gifts. However, the operation of these rules will be closely monitored and the Government will not hesitate to act to prevent any tax avoidance through other gifts."

[4] See FA 1986, Sch.20, para.6(1)(a): actual enjoyment of a chattel "if it is for full consideration in money or money's worth" is disregarded in applying the reservation of benefit rules.

[5] See generally *Christie's Bulletin for Professional Advisers*, Autumn 1995 (Manisty) and Autumn 1998 (McCall).

[6] TCGA 1992, s.262(1): note that there are special rules for sets: *ibid.*, s.262(4). In the case of more valuable chattels the gift could be into a discretionary trust taking advantage of holdover relief under *ibid.*, s.260(2)(a) provided that the value was limited to the donor's available IHT nil rate band (so as to avoid an immediate IHT charge).

machines, animals and all plant and machinery, the latter term to include, in the Revenue's view, such assets as antique clocks and watches, certain vintage cars and (generally) shotguns.[7]

Impact of the Regime

Stated objectives

The December consultation paper made it clear that a main target of **18–05** the new charge was chattel schemes: it referred to tax being charged at a specified percentage of capital value in cases where there was no market evidence of an appropriate rent as in the case of "art or antiques".

Ingram schemes

The charge under para.6[8] will apply (in essence the analysis is much **18–06** the same as in the case of *Ingram* arrangements affecting the land: see 14–08). Hence the options open to the taxpayer are much the same.

Gift and leaseback arrangements

It is considered that the Regime does not apply for the following **18–07** reasons:

(i) the para.6 charge does not apply if the relevant property falls within para.11(5): see para.11(3); and

(ii) para.11(5) includes (*inter alia*) property which would fall within the reservation of benefit rules "but for s.102C(3) of, and para.6 of Sch.20 to, the 1986 Act." The latter provision

---

[7] *Tax Bulletin*, October 1994 and February 2000: TCGA 1992, s.44.
[8] See Chapter 4, *ante*. Note that para.6(2)(b) refers to a disposal of all **or part** of his interest in the chattel and para.6(4) treats the creation of a new interest out of an existing interest as the disposal of part of the existing interest. The authors are not aware of reversionary leases being used for chattels.

deals (*inter alia*) with full consideration arrangements in relation to the enjoyment of chattels.[9]

It is not clear whether this represents a change of policy of the part of the Revenue and that, whilst the original intention (as manifested in the December consultation paper) had been for the Regime to apply to both chattel schemes, it was subsequently accepted that there should be consistency between the treatment of land and chattels. Given that taxpayers had been encouraged to enter into market rental agreements in both cases by the inclusion of the statutory exemption it would be inequitable for the Regime to apply at all or in one case (chattels) but not the other (land).[10]

Current attitude of the Revenue

18–08 A number of gift and leaseback schemes are under consideration by the IR Capital Taxes Division which is concerned to ascertain whether full value has been paid in "rent". Bear in mind that if it can be shown that there is **any** element of undervalue the protection of Sch.20, para.6(1)(c) will be lost and the taxpayer will have reserved a benefit in the chattels. The pre-owned assets charge will not therefore apply.[11]

Practical advice

18–09 (i) Consider what steps should be taken to deal with the para.6 charge in the case of *Ingram* chattel schemes. It will not usually be attractive to pay the charge (apart from the cost, the valuation difficulties and expenses are likely to be considerable), although in a case where the gift of the freehold (the PET) has been made more than seven years ago (so that there is an accrued IHT benefit) it ought to be considered. This will be especially so if the taxpayer is in poor health so that paying for a few more years use of the chattels may be sensible. In some cases the taxpayer may be prepared to give up possession or use of the chattels so that

---

[9] The wording of para.11(5) is unsatisfactory in running together s.102C(3) with para.6 given that the former provision is concerned with occupation of land in hardship cases (dealt with also in para.6(1)(b)) whereas para.6 deals with other matters such as full consideration. It is therefore considered that "and" must be read disjunctively. See 7–17 to 7–19.

[10] The consultation paper is in Appendix II.

[11] Para.11(5)(a).

the Regime will not apply. More generally, it may be attractive for the donor to exercise the election for the reservation of benefit rules to apply and then to bring the reservation to an end by paying full consideration for the use of the chattels within FA 1986, Sch.20, para.6(1). This will, of course, result in him making a deemed PET within s.102(4) but if the *Ingram* scheme was only recently entered into nothing much may be risked by adopting this course.

(ii) In the case of existing gift and leaseback arrangements, make sure that arguments can be adduced to defend the level of rent paid (in particular make sure that the terms of the lease—and especially the level of rent—have been reviewed periodically).

(iii) Given that the exclusion of the Regime is apparently deliberate, taxpayers and their advisers may in the future consider entering into new gift and leaseback arrangements.

CHAPTER 19

INSURANCE-BASED ARRANGEMENTS

19–01 There are a wide variety of arrangements involving insurance policies held in trust which, in one form or another, avoid the reservation of benefit provisions by relying on the carve-out principle.[1] It is beyond the scope of this discussion to consider all these arrangements, but the following comments should provide some guidance.

Qualitative carve-outs

19–02 Under one kind of arrangement a policy is held by trustees on trusts to hold certain rights under the policy for the settlor absolutely and other rights on trust for other beneficiaries. For example, under a critical illness policy, the trustees would hold the critical illness benefit on trust for the settlor absolutely and the death benefit on trust for his family.

This is thought to be effective to avoid a reservation of benefit.

So far as the Regime is concerned the requirement under para.8 is that:

(a) the terms of a settlement, as they affect any property comprised in the settlement, are such that the settlement is a settlor-interested settlement (note, however, that a trust which can benefit the spouse of the settlor but not the settlor is not settlor-interested for the purposes of the Regime); and

(b) that property includes any property which is intangible property settled by the settlor or representing such property.

---

[1] The carve out principle is discussed in the context of *Ingram* schemes: see Chapter 14.

172

For this purpose, "settlement" and "settled property" have the same meanings as for IHT. Property held on trust for a person absolutely is not settled property for IHT purposes.

What is the settled property for this purpose? On one construction, it is the insurance policy, which is the property comprised in the settlement. On that analysis, such arrangements are within para.8.

On another construction: **19–03**

(a) the rights held on trust absolutely for the settlor are not settled property; and

(b) the rights held on trust for the other beneficiaries are settled property but are not held on settlor-interested trusts.

This is understood to be the construction which the Revenue has indicated it would adopt in discussions with the Association of British Insurers. Although this is consistent with the IHT treatment of such arrangements, so far as the Regime is concerned it is arguable that the policy is the relevant property for purpose of para.8.

An alternative construction is that even if the critical illness is "settled property" this is the only part of the trust property to which s.660A applies and therefore to which the Regime could apply.[2] The death benefits are held in a separate fund from which the settlor is excluded. Therefore the Regime cannot apply to the death benefits.

Quantitative carve-outs: immediate drawdown

Under another kind of arrangement the settlor's entitlement is **19–04** defined quantitatively, *e.g.* he is entitled to have returned to him each year a fixed portion of the trust fund, usually funded by the trustees making a partial surrender of the policy within their annual 5 per cent tax-free allowance. This is thus a form of reverter to settlor trust. The other beneficiaries get what is left of the trust fund after the payments made to the settlor.

Although this is thought to be effective for reservation of benefit purposes, it would seem to be caught by para.8 on the basis that there is no segregation of the rights under the policy: the only intangible property is the policy. It appears, however, that the Revenue proposes to treat such arrangements in the same way as qualitative carve-outs.

---

[2] See 6–02 for a fuller discussion on sub-funds. Of course, rights held in trust for the settlor absolutely are part of his estate for IHT purposes and so outride the para.8 charge (see para.11(1)(b)).

Reversionary interests: deferred drawdown

19–05 Under these arrangements the trust is divided into a number of funds. The settlor retains a contingent reversionary interest in each of the funds. The reversions are timed to vest serially if he survives to certain dates so that he is effectively entitled to a series of payments. Until his interest in a fund vests, the fund is held on interest in possession trusts for the beneficiaries. This is another form of reverter to settlor trust. Again, the only intangible settled property is the one or more policies held on trust.

It appears that the Revenue will also treat these arrangements in the same way as qualitative carve-outs.

Eversden-based arrangements

19–06 *Eversden*-based arrangements are within para.8 and the Revenue has indicated that such arrangements are among the targets of the Regime.[3]

Loan arrangements

19–07 Under some arrangements the settlor funds a trust by an interest-free loan repayable on demand. The Revenue has now accepted that such an arrangement is not within para.8 because any benefit accruing to the settlor from the repayment of the interest-free loan will arise to him as a creditor, not under the terms of the settlement (*Jenkins v IRC*[4] had been quoted by the Revenue to refute this view).

Personal pensions

19–08 It is common for an individual to settle a personal pension on trusts under which the pension rights are held absolutely for the individual and the death benefit is held on discretionary trusts for his family. It is understood that the Revenue propose to treat such arrangement in the same way as qualitative carve-outs (*i.e.* there is no charge under the Regime).

---

[3] For a fuller discussion see Chapter 16.
[4] [1944] 2 All E.R. 491. See 2004 SWTI, p.2160.

Partnership death benefits

It is common for all the partners in a firm to take out policies on their **19–09**
own lives and to transfer them to a discretionary trust for all the
partners, the trustees holding all the policies as a buy-out fund in the
event of the death of a partner. Strictly, such arrangements appear to
be within para.8. In particular the "no-bounty" defence will not be
available because the definition of "settlement" for these purposes is
the IHT definition, not the income tax definition (see 6–09). It is
understood that the Association of British Insurers is making strong
representations to the Revenue that such arrangements should not be
within the Regime.

Double taxation

If para.8 does apply and charges are imposed under the insurance **19–10**
policy "chargeable events" legislation, the tax paid under the
chargeable events legislation reduces the chargeable amount under
the Regime.[5] However, tax charges on chargeable events (*e.g.* on the
surrender of a policy) are likely to arise subsequent to most of the
charges imposed under the Regime so that this will be of little, if any,
comfort.

---

[5] See 6–11.

CHAPTER 20

FOREIGN DOMICILIARIES

20–01 Foreign domiciliaries are in most cases protected from the effects of the pre-owned assets legislation. There are two mechanisms—the let-outs given specifically to foreign domiciliaries contained in para.12[1] and the para.11 exemptions available to taxpayers generally.[2] Those reliefs and exemptions will be reviewed and then applied to various situations of concern to foreign domiciliaries.

Relief relevant to all non-residents wherever domiciled: under para.12(1) the Regime does not apply to any person for any year of assessment during which he is not UK resident.

Reliefs relevant only to foreign domiciliaries

20–02 These are contained in para.12(2) and (3) and discussed in detail at 8–09 *et seq.* They are briefly as follows:

The *basic relief* under para.12(2): where an individual is not domiciled or deemed domiciled in the United Kingdom for IHT purposes, the Regime does not apply to him unless the property by reference to which the Regime operates is situated in the United Kingdom.[3]

The settled property relief—para.12(3)

20–03 In applying the Regime to a person who was at any time domiciled outside the United Kingdom for IHT purposes, no regard is had to

---

[1] Discussed in Chapter 8.
[2] Discussed in Chapter 7.
[3] See Sch.15, para.12(2).

foreign *situs* property which is excluded property by reason of being comprised in a settlement made by a settlor who was not domiciled in the United Kingdom when he made the settlement.[4]

Exemptions relevant to all taxpayers—The para.11 and para.16 exemptions

These are discussed in detail at 7–01 *et seq.* They apply regardless of **20–04** the taxpayer's domicile and regardless of the *situs* of the Regime property. They are briefly as follows:

Ownership exemption under para.11(1)(a)

The Regime does not apply to an individual in respect of property **20–05** already included in his IHT estate. A person's estate for IHT purposes includes settled property in which the person concerned has an interest in possession—see s.49(1)—as well as property he owns directly. Although the settled property held in trust for foreign domiciliaries is excluded property and not generally subject to inheritance tax on a person's death, it is nevertheless within para.11(1). This is subject to the "excluded liabilities" rule.[5]

Derived ownership exemption—para.11(1)(b)

As discussed at 7–06, the Regime also does not apply to an **20–06** individual in respect of relevant property if that individual's estate includes property which derives its value from that relevant property (para.11(1)(b)). This is subject to the "excluded liabilities" rule and the "substantially less" rule.[6] For the purposes of this Chapter, this is called the derived ownership exemption.

Reserved benefit exemption—paras 11(3)(a) and (5)(a)

The Regime does not apply to an individual by reference to any **20–07** property in which he has reserved a benefit. Neither the "substantially less" nor the "excluded liabilities" rules apply.

[4] See Sch.15, para.12(3).
[5] See 7–03, *et seq.*
[6] See 7–06, *et seq.*

Example:
Assume X dies deemed domiciled in the UK, having reserved a benefit in respect of excluded property held on discretionary trusts set up when he was not domiciled in the UK. Revenue practice in such a case is not to impose a charge on the settled property on the basis that, as excluded property, it does not form part of X's estate immediately before he died. But this does not prevent the property from being property subject to a reservation while he is alive and thereby obtaining the protection of para.11(5)(a).

Derivative reserved benefit exemption (para.11(3)(b))

20–08 As discussed at 7–12, the reservation of benefit exemption is extended by para.11(3)(b) to exempt property in which the donor reserves a benefit which **derives its value** from relevant property.[7] In this chapter this is called the derivative reserved benefit exemption.

Posthumous arrangements under para.16

20–09 The Regime does not apply in respect of certain posthumous arrangements.[8]

Hierarchy of let-outs and exemptions

20–10 The legislation does not establish any hierarchy between the para.12 let-outs and the para.11 exemptions. In practice, it is simpler to apply the para.12 reliefs first because they are easier to apply conceptually than the para.11 exemptions and, unlike the para.11 exemptions, are not subject to any qualifications.[9]

---

[7] See 7–08.
[8] See 7–08, *et seq.*
[9] There has been some question as to whether para.12(3) causes a problem by disapplying the Schedule in relation to excluded property of a former foreign domiciliary. "In the application of this Schedule to a person who was at any time domiciled outside the UK, no regard is to be had to any property which is . . . excluded property . . . " In these circumstances, can such a person rely on the para.11(1) exemption if the Schedule does not apply to excluded property—arguably the excluded property is not then part of the person's estate and therefore the underlying property cannot obtain the benefit of the derived ownership exemption. It is not thought this is the correct interpretation of para.12(3), which should be read more narrowly. See 8–12.

Application in practice

The best way of explaining how the para.11 reliefs and para.12 **20–11**
exemptions work is by example. The examples chosen begin with
simple arrangements and then proceed to more sophisticated structures. In all the examples, references to a person's domicile are
references to their domicile for IHT purposes, *i.e.* applying both the
general law and the IHT deemed domicile provisions.

**Non-trust and non-corporate structure: assets owned by
another individual**

These divide into two categories: **20–12**

(a) foreign land or chattels owned by another individual but
which the taxpayer occupies or enjoys; and

(b) United Kingdom land or chattels owned by another individual
but which the taxpayer occupies or enjoys.

Foreign land/chattels owned by another individual

Alexis, a foreign domiciliary, owned land and chattels and gave these **20–13**
away post-March 17, 1986. He occupies the foreign *situs* land or uses
a foreign *situs* chattel owned outright by another individual. The
basic relief under para.12(2) for foreign domiciliaries will apply. If
the circumstances are such that Alexis has reserved a benefit,
para.11(3)(a) (reserved benefit exemption) will also apply. If Alexis
becomes domiciled in the United Kingdom he loses any relief under
para.12(3) but the reserved benefit exemption (paras 11(3) and
11(5)(a)) will still apply. There is therefore no charge under the
Regime.

United Kingdom land/chattel owned by another individual

Boris, a foreign domiciliary, occupies United Kingdom *situs* land or **20–14**
uses a United Kingdom *situs* chattel owned by another individual.
The basic relief under para.12(2) for foreign domiciliaries will not
apply. Paragraph 12(3) is not applicable because the property is not
settled. If the circumstances are such that Boris has reserved a

benefit, paras 11(3)(a) and (5)(a) (reserved benefit exemption) will apply wherever Boris is domiciled.

Corporate non-trust structures:

20–15 These divide into four categories:

(a) foreign land or chattels owned by a company (whose shares are not owned by the taxpayer) which the taxpayer occupies or enjoys;

(b) United Kingdom land or chattels owned by a company (whose shares are not owned by the taxpayer) which the taxpayer occupies or enjoys;

(c) foreign land or chattels owned by a company owned by the taxpayer and which the taxpayer occupies or enjoys; and

(d) United Kingdom land or chattels owned by a company owned by the taxpayer and which the taxpayer occupies or enjoys.

In all cases it is assumed that the company is not funded by way of loan but by share capital: otherwise there may be problems in claiming any derivative exemption.

Foreign land/chattel owned by company not owned by the taxpayer

20–16 Cyrus, a foreign domiciliary, occupies foreign *situs* land or uses a foreign *situs* chattel owned by a company the shares of which he does not own. The basic relief under para.12(2) will apply so long as Cyrus does not become domiciled in the United Kingdom. If Cyrus has reserved a benefit in respect of the shares para.11(3)(b) (derivative reserved benefit exemption) will apply to the land and chattels wherever he is domiciled.

United Kingdom land/chattel owned by company not owned by the taxpayer

20–17 Dimitri, a foreign domiciliary, occupies United Kingdom *situs* land or uses a United Kingdom *situs* chattel owned by a company the shares of which he does not own. Since United Kingdom *situs* assets are involved, neither of the para.12 reliefs will apply wherever Dimitri is domiciled. If Dimitri has reserved a benefit in respect of the shares paras 11(3)(b) and (5)(a) will apply wherever he is domiciled and under the derivative reserved benefit exemption the protection extends to the land and chattels, even though he has only reserved a benefit in the company shares.

Foreign land/chattel owned by company owned by the taxpayer

Erik, a foreign domiciliary, owns all the shares in a company which **20–18** owns foreign *situs* land which he occupies or a foreign *situs* chattel which he uses and which was purchased with funds he provided. The para.12(2) basic relief and the para.11(1)(b) (derivative ownership exemption) will both apply. If Erik becomes domiciled in the United Kingdom the para.12(2) relief will not be available but para.11(1)(b) (derivative ownership exemption) will still apply.

United Kingdom land/chattel owned by company owned by the taxpayer

Franz, a foreign domiciliary, owns all the shares in a company which **20–19** owns United Kingdom *situs* land which he occupies or a United Kingdom *situs* chattel which he uses and which was purchased with funds he provided. Neither of the para.12 reliefs will apply. However, para.11(1)(b) (derivative ownership exemption) applies wherever he is domiciled.

Trust structures—land and chattels; no corporate structure

This involves two basic scenarios: **20–20**

(a) the land/chattel is owned by a trust in which the taxpayer has an interest in possession; and

(b) the land/chattel is owned by a discretionary trust under which the taxpayer can benefit at the discretion of the trustees.

181

Land/chattel owned directly by interest in possession trust; no corporate structure

20–21 Gregor, a foreign domiciliary, occupies land or uses a chattel owned directly by the trustees and he has an interest in possession.

If the land/chattel is situated abroad the basic relief under para.12(2) will apply so long as Gregor is domiciled abroad, but not thereafter. The settled property relief under para.12(3) will also apply if Gregor was domiciled abroad when he made the settlement, and this is so even if Gregor becomes domiciled in the United Kingdom. The para.11(1) ownership exemption also applies wherever the land/chattel is situated and wherever Gregor is domiciled.

If the land is situated in the United Kingdom only the para.11(1) ownership exemption will apply. (The UK land is not excluded property so cannot qualify for relief under para.12(3)).

Land/chattel owned by discretionary trust

20–22 Henrik, a foreign domiciliary, occupies foreign *situs* land or uses a foreign *situs* chattel owned directly by trustees of a discretionary settlement made by him and under which he can benefit. The position is the same as in the previous example concerning Gregor and there is no charge under the Regime, save that, if Henrik has reserved a benefit in respect of the land or chattels the para.11(3)(a) and (5)(a) (reserved benefit exemption), rather than the para.11(1) ownership exemption, applies.

If the land or chattel is situated in the UK then para.11(3)(a) will apply.

Land/chattel held in two tier trust structure

20–23 This involves four basic scenarios:

(a) foreign land or a foreign chattel is owned by a company the shares in which are owned by a trust in which the taxpayer has an interest in possession;

(b) United Kingdom land or a United Kingdom chattel is owned by a company the shares in which are owned by a trust in which the taxpayer has an interest in possession;

(c) foreign land or a foreign chattel is owned by a company the shares in which are owned by a discretionary trust under which the taxpayer can benefit; and

(d) United Kingdom land or a United Kingdom chattel is owned by a company the shares in which are owned by a discretionary trust under which the taxpayer can benefit.

Foreign land/chattel owned by company owned by trust in which taxpayer has an interest in possession

Ivan, a foreign domiciliary, occupies foreign *situs* land or uses a **20–24** foreign *situs* chattel owned by an offshore company all the shares of which are owned by trustees of a settlement made by him. He has an interest in possession in all the shares which comprise the trust fund. Under the Regime, there are two relevant assets—the shares (as intangible settled property) and the land/chattel.

As regards the shares, the basic relief in para.12(2) will apply and the settled property relief in para.12(3) will also do so if Ivan was domiciled outside the United Kingdom when he made the settlement. If Ivan becomes domiciled in the United Kingdom the basic relief in para.12(2) will cease to apply, but the settled property relief under para.12(3) will continue to do so if Ivan was domiciled outside the United Kingdom when he made the settlement. The ownership exemption in para.11(1) will apply wherever Ivan is domiciled. If the shares were United Kingdom *situs* shares neither of the para.12 reliefs would apply but para.11(1) ownership exemption would still apply.

As regards the foreign land/chattel, the basic relief will apply under para.12(2) and so will the derived ownership exemption under para.11(1)(b). If Ivan becomes domiciled in the United Kingdom, neither of the para.12 reliefs will apply but para.11(1)(b) (derivative ownership exemption) will continue to apply.

United Kingdom land/chattel owned by offshore company owned by an interest in possession trust

Janek, a foreign domiciliary, occupies United Kingdom *situs* land or **20–25** uses a United Kingdom *situs* chattel owned by an offshore company all the shares in which are owned by trustees of a settlement made by him, and under which he has an interest in possession.

As regards the shares, the analysis is the same as it was in the previous example concerning Ivan. As regards the land/chattel, neither of the para.12 reliefs will be available, but the derivative ownership exemption in para.11(1) will still apply, and that is so even if Janek becomes domiciled in the United Kingdom.

Foreign land/chattel owned by company owned by discretionary trust

20–26 Mischa, a foreign domiciliary, occupies foreign *situs* land or uses a foreign *situs* chattel owned by an offshore company all the shares of which are owned by trustees of a discretionary settlement made by him and under which he is a discretionary beneficiary.

As regards the shares, the basic para.12(2) relief will apply, as will the settled property relief in para.12(3) if Mischa was domiciled outside the United Kingdom when he made the settlement. If Mischa has reserved a benefit in respect of the shares, the para.11(3)(a) and (5)(a) exemption (derivative reserved benefit exemption) will also apply.

If Mischa becomes domiciled in the United Kingdom para.12(2) will not apply but para.12(3) (the settled property relief) will continue to apply in relation to the shares if Mischa was domiciled outside the United Kingdom when he made the settlement. The para.11(3) and (5) reservation of benefit exemption will still apply if Mischa has reserved a benefit in respect of the shares. If the shares were United Kingdom *situs* shares neither para.12 relief would apply but the reservation of benefit exemption under para.11(3)(a) and (5)(a) would still apply wherever Mischa was domiciled.

As regards the foreign land/chattel, para.12(2) basic relief will apply as will the derivative reserved benefit exemption (para.11(3)(b)). If Mischa becomes domiciled in the United Kingdom, the derivative reserved benefit exemption will apply to the land/chattels under para.11(3)(b).

United Kingdom land/chattel owned by company owned by discretionary trust

20–27 Nina, a foreign domiciliary, occupies United Kingdom *situs* land or uses a United Kingdom *situs* chattel owned by an offshore company all the shares in which are owned by trustees of a discretionary settlement made by her and under which she is a beneficiary.

As regards the shares, the analysis is as in the previous example of Mischa. As regards the land/chattel, neither para.12 relief will be available even when she is not domiciled here because the settled property which is excluded is not as such the land/chattels (albeit the latter are not subject to IHT). The settled property is the shares. However, the para.11(3)(b) (derivative reserved benefit exemption) will apply if Nina has reserved a benefit in respect of the shares, because the shares will derive their value from the land/chattel. If Nina becomes domiciled in the United Kingdom, the para.11(3)(b) exemption will still apply.

Summary

The conclusion is that relevant property contained in a settlement **20–28** where the donor retains an interest in possession wherever situate and whether or not owned through a corporate structure should be outside the Regime, due either to the direct or derived property exemption in para.11(1) even if the donor is deemed domiciled here. This is irrespective of the settlor's domicile assuming that there is no excluded liability problem.

Similarly discretionary trusts set up by non-UK domiciliaries are likely to be outside the Regime even where the land or chattels are UK *situs* and owned through offshore companies and even where the foreign domiciliary is now deemed domiciled.

This is because even if the para.12 reliefs are not available, the para.11(1) exemption will generally assist interest in possession trusts and the para.11(3) exemption will generally assist discretionary trusts. Where the company has been funded by way of loan there are greater difficulties in claiming the derivative exemptions and consideration should be given to capitalising the loan.

Special trust situations

Two trust situations remain to be considered where the reservation of **20–29** benefit rules do not apply even though the trust is a discretionary settlor-interested trust under which the settlor can benefit. This occurs where:

(a) the settlor has retained a reversionary interest in circumstances such that the carve-out principle prevents him from reserving a benefit (and he is not deemed to have done so by the anti-*Ingram* legislation); or

(b) the trust is part of an *Eversden* arrangement not caught by the reservation of benefit provisions.

Assume Olga, a foreign domiciliary is the settlor and beneficiary of a discretionary settlor-interested trust under which she can benefit but which is not caught by the reservation of benefit provisions and that the trust owns an insurance policy. None of the para.11 exemptions will apply. If the insurance policy is situated abroad the basic relief under para.12(2) will apply so long as Olga does not become domiciled in the United Kingdom. The settled property relief under para.12(3) will apply if Olga was not domiciled in the United Kingdom when she made the settlement, even if she becomes domiciled in the United Kingdom.

If the policy is situated in the United Kingdom neither of the para.12 reliefs will apply. None of the para.11 exemptions will apply wherever the policy is situated. The trust would need to be converted into an interest in possession trust.

Accommodation arrangements

20–30 For many years a foreign domiciliary who wished to own, *e.g.* a house in London, was advised to establish a trust which owned all the shares in an offshore company which in turn owned the house. The thinking was that the relevant asset for IHT purposes would be the shares in the company which would be excluded property for IHT purposes. There then developed a protracted controversy with the Revenue concerning the possible exposure of the foreign domiciliary to a charge to income tax under what was then Sch.E (now ITEPA 2003, ss.97–113) by reason of the benefit of the occupation conferred upon the foreign domiciliary if he was an actual or a shadow director of the company. The *Dimsey*[10] and *Allen*[11] cases exacerbated this situation and new approaches were developed which did not involve a company owning the house.

Offshore "home loan" arrangements

20–31 Often a two trust solution was used which was a variant of the home loan schemes discussed in Chapter 17. The essence of the arrangement was that the foreign domiciliary created two trusts. He funded the first trust, which was often discretionary, which in turn funded a company wholly owned by that trust. The company lent the funds to the second trust, under which the foreign domiciliary had an interest in possession trust, which used the funds to purchase the house. The loan, which was secured on the house, was left outstanding interest-free and repayable on demand.

Alternatively, due to worries about whether there was still a taxable benefit on the settlor by virtue of the loan from the company, the discretionary trust lent the cash direct as a specialty debt to the interest in possession trust and there was no charge taken over the house. This kept the loan non-UK situated but in order to ensure the

---

[10] *R v Dimsey* [2001] S.T.C. 1520.
[11] *R v Allen* [2001] S.T.C. 1537.

deductibility of the debt by the interest in possession trustees, the interest in possession trust held no other property.[12]

Assume the company (or discretionary trust) lent to the interest in possession trust £1,500,000 all of which the trust used to purchase the house and that 10 years later, when the foreign domiciliary died, the house was worth £2,000,000. For IHT purposes the property would have been reduced by the debt owed to the company and so worth £500,000. The debt could be structured as a non-United Kingdom *situs* asset so that it remained excluded property in the hands of the discretionary trustees. The net result was to take the amount of the debt outside the scope of IHT. In many cases the foreign domiciliary and his spouse had successive life interests in the property, so that if the foreign domiciliary's spouse survived him any charge on the excess value on his death was deferred until the death of his spouse.

20–32

The Regime has adversely affected the tax effectiveness of some of these arrangements. Although both the para.12(2) basic relief and the settled property para.12(3) relief will operate in respect of the shares in the company (or the debt if held direct and non-UK *situs*), neither of those reliefs will be available in respect of the house, because it is situated in the United Kingdom and is not excluded property. If, as is normally the case, the foreign domiciliary has an interest in possession in the house, the para.11(1) ownership exemption will *prima facie* be available in respect of the house but only to the extent that the value of the house exceeds the "excluded liability" of, returning to the above example, £1,500,000. The effect (assuming that the debt is indeed an excluded liability)[13] is that the first £1,500,000 of the house will be within the Regime and be subject to annual income tax charges. Such structures need reviewing. However, para.11(6) provides that there is a Regime charge on the debt only "where the value of someone's estate for the purposes of IHT is reduced by an excluded liability affecting any property". If the discretionary trust holding the debt is converted into an interest in possession trust, the effect is presumably that the debt is now part of the foreign domiciliary's estate for IHT purposes so that the value of his estate is not reduced. Although the debt excludes property and therefore no inheritance tax is payable on his death in respect of that property, nevertheless the income tax charge does not apply under the Regime to the value of the debt because the condition in para.11(6) is not satisfied. Thus foreign domiciliaries should consider amending their double trust structure by converting the discretionary trust into an interest in possession trust.

---

[12] See s.162 of the IHTA 1984.
[13] see Chapter 17—Home loan arrangements.

Summary

20–33 The traditional property owning structure of trust/company/house is generally unaffected by the Regime: *i.e.* where the United Kingdom house is occupied by the foreign domiciliary or deemed domiciliary owned by an offshore company all the shares in which are owned by a settlement which was made by a foreign domiciliary, there is no income tax charge under the Regime. This is the case whether or not the trust is discretionary or interest in possession.

The *Dimsey* income tax charge as well as the corporation tax charge on a disposal of the house by the company if there is a shadow director problem and/or the company becomes UK resident, nevertheless remains a risk.

Where these sorts of traditional arrangements have not been adopted or have been unravelled, with debt structures set up it, would appear that there could be a problem for foreign domiciliaries in respect of UK property that they occupy irrespective of whether or not they are deemed domiciled here. It may be sensible to ensure that both trusts are interest in possession.

PART IV: PLANNING IN PRACTICE: PROACTIVE PLANNING

What can still be done to mitigate or avoid the imposition of Inheritance Tax? This Part considers the possibilities in the light of the introduction of the Pre-Owned Assets charge and the Government's antipathy to "schemes".

CHAPTER 21

REGIME IMPLICATIONS FOR TAX PLANNING
GENERALLY

In retrospect the tax planning opportunities available pre-December **21–01** 10, 2003, resemble a "golden age": by contrast the current opportunities and, equally significant, the climate suggests that we are back to "stone age" planning.

Considering capital tax planning opportunities in the wake of the Regime is only part of the story and the introduction of the Regime needs to be seen as part of a wider picture which should be taken into account in effecting future tax saving exercises.

THE CHANGES OF DECEMBER 10, 2003

The changes announced in the Chancellor's Autumn Statement, **21–02** delivered rather late on December 10, 2003, dealt a severe blow to capital tax planning in that:

  (i) the pre-owned assets regime was announced with retrospective (or at least retroactive) effect which struck at the heart of schemes designed to circumvent the reservation of benefit rules[1]; and

  (ii) restrictions on CGT hold-over relief were introduced which, above all, destroyed the basis of *Melville* schemes which had become an essential adjunct to much lifetime IHT planning.[2]

---

[1] See 1–21, *et seq.*

[2] See the restrictions on CGT hold-over relief in ss.165 and 260 of the TCGA 1992 introduced by FA 2004, s.116 "*Melville* schemes" enabled the CGT that would otherwise have been payable on lifetime gifts to be held over by utilising a discretionary trust under which the settlor was interested.

21–03 The introduction of a requirement that marketed tax schemes in relation to financial and employment products should be disclosed to the Revenue (with effect from August 1, 2004, subject only to transitional provisions) represents a radical step into the unknown.[3] Exasperation in government circles with the scale, growth and success of tax saving schemes (notably in the area of income and corporation tax) appears to have driven Ministers to seek early disclosure of such arrangements, doubtless with an eye to producing appropriate anti-avoidance legislation that much sooner. For the present, IHT schemes are not generally subject to disclosure but, if the disclosure regime is considered to be a success, the provisions will doubtless be extended to cover all taxes.

RAMSAY

21–04 Tax saving schemes—especially highly artificial pre-packaged schemes—not only infuriate Ministers, they also present problems for the judiciary in deciding how the tax legislation is to be applied in such cases. For instance, should CGT loss relief be given in a case where, by a manipulation of a gap in the legislation, a loss appears to have arisen albeit that, in economic terms, the taxpayer has suffered no loss (although he will have paid substantial fees to the scheme promoters). The so-called *Ramsay* principle was developed in an attempt to limit the effectiveness of the pre-planned scheme by excising artificial steps and attempting to look at the transaction in the real world. The scope of the doctrine has waxed and waned over the years: the most recent decision of the House of Lords, for instance, had been thought to impose severe restrictions on its scope, so much so that it was widely thought not to have much impact in the realm of IHT planning.[4]

This position is, however, changing[5] and the doctrine appears likely to be about to go through a further expansionist phase. It is

---

[3] See FA 2004, ss.307–318, the Tax Avoidance Schemes (Prescribed Descriptions of Arrangements) Regulations 2004; Tax Avoidance Schemes (Promoters and Prescribed Circumstances) Regulations 2004 and the Tax Avoidance Schemes (Information) Regulations 2004.

[4] See *MacNiven v Westmoreland Investments Ltd* [2001] UKHL 6, in which Lord Hoffmann appeared to draw a distinction between commercial concepts (when the *Ramsay* doctrine would apply) and legal—or juristic—concepts when it would not.

[5] See, for instance, *Barclays Mercantile Business Finance Ltd v Mawson* [2003] S.T.C. 66; *Scottish Provident Institution v IRC* [2003] S.T.C. 1035; *Stamp Commissioner v Carreras Group Ltd* [2004] UKPC 16; *Collector of Stamp Duty v Arrowtown* 6 I.T.L. Rep. 454, CFA (HK).

likely that their Lordships will attempt in forthcoming appeals to restate the principle on a widened basis so that it will again become a factor to be considered when evaluating the chances of tax saving arrangements (especially aggressive arrangements) succeeding.

STOPPING THE SCHEMES—THE GOVERNMENT'S RESPONSE

There is now a willingness—certainly on the present Government's **21–05** part—to stop tax saving schemes by whatever means are necessary. References to fighting fire with fire and that those who play with fire must expect to get burnt abound. The rhetoric is, of course, designed to seize the moral high ground and to provide a justification for measures that in another age might have been rejected on the grounds of "not playing the game" or, more importantly, as being retro-spective. Such issues are rarely understood, however, and there is a general perception that anyone who avoids tax is damaging the community (taking a shovel to the cash that should be in the Exchequer). Thus when retrospective changes were made to the CGT treatment of offshore trusts last year, the principle at stake was lost amid the condemnation of the actions of the wealthy few in establishing the offshore structures in the first place. The general climate that now exists is well encapsulated in the Paymaster General's comments quoted above at 1–06.

Where does this leave the professional adviser charged with doing his best to mitigate a client's IHT liability? If all that is involved is taking advantage of statutory exemptions **for their intended purpose** he may feel that this will not be attacked by future legislation: more aggressive tax planning, however, may well (when discovered) provoke the wrath of an easily enraged Exchequer. This needs to be discussed with clients, given that the response of government may be to leave the taxpayer in a worse position than if he had done nothing. The Pre-Owned Assets charge on *Ingram* schemes is a particularly striking illustration.[6] The easy assumption of some Ministers that schemes can be undone (unravelled) because they lack substance is normally far from being the reality.

SAFE PLANNING

Using the basic IHT exemptions and reliefs (annual exemption; small **21–06** gifts and PETs) is hardly exciting but it is safe. Making larger gifts

[6] See 14–14 *et seq.*

is obviously still possible provided that the donor retains no benefit or interest in the gift. Make sure both husband and wife use their exemptions. More interesting is the normal expenditure out of income exemption which, the courts have decided, has a wider application than had originally been thought to be the case. For a taxpayer in his 50s with substantial surplus earnings it is to be recommended as a way of controlling the growth in value of his estate.[7]

Business property (as defined) and farming can attract IHT relief at 100 per cent irrespective of the value of the enterprise. This is a striking valuation relief and should be safeguarded at all costs. Do not, for instance, depress the value of business property by raising mortgages against it[8] and do not rush into *inter vivos* tax planning given that full relief will be available on death.[9]

A well-drafted Will may, as we will see in Chapter 28, provide a reasonable solution for the married couple.

RUNNING THE RISK

21–07 Suppose there is a loophole in the legislation—which may or may not be intended—do you exploit it? This is the area of risk where a health warning should certainly be given to clients. A good example is chattel schemes involving a gift and "commercial" lease back. Originally there seems no doubt that the Regime was intended to apply to these but in the legislation it does not. Should new arrangements be entered into? Only with a warning that it would be a simple matter for the Government to introduce amending legislation to bring them within the income tax net.[10]

One practical point about future legislation is to note that it can be made to impact upon a continuing state of affairs (doubtless in a "retroactive" way) but that a "done deal" is far more difficult to attack without imposing a blatantly retrospective tax charge.[11]

---

[7] See IHTA 1984, s.21 and see *Bennett v IRC* [1995] S.T.C. 54 and *McDowell v IRC* [2004] S.T.C. (SCD) 362. However, gifts made under the normal expenditure out of income exemption are potentially within the Regime. It would seem that many insurance schemes may be considered "safe" given that the Revenue has suggested that, despite arguments to the contrary, the Regime will not apply to them: see Chapter 19.

[8] See IHTA 1984, s.162(4).

[9] A good example is a gift by a farmer of his farmland and retention of the farmhouse. On his death, because the house will no longer be a farmhouse, relief will not be available: see *Rosser v IRC* [2003] S.T.C. (SCD) 311.

[10] See 18–07.

[11] For the distinction between retrospectivity and retroactivity, see 1–21 *et seq*. Exploiting the gift/transfer of value dichotomy through a flexible trust (see Chaper 24) must be vulnerable to future legislative changes but may be arranged in a way which enables it to be unscrambled.

The authors feel that the following arrangements—considered in detail elsewhere—can be considered "safe":

   (i) sharing arrangements for the family home;[12]

  (ii) cash gifts and the seven-year "window";[13]

 (iii) tax planning *via* deeds of variation;[14]

 (iv) commercial sales (equity releases);[15] and

  (v) Will planning.[16]

---

[12] Chapter 22 though beware gifts of more than 50 per cent (unequal shares).

[13] Chapter 25.

[14] Chapter 29: are there signs of a Revenue crack-down? "Real world" debates in connection with life interest trusts being varied after the death of the life tenant may point to a more rigorous consideration of how the variation operates in reality.

[15] Chapter 26.

[16] Chapter 28.

CO-OWNERSHIP/SHARING ARRANGEMENTS

Background

22–01 During the consultation period on the Regime, it became apparent that the Government was anxious not to disturb "genuine" house sharing arrangements, which have always qualified for protection from the reservation of benefit rules provided that certain conditions are satisfied. The question of whether such arrangements would now be caught by the Regime was raised on several occasions at both the Committee and Report Stages of the Finance Bill by both Liberal Democrats and the Conservatives.

> *Example:*
> An elderly mother living with her daughter has given a share in the property to daughter. Will mother be caught by the Regime in respect of the gifted share? Generally the answer will be no. The principle is that since such arrangements are "approved" for inheritance tax purposes, they should not be subject to an income tax charge under the Regime.

Since co-ownership arrangements have statutory protection, they are always worth considering first when advising clients who want to carry out lifetime inheritance tax planning.

Inheritance tax position

22–02 The IHT treatment of co-ownership arrangements is not entirely straightforward. Prior to March 9, 1999, the so-called "Hansard Statement" governed the position as stated by Mr Peter Brooke on June 10, 1986:

"It may be that my Hon Friend's intention concerns the common case where someone gives away an individual share in land, typically a house, which is then occupied by all the joint owners including the donor. For example, elderly parents may make unconditional gifts of undivided shares in their house to their children and the parents and the children occupy the property *as their family home*, each owner bearing his or her share of the running costs. In those circumstances, the parents' occupation or enjoyment of the part of the house that they have given away is in return for similar enjoyment of the children of the other part of the property. Thus the donors' occupation is for full consideration.

Accordingly, I assure my Hon Friend that the gift with reservation rules will not be applied to an unconditional gift of an undivided share in land merely because the property is occupied by all the joint owners or tenants in common, including the donor".[1]

This is a somewhat puzzling statement. The parents' occupation is surely by virtue of their owning a share in the property: the children are not "allowing" them to live there. The statement also suggests that the house is divided into discrete parts so that the parents' use of the children's part is in return for the parents letting the children use their part. In reality, the parents have the right to occupy the entire property as the owners of an undivided share. Presumably the "full consideration" referred to in the above statement is intended to be that "I will let you use my 50 per cent in consideration for you allowing me to use your 50 per cent". This is presumably the basis of the supposed 50 per cent ceiling in the size of the gift.

However, it is arguable that this sort of arrangement is more in the nature of a carve out—the parents' right to occupy the entire property is derived from the interest they have retained and does not amount to a reservation in the gifted share. This carve out argument was considered in the *Eversden* case at first instance (of course the taxpayer was not in joint occupation and therefore could not rely on the full consideration argument or on the *Hansard* statement). The Special Commissioner and Lightman J. appeared to accept it, at least in relation to the original property, although the latter did not agree there was a carve out in relation to the replacement property.[2]

If the carve out argument is right, then the full consideration argument and therefore the precise interest retained is irrelevant under pre-1999 arrangements since even a 5 per cent retained share would confer the right to occupy the property in its entirety. In correspondence between the Law Society and the Revenue in 1987, the Revenue accepted that an arrangement would not necessarily be jeopardised simply because it involved a gift of an unequal share in the home. However, that statement made it clear that the owners had to remain in joint occupation and that the donee should not pay the donor's share of running costs. It was also seen as important that the

<hr>

[1] Statement of Mr Peter Brooke, Minister of State, Treasury Standing Committee G; Hansard, June 10, 1986, col.425.

[2] For the facts of the case, see 2–09 and 16–10 *et seq*.

donee occupied as the family home; contrast the position under the 1999 legislation.

Position post-March 8, 1999

22–03 For gifts of undivided shares in land from March 9, 1999, the position is now regulated by s.102B of the FA 1986. Subsection 102B(4) gives relief from a charge under the reservation of benefit rules in the following circumstances:

1. the donor disposes by way of gift on or after March 9, 1999 of an undivided share of an interest in land;

2. the donor and the donee occupy the land; and

3. the donor does not receive any benefit, other than a negligible one, which is provided by or at the expense of the donee for some reason connected with the gift.

Note that post-*Hansard* there is no longer any requirement for occupation by the donor and donee as *the family home*. Further, there is no reference to full consideration as the basis for the exemption, so it is thought that the donor is able to give away more than a 50 per cent interest.

It should be said, however, that the Revenue is known to dislike arrangements where the donor gives away (say) 90 per cent and retains 10 per cent, and is likely to investigate carefully the third head condition set out above—*i.e.* has the donor received any connected benefits from the donee? That in turn may well involve scrutinising how expenses have been split between them.

Expenses

22–04 Under both *Hansard* and s.102B there has been some misunderstanding of precisely how the running costs should be split. A cursory reading of the *Hansard* statement might suggest that running expenses should be split in proportion to the *beneficial* interests each has in the property. However, "his share of the running costs", as the Revenue subsequently confirmed in 1987, is referring to the donor and donee's *actual* expenses incurred. Thus if there is a 90/10 beneficial split in the property, the donee arguably should not pay 90 per cent of the expenses but instead no more than the expenses he has actually incurred; where donor and donee live together full-time, this will generally mean a 50 per cent split.

In summary, the Revenue argument is that just because a person owns 90 per cent of a property does not mean that he uses 90 per cent of the gas, electricity and water, and if the donee agrees to pay 90 per cent of such expenses he is therefore conferring a benefit on the donor. The Revenue is focusing more closely on what collateral benefits, if any, are being provided by the donee in connection with the gift. It does not seem to distinguish between capital and living expenses.

Example:

In 1997, Barry gave 50 per cent of his house to his son, David. David does not occupy the house full-time. He occupies a flat in town during the week but spends most weekends at the property. On these facts, are the donor and donee both "occupying" the land? This is a question of fact and degree. However, if David pays 50 per cent of the outgoings but is using the property less than Barry, arguably a benefit is being conferred on Barry by David in connection with the gift and s.102B(4) is not satisfied so that the gift is caught by the reservation of benefit rules.

The correct course is for Barry as donor to pay at least his share of the outgoings reflecting his *actual* use. So as he is there more often than David, one would expect him to pay a significantly greater share of the running costs. Indeed to be safe, he may want to consider paying almost all the outgoings, including capital expenditure on the property. (Capital expenditure may be split differently from day-to-day running expenses, although the Revenue does not necessarily distinguish between the two.)

Position under the Regime

Whilst the Revenue may not like co-ownership arrangements which **22–05** involve the donee taking a larger share than the donor, nevertheless Sch.15 does not stop such planning. *Prima facie* the Regime can, of course, apply to co-ownership arrangements because there has been a disposal of an interest in land and the donor continues to occupy the property. Thus, the basic disposal and occupation conditions in para.3 of Sch.15 are satisfied.

However, para.11(5)(c) provides a rather tortuous exemption. If property "would fall to be treated as property which is subject to a reservation of benefit" but for s.102B(4), such a disposal is protected from a POA charge. Since s.102B(4) can only apply to, and therefore protect, post-March 8, 1999 arrangements, the legislation also provides that a gift made before March 9, 1999 will not be subject to the POA Regime if one assumes it had been made on or after that date and would then have qualified for s.102B(4) protection.

Thus, in the above example, Barry would not be subject to a charge in respect of the gift made in 1997, whilst David continues in occupation because para.11(5)(c) gives protection. What is slightly odd about this is that of course in the case of Barry, the gift made prior to March 9, 1999 might not have had *Hansard* protection given that the donee was not occupying as his family home, albeit it would qualify for s.102(B)(4) protection if made now. The Regime does not seem to distinguish between the slightly different conditions required under *Hansard* as opposed to s.102(B)(4) and it may be, particularly in the light of the comments in 22–04, above, that the Revenue does not in practice require occupation as a *family home* in relation to pre-March 1999 arrangements, even in the inheritance tax context. Of course, if the pre-1999 gift was *not* protected under *Hansard* then there would be a reservation of benefit so that the Regime should not apply anyway (see Sch.15, para.11(5)(A)).

Sales of part

22–06 It is also odd that *gifts* of part are protected from the Regime but sales of part at *full* value (albeit such transactions are not gifts and therefore are not subject to the gifts with reservation rules) are not so protected. This is discussed further in Chapters 5 (excluded transactions) and 26 (sales and equity release schemes). It is assumed, although it is not entirely clear at present, that sales of part at an *undervalue* are gifts and may still qualify for protection from the reservation of benefit rules under s.102B(4) and therefore protection under the Regime.[3]

Cash gifts

22–07 What happens if Barry does not give an undivided interest in the land to his son but instead gives him cash? For example, suppose Barry gives cash of £100,000 to David and together they buy a house worth £200,000, owning it in equal shares and both living there. Section 102B(4) is not satisfied because Barry has not satisfied the first condition—he has not made a gift of an undivided share in land. He has, however, not made a gift with reservation unless perhaps the cash was conditional on David purchasing the property (see 25–03).

---

[3] The Revenue accepts in the Advanced Instruction Manual that sales at an undervalue are gifts.

Does Barry then have a problem under the Regime? He has clearly satisfied the contribution and the occupation conditions and therefore *prima facie* is caught by para.3. He is not directly protected under the para.11(5)(c) exemption as he does not have s.102B(4) protection.

An amendment at Committee Stage tried to deal with this problem—para.11(8) provides that in determining whether any property falls within para.11(5)(c) in relation to cash gifts, para.2(2)(b) of Sch.20 (exclusion of gifts of money from the tracing rules) is to be disregarded. Thus, one has to pretend that there is a reservation of benefit for the purposes of Sch.15 and then argue that s.102B(4) protection applies.[4]

It is not clear that the wording in para.11(8) actually achieves this: just because para.2(2)(b) of Sch.20 is to be disregarded does not necessarily mean that one can deem a gift of cash to have the protection of s.102B(4), which specifically refers to a gift of a share in land as the basic requirement. There is nothing present to deem a gift of cash to be a gift of land. However, this seems to be the intention of para.11(8).

Donee moves out

What happens if, in the above example, David moves out? Would **22–08** Barry then face a charge under the Regime? The answer is that he would not: if David moves out and Barry does not pay full consideration for his continued occupation, the reservation of benefit rules would apply at that point anyway and therefore the gift would have the protection of para.11(5)(a) and would not be subject to a Regime charge as well. The position would be different if Barry had given David cash to buy the property with him, rather than a share in the property. In that case there would not be a reservation of benefit and once David moves out there is no longer para.11(5)(c) protection and para.11(5)(a) does not apply.

If having been given a share in the property David moved out and Barry wanted to preserve the inheritance tax savings, he might consider paying full consideration for his continued occupation (see Chapter 7). In these circumstances he would not be subject to the reservation of benefit rules because he would have the protection of para.6, Sch.20 to the 1986 Act; nor would he be subject to the Regime which gives protection under para.11(5)(d).[5] There are, of course, difficulties in determining what would be full consideration for these purposes where Barry is already entitled to occupy the property as a co-owner. Does he pay the rent that a lodger would

---

[4] See Chapter 7 for further details.
[5] See Chapter 7.

have to pay to share with him or does he have to pay 90 per cent of the full market rent he would have to pay if the property were let with vacant possession (assuming that he gave 90 per cent of the property away to his son)? The former rent is likely to be much lower than the latter!

It is noteworthy that under the Regime the rental value is the full market rent if the property were let with vacant possession; the only unknown factor to determine is the DV—the value of what Barry has given away to his son.[6] By contrast, in the case of Sch.20, para.6 arrangements, full consideration is not defined and could be different from rental value.

An alternative strategy would be for David to settle his share in the property on a reverter to settlor trust for Barry for life. The tax treatment of these trusts is considered in Chapter 23 but the advantage in this case is that whilst David's share is property comprised in Barry's estate when he dies (so that neither the reservation of benefit provisions will apply at that time and nor will the POA charge during his life) its value will not attract an IHT charge provided, of course, that the trust property then passes to David (see IHTA 1984, s.54(2)).

Practical issues

22–09 There are a number of practical issues that should always be considered before advising clients to enter into this sort of arrangement. For example, what happens if David marries someone whom Barry does not like? The spouse may then move in with David. Supposing Barry wishes to sell and move somewhere smaller, does he have sufficient funds from his retained share to rehouse himself? If David dies, tax will be charged on his share in the house and it may be appropriate to take out life insurance to cover this eventuality.

A particular concern is whether a gift of a share to one child will disadvantage the other child. In the above example, Barry has given a share in his house to David. Suppose he made the gift today and that share is worth £270,000. That is in excess of his nil rate band but more or less covered by two years' annual inheritance tax exemptions. However, if Barry dies within seven years of the gift, although David suffers no extra inheritance tax as donee, John Barry's other son, who has been left the rest of Barry's estate will find that his tax bill is much higher—the benefit of the nil rate band has been allocated entirely against David's gift and John suffers 40 per cent inheritance tax on the residue.

---

[6] See 16–38 for a fuller discussion of the problem of valuing what has been given away.

Other problems in these arrangements can arise where the house increases in value faster than the rest of the estate or the remaining estate has to be used to pay nursing home fees. Suppose in our example Barry gives David a 90 per cent interest in the house and retains 10 per cent. The 90 per cent share is worth £270,000 and the 10 per cent share £30,000. Barry's other investments such as cash and equities are worth around £300,000 at the time of the gift. He leaves all these to John by will.

Unfortunately within three years of the gift Barry becomes ill and has to move into a nursing home. (The Revenue accepts that although s.102B(4) will thereupon cease to be satisfied, Barry will not fall within the reservation of benefit rules given that he no longer occupies the property.) David remains in the property but all the liquid assets of Barry are used to pay the nursing home fees. Three years later Barry dies and his remaining liquid investments are by then worth only £150,000. In addition, John has to pay tax at 40 per cent. He has received significantly less than David. While there may be ways round some of these practical issues, they shall be discussed with the client fully.

Who is the donee?

An outright gift of an undivided share is the most common situation **22–10** but assume, for instance, that Barry would prefer to settle an interest in the property for the benefit of David (perhaps because David is a disabled child in receipt of state benefit). A gift into a flexible life interest trust for David is considered to fall within the protection of s.102B(4) on the basis that, as life tenant, David is treated as owning the property in the settlement (by virtue of IHTA 1984, s.49(1)) and hence is the donee. The flexibility given to the trustees and which enables them to terminate David's interest in whole or part gives Barry some protection against David contracting an unsuitable marriage whilst (it may be) preserving any entitlement to state benefits.

In cases where it is desired to gift a share in a second home not attracting principal private residence relief to David (which it is considered may be protected by s.102B(4) provided that both Barry and David occupy the property), a problem which frequently arises is the CGT charge on the disposal of the share in the property. To deal with that problem the gifted share may be put into a discretionary trust (in order to obtain the benefit of CGT holdover relief under TCGA 1992, s.260(2)(a)) and subsequently appointed out to the intended donee, David (again with the benefit of holdover relief). The difficulty with this arrangement is reconciling it with the wording of s.102B(4) since David will not be the donee of the gift.

That will be the discretionary trustees and hence it is considered that s.102B(4) will not afford protection so that the share settled by Barry will be caught by the reservation of benefit rules and therefore taxed as part of his estate when he dies.

Conclusions

22–11 Co-ownership arrangements may be regarded as one of the safer lifetime inheritance tax planning options provided that the donee continues to occupy the property and the various family and practical issues mentioned above can be resolved.

The result is that the donor can avoid both the reservation of benefit rules and the Regime. Of course, this let out will have relatively limited application (as the Government no doubt intended).

It is also of some comfort that these exemptions under both the IHT legislation and the Regimes are unlikely to be removed: in effect they have been given statutory protection.

The one area that may be vulnerable to attack is gifts of unequal shares, for example, where the donor gives a 90 per cent interest away. Hence the cautious might wish to limit their gifts to a 50 per cent share in the property.

CHAPTER 23

REVERTER TO SETTLOR TRUSTS

Reverter to settlor trusts have proved popular in recent years. **23–01** Typically as a tax efficient way of providing for an elderly relative but also as part of tax saving arrangements: for instance, as a part of an arrangement a testator's nil rate band on death whilst ensuring that his surviving spouse is both well provided for and secure. Although relatively simple in concept, in practice there are a number of problems and pitfalls which should be drawn to the settlor's attention.

INHERITANCE TAX POSITION

Sections 53(3) and 54(2) of the IHTA 1984 provide that IHT is not **23–02** chargeable on the termination of an interest in possession (whether on the death of the life tenant or otherwise) if, when the interest comes to an end, the property in which the interest subsisted reverts to the living settlor.[1] Similarly, reverter to settlor relief is extended where the property in which the interest in possession subsisted reverts to the spouse of the settlor while the settlor is alive or to the widow/widower of the settlor within two years of the settlor's death.[2]

The result if these conditions are satisfied is that:

(i) IHT is not chargable if the interest in possession ends during the lifetime of the beneficiary; and

---

[1] The reversion in these cases may be absolute or on interest in possession trusts for the settlor.

[2] See IHTA 1984, s.53(4) and s.54(2).

(ii) on death the value of the settled property is left out of account in determining the value of the deceased's estate immediately before his death.[3]

Example:

Angela sets up a trust in 2000 for her father Fred for life reverter to Angela on the death of Fred or on earlier termination of Fred's interest. Fred dies and the property passes back to Angela.

There is no IHT on the death of Fred. If the property reverts to Angela's spouse while Angela is alive or to her widower within two years of her death there is still no IHT payable on the ending of Fred's interest. However, if Angela dies while Fred is still alive, his interest must revert to Angela's widower within two years of her death in order to secure the relief.[4]

The exemption is often used (as in the above example) where children want to provide for their parents or for other elderly relatives. It can also be useful where a settlor wants to make provision for a minor child but wishes to ensure that if the child dies before becoming absolutely entitled, the funds will revert to him.[5] The trust can also be used in a matrimonial context where one spouse is providing for another but wishes to retain some long term interest in the assets being transferred.

The exemption is only available if the property that reverts to the settlor is settled property in which an interest in possession subsisted. Thus if A settled property on discretionary trusts for aunts Doris and Dotty, with reverter to him on the last of these to die, the exemption is not available.[6]

The exemption is only applicable at the point when the settled property reverts to the settlor. Thus if property is settled for A for

---

[3] Does this mean that the property is in his estate but the value is ignored? Reverter to settlor trusts are sometimes seen as a way of escaping from a sharing arrangment in which the donee has ceased to occupy the property: see 22–08. The argument is that on the death of the original donor he may have reserved a benefit but since he has an interest in possession in the property, s.102(3) in effect is disapplied. However, despite the fact that A has an interest in possession and thus the property is in his estate for both IHT and POA purposes, its value is ignored on A's death if the property then reverts to the settlor so there is no IHT. Note that the reservation of benefit rules would not be disapplied in this case if A's interest in possession ended during his lifetime because of the different wording in IHTA 1984, s.52(3).

[4] This is an important practical point: whilst children may assume that parents die first it does not always happen. Deaths in the wrong order can result in multiple IHT charges.

[5] As discussed below, for relief to be available, the trust for the child must be interest in possession: it cannot, for instance, be in the form of an accumulation and maintenance trust.

[6] The position would be different if the trust had been converted into an interest in possession trust before the property reverted (relief would then be available).

life, then to B for life with a reverter to settlor C there is no IHT on the death of B when the property reverts to C but there will have been IHT (subject to the availability of any other reliefs) on the death of A when it passed to B.

Reservation of benefit and reverter to settlor trusts

By retaining a reversionary interest has the settlor reserved a **23–03** benefit? The answer is no: the interest retained is not a reservation of benefit but a carve-out. The settlor has retained his interest in reversion and merely given away the immediate enjoyment of those funds (*viz* the interest in possession).[7] It is for this reason that such trusts have proved useful in connection with insurance bonds.[8]

If the trustees have power to appoint the settled funds back to the settlor at any time, then the carve out argument is less persuasive —see recent statements of Lightman J. in the *Eversden* case confirming that a settlor reserved a benefit when he was an object of his discretionary trust.[9]

The remainder interest will have some value in the settlor's estate because it is not excluded property.[10] However, if his interest can be defeated by the exercise of overriding powers of appointment this will devalue the remainder interest.

Failed PET

If the settlor dies within seven years of making the settlement, he has **23–04** made a failed PET. In calculating the transfer of value, the value (if any) of his reversionary interest will be taken into consideration.

Example
Alan settles a house worth £100,000 on interest in possession trusts for his mother Mischa remainder to him. His mother has a life expectancy of 10 years. Alan dies two years after the settlement was made. At the date of the settlement Alan's reversionary interest was worth £20,000 and therefore the loss

---

[7] This was confirmed in a Revenue letter to the Law Society dated May 18, 1987. See also the *Advanced Instruction Manual* at D73 and *Re Cochrane* [1906] 2 I.R. 200.

[8] See Chapter 19.

[9] The whole concept of a carve-out in such cases is difficult to reconcile with the decision of the Court of Appeal in *Eversden* that there is only a single gift to the interest in possession beneficiary. See generally Chapter 16.

[10] See IHTA 1984, s.48(1)(b).

to his estate in making the transfer into trust was £80,000. By the time A has died, however, his reversionary interest is worth £40,000.

A is taxed on a failed PET of £80,000 and on the reversionary interest worth £40,000. He has retained in his estate an appreciating asset.

A settlor-interested trust for income and capital gains tax

23–05 The settlor has retained an interest in the settlement for the purposes of s.660A of the TA 1988 and s.77 of the TCGA 1992, and therefore he (rather than the trustees or life tenant) will be subject to tax on any settlement income and chargeable gains. Reverter to settlor trusts are therefore commonly used to hold property which produces neither income nor chargeable gains, *e.g.* a family home which is occupied by the life tenant or an insurance bond.

PUTTING A HOUSE IN THE TRUST

23–06 A reverter to settlor trusts is often used to obtain principal private residence relief on what is effectively a second home of the settlor.

> ***Example:***
> Eric wants to purchase a property for the use of his mother. He settles the funds on interest in possession trust for his mother, reverter to himself. The trustees purchase the property.
> On the death of the mother there is no charge to IHT as a result of the reverter to settlor exemption.[11]

If the house is sold during the mother's lifetime (while she is in occupation) then the principal private residence relief under s.225 of the TCGA 1992 will be available to the trustees. Therefore no chargeable gains arise which can be assessed on the settlor under s.77. This is a better position than if Eric had bought the property personally since, unless he is in occupation, no principal private residence relief would have been available.

CGT on termination

23–07 On the life tenant's death, if the trust then ends, the property is deemed to be disposed of at no gain no loss the normal death uplift

---

[11] See IHTA 1984, s.53(3).

will *not* apply. The settlor will therefore receive back the trust assets without a CGT charge but (broadly speaking) at a base cost equal to the market value of the assets when he first put them into trust.[12]

For this reason it is often preferable to ensure that on the death of the life tenant the settlor becomes entitled to an interest in possession with the trustees having power to advance him capital. This still secures the IHT reverter to settlor relief but ensures that the death uplift is available for CGT purposes when the life tenant dies.[13]

A recent concern was whether this favourable capital gains tax treatment would end as a result of the review of the taxation of trusts announced on December 10, 2003. In fact, it appears from the recent consultation document published in August 2004 that proposals to treat settlor interested trusts as fiscally transparent have been abandoned. Accordingly, principal private residence relief and the death uplift will continue to be available even if the settlor is not in occupation of the property.

THE EFFECT OF THE REGIME

In the example of Eric and his mother (see 23–06) there will be no **23–08** charge under the Regime. Eric is not in occupation of the property and so para.3 has no application.[14]

If Eric later moved into the property with Mum, then para.3 might prove to be a problem. The remainder interest has value in his estate and will provide a partial exemption from the Regime within para.11(1).[15] Of course his occupation arguably involves a reservation of benefit so that the whole property is in his estate for IHT purposes, in which case the Regime will not apply. Alternatively, the trustees could (assuming they have the necessary power) appoint him an interest in possession.[16]

A more likely scenario would be for the mother to move out into a nursing home and the trustees to sell the house. At that point the trust holds intangibles (cash) and all the other conditions in para.8 are satisfied.[17] If Eric wishes to keep the trust going to provide income

---

[12] TCGA 1992, s.73(1)(b) which applies if the settlement ends on the death of the interest in possession beneficiary.

[13] TCGA 1992, s.72: there is no logic in the different CGT treatment of a continuing trust which is thought to result from a legislative oversight.

[14] For the requirements of this paragraph, see Chapter 3. If mother had originally given Eric funds to purchase the property she will then have met the contribution condition and, of course, she is in occupation. The property, however, is comprised in her estate (*qua* life tenant) and so exempt from the charge under para.11(1).

[15] See 7–08.

[16] Once Eric is either caught by the reservation of benefit rules or enjoys an interest in possession the Regime does not apply: see para.11 and Chapter 7.

[17] For the para.8 charge, see Chapter 6.

for Mum (although he derives no income tax benefit from this) the trustees should invest in assets **other than** intangibles.

Once the trust holds land or chattels (which are not occupied by Eric), Eric is only taxed on actual income arising. There is no charge under the Regime based on a percentage of capital values. It is unclear at present precisely what will happen if the trustees hold cash for say a month before investing it in chattels or land. It appears that para.8 applies for that month of the tax year and therefore the calculation of the chargeable amount under para.9 has to be made and the tax paid.

Example:
If the cash from the sale of the house is (say) £1 million, the chargeable amount for the whole year at 5 per cent = £50,000. The chargeable amount for the taxable period of one month is £4,166. If the cash also produces income (*e.g.* £1000 in the relevant month), Eric (a 40 per cent taxpayer) will end up paying income tax as follows:

Trust income

£400 income tax under TA 1988, s.660A

Regime charge

Chargeable amount is

£4,166 less £400 = £3,766 × 40 per cent = £1,506.

Total income tax liability is £1,906 (£1,506 + £400)

This is not a huge liability but Eric may prefer to avoid the hassle of compliance and valuation. In these circumstances it would be preferable to appoint him an interest in possession to take effect immediately on the sale of the house.

USING REVERTER TO SETTLOR TRUSTS TODAY

23–09 Apart from their use in providing for aged relatives consider the following:

(i) **As part of a property purchase arrangement**[18]: Dad retains a lease and will sell the encumbered freehold to his children. Funds for its purchase are settled by the children on a reverter to settlor trust which purchases the interest. Provided that the trust is

[18] See 26–08.

correctly drafted, the CGT death uplift will be available on Dad's death. Of course, the entire property could be bought by such a trust if the children have sufficient funds.

(ii) **As part of post-death planning**[19]**:** On Dad's death his half share in the family home is left in his Will to his daughter Clara. She settled that interest on reverter to settlor trusts for her Mum.[20] Main residence relief for CGT purposes should be available on the share held in trust.

Finally, a warning! CGT may present a problem if the property to be settled is pregnant with gain. It was formerly the case that the trust could first be established in discretionary form (to obtain CGT hold-over relief) and then converted into a reverter to settlor interest in possession trust. This arrangement is no longer possible since December 10, 2003, because the discretionary trust will be "settlor-interested" and so hold-over relief will no longer be available.

---

[19] See Chapter 28.
[20] There should be no "understanding" that this will happen: see IHTA 1984, s.143 and 28–04.

CHAPTER 24

TRUST REORGANISATIONS

24–01 For IHT purposes, a beneficiary entitled to an interest in possession in settled property "is treated for the purposes of this Act (*viz.* IHTA 1984) as beneficially entitled to the property in which the interest subsists".[1] As a result it may be desirable to take steps to reduce the eventual IHT bill on the settled property.[2] In this chapter it is assumed that we are discussing trust arrangements where the person entitled to an interest in possession is **not** the settlor nor a person who made the disposal of the relevant property into trust.[3] Alternatively, we are considering arrangements under which the property was settled pre-March 18, 1986.

There will be cases where the beneficiary is content to surrender or assign the benefit of his trust interest: normally the result will be a PET and care may need to be exercised to ensure that CGT does not arise.[4]

POSITION IF THE TRUST INCLUDES THE BENEFICIARY'S RESIDENCE

24–02 The ideal in such a case is likely to be an arrangement under which:

---

[1] See IHTA 1984, s.49(1). In practice, it is the net value of the property in the settlement which is comprised in the estate of that beneficiary although the legislation is silent about the position of the trustee liabilities. Any other result would have potentially grotesque consequences.

[2] On the death of the interest in possession beneficiary, liability for the IHT rests primarily with the trustees: see IHTA 1984, s.201.

[3] Otherwise the Regime would *prima facie* apply when the settlor's interest in possession is terminated if the reservation of benefit rules were not then in point.

[4] See IHTA 1984, s.52 deals with the situation where an interest in possession ends during the lifetime of the beneficiary. Note that the **amount** of the deemed transfer of value is specified in s.52(1) which precludes an application of the general principle measuring the amount by reference to the fall in value of the transferor's estate (see *ibid.*, s.3(1)). CGT may arise on the ending of a settlement: see TCGA 1992, s.71.

(a) the beneficiary continues to occupy the property under the terms of the settlement; *but*

(b) the value of the property remaining subject to his interest in possession is reduced.

For instance, if the property were to be split into:

(a) a leasehold interest which remained subject to the interest in possession trusts; **and**

(b) the remaining **freehold** interest which ceases to be held on the interest in possession trusts,

then the above objectives would appear to be met.

Arrangements of this type, involving the division of a freehold interest in land into two separate property interests (the leasehold and the freehold), have been considered in the context of "*Ingram* schemes": see especially 14–01. Those arrangements were, of course, rendered ineffective for IHT purposes by the FA 1999 amendments to the reservation of benefit provisions.[5] All that, however, is in the context of gifts of unsettled property: what is the position if the house is already held in trust?

MEANING OF GIFT

The operation of the reservation of benefit rules is dependent upon **24–03** the taxpayer making a gift of property. The absence of any gift means that these rules do not apply. It is, of course, curious that this mini-code uses the word gift rather than transfer of value (which is employed throughout the rest of the IHT legislation)[6] but the result is considered to be that whilst most transfers of value will also be gifts there are circumstances, notably "deemed" transfers of value, which do not involve any element of donative intent on the part of the taxpayer.

The upshot is that if the trustees have overriding powers which enable them to terminate the interest in possession beneficiary's interest in property, it is difficult to see any basis for arguing that the beneficiary has made a gift of that property. He has no donative intent and indeed has "suffered" a diminution in the value of his trust interest.

[5] Considered at 14–09, *et seq.*

[6] The simple explanation is doubtless that the reservation of benefit legislation in FA 1986 was lifted wholesale from the estate duty legislation without ensuring that the concepts used fitted in with the rest of the capital transfer tax legislation (then rechristened inheritance tax).

The relationship between the concept of a gift and a transfer of value is considered in detail in the chapter dealing with *Eversden* schemes to which the reader is referred.[7] At this point, the authors would merely confirm that they remain firmly of the opinion that a gift requires donative intent and so it does not follow that because the taxpayer has made (or is treated as making) a transfer of value that he has also made a gift.

APPLICATION OF THE PRE-OWNED ASSET LEGISLATION

24–04 The trigger for the application of this legislation is the satisfaction of the disposal or contribution condition (in the case of land and chattels) or a settlement of property (in the case of intangibles). A life tenant who suffers a termination or partial termination of his life interest does not satisfy any of these requirements provided that he did not originally own the property or property it represents or he made and funded the settlement pre-March 18, 1986. Hence it is considered that the pre-owned assets charge will not apply to a trust reorganisation.

EFFECTING A TRUST REORGANISATION

24–05 A reorganisation will not be possible in all cases since it depends upon the trustees possessing (and exercising) overriding dispositive powers. These may be of two types: first, an overriding power of appointment which will permit them to declare new trusts of the appointed property as well as make outright appointments in favour of a beneficiary.[8] Secondly, a power to pay or apply capital to or for the benefit of a beneficiary and which may be exercised to "resettle" the relevant property (commonly known as a "settled advance").[9]

If a suitable power exists then the procedure would be:

(i) For the trustees to carve out a lease (*e.g.* for 20 years) in the property.[10]

---

[7] See especially 16–17. It is understood that the Revenue accepts the views expressed in the text.

[8] A good example is the power in cl.2 of Precedent I contained in Chapter 28.

[9] See, for instance, the statutory power of advancement in Trustee Act 1925, s.32, although note that (unless widened in the trust document) this is limited to one half of the beneficiary's presumptive share.

[10] For the mechanics of carving out such a lease, see 14–02 and 14–04.

(ii) The trustees then appointing or making a settled advance (depending upon the type of dispositive power possessed by the trustees) of the now encumbered freehold to the remainder beneficiaries (*e.g.* the children of the life tenant) on continuing trusts.

Diagrammatically the position is then as follows—

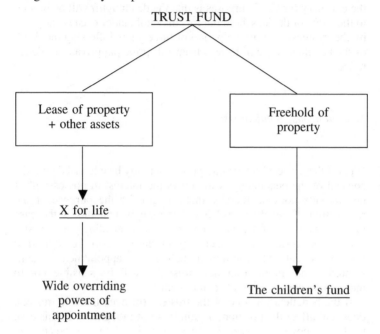

CGT aspects

Given that the overriding power will be exercised to create continuing trusts in respect of the property in question, no charge to CGT should arise on the reorganisation.[11] One reason for retaining the encumbered freehold in trust is to ensure that on any future sale of the property principal private residence relief, under TCGA 1992, s.225, will be available to the trustees. The crucial point in connection with this section is that there is a single trust (albeit comprised **24–06**

---

[11] The relevant chargeable occasion would be the ending of the settlement which will not happen unless the relevant power has created a new settlement (TCGA 1992, s.71 and see SP 7/84). In any event principal private residence relief is likely to be available given the use of the property as a main residence by the interest in possession beneficiary.

of two funds) so that the trustees own the property (both leasehold and freehold interest) which is being occupied by a beneficiary under the terms of the trust. Hence relief will be due.

On the death of the interest in possession beneficiary, IHT will only be payable on the then value of the property in his fund (*viz.* the leasehold interest): provided that he has survived the reorganisation by seven years the freehold interest will not be charged. Of course the corollary for CGT purposes is that the death uplift will be limited to the value of the leasehold but this may not matter because any sale by the trustees—within the period of three years following the death of the beneficiary—will benefit from full principal private residence relief.

Miscellaneous technical issues

24–07 What if the trustees' overriding power can only be exercised with the consent of the beneficiary who enjoys the interest in possession? If he consents does he thereby make a gift for the purpose of the reservation of benefit rules? It is not thought that this is the case given that the actual decision to exercise the overriding power is still one for the trustees. The beneficiary might, however, be advised to release the consent requirement before any appointment is considered[12] and, in drafting new trusts, it will be sensible not to incorporate such a consent requirement.[13]

If the beneficiary is one of the trustees (or even the sole trustee), does that affect the position? Again it is not thought so: in this case the trustee powers are vested in that person in a fiduciary capacity so that any exercise cannot be said to involve him making a gift or disposal in his personal capacity.[14]

If the beneficiary was also the settlor then different issues arise. For instance, on the termination of his interest in possession there may be a reservation of benefit problem.[15] In addition he has made the original disposal of relevant property into trust and so, even if he is not caught by the reservation of benefit provisions, the Regime can apply.

---

[12] See 16–17.

[13] See, for instance, Precedent I in Chapter 28.

[14] This is not, of course, to say that having the beneficiary as sole trustee is recommended. It may be considered prudent in all cases for the beneficiary to be replaced as a trustee (under s.36 of the Trustee Act 1925) before the dispositive power is exercised.

[15] See 16–18.

The mechanics, and advantages, of setting up a flexible interest in **24–08** possession trust over residue in favour of the testator's surviving spouse are discussed at 28–07 *et seq.* Terminating the interest in possession and establishing a discretionary trust under which the beneficiary whose interest has been terminated can benefit is also considered.

CHAPTER 25

CASH GIFTS

SETTING THE SCENE

25–01 Jason has lived abroad for many years and plans to return home. He gives his daughter, Laos, £250,000 which she uses to purchase a Suffolk property ("the Crow's Nest"). On his return to England, Jason occupies the property with Laos.

RESERVATION OF BENEFIT

25–02 Jason has made a gift to his daughter and now occupies the property purchased: is he caught by the reservation of benefit rules in FA 1986? The relevant provisions are as follows:

(i) Section 102(1) of the FA 1986 provides that there is a gift with reservation if an individual disposes of any property (here the cash) by way of gift and either: (a) possession and enjoyment of the property is not *bona fide* assumed by the donee, or (b) at any time in the seven years prior to the donor's death the property is not enjoyed to the entire exclusion of the donor and of any benefit to him by contract or otherwise.

(ii) Paragraph 6(1)(c) of Sch.20 to the FA 1986 is also relevant. This provides that in determining whether any property which is disposed of by way of gift is enjoyed to the entire exclusion of the donor and of any benefit to him by contract or otherwise, a benefit which the donor obtained by virtue of any associated operations of which the disposal by way of gift is one shall be treated as a benefit to him by contract or otherwise.

(iii) Associated operations are defined by s.268 of the IHTA 1984 to mean any two or more operations of any kind being: (a) operations which affect the same property or one of which affects some property and the other or others of which affect property representing that property or (b) any two operations of which one is effected with reference to the other or with a view to enabling the other to be effected or facilitating its being effected.

(iv) Finally Sch.20, para.2 ("substitutions and accretions") deals with substitutions but the paragraph does not apply if the property is a gift of cash.[1]

Has Jason reserved a benefit in the cash gifted?

Prima facie it does not appear that there is any reservation of benefit **25–03** in the cash itself because the cash has gone and Sch.20 provides no tracing provisions for gifts of cash. There is no direct link between the benefit received (donor living in the property) and the gift of cash. The benefit to Jason of occupying the house does not arise from the gift of cash **unless that gift was in some way made conditional**.

The property gifted (*i.e.* the cash) has been enjoyed to the entire exclusion of Jason provided that the gift had not been made **conditional** on being used to purchase the property: otherwise there is a risk that the gift is in fact of an interest in land or alternatively (and more likely here) that he is treated as receiving a benefit in the cash gifted because it was made on the basis and on the understanding that he should be allowed to continue in occupation. (The benefit does not need to come from the gifted asset as such if it arises out of the gift). So, the Revenue might argue that Laos is estopped from denying Jason's occupation once the gift has been made, because he had made it solely under an agreement that she would use the funds to purchase the property and so she is estopped from changing her mind later.

---

[1] Paragraph 2(2)(b). Note also that different rules apply if the original property disposed of by the gift is not cash or is cash which "becomes settled property by virtue of the gift": *ibid.*, para.2(2)(a). The rules affecting settled gifts are in para.5 which treats the gift as being of property comprised in the trust fund from time to time. There is therefore no exemption for settled cash gifts.

Position of Jason

25–04 In this case, however, it seems difficult to argue that the gift of cash was in reality a gift of the Crow's Nest. On the basis of the estate duty cases such as *Sneddon v Lord Advocate*[2] (gift of cash used to purchase shares three days later) and *Potter v Inland Revenue*[3] (gift from donor of cash expressed to be to enable the donee to purchase shares), the subject matter of the gift was nevertheless still the cash not the property purchased, and this is important in the context of reservation of benefit. The fact that the money was given for a particular purpose does not mean that the gift was subject to a legally enforceable condition.

Effect of the associated operations rule

25–05 It is not thought that the associated operations rule will affect the conclusion: either the arrangement involves a reservation in the gifted property or the reservation of benefit provisions are inapplicable.

It might be argued that the gift of cash and the purchase of the freehold are associated transactions in that the gift of cash was made at least with reference to the subsequent purchase and questions of estoppel and conditional gifts are not relevant. But is para.6(1)(c) of Sch.20 wide enough to deem the benefit from the associated operation (the purchase) to be a benefit to the donor in the property disposed of (the gift of cash)? If, as is thought, the benefit enjoyed from the associated operation must entrench in some way upon the possession of the actual gifted property in order for there to be a reservation of benefit, then associated operations do not cause an additional reservation of benefit problem. The benefit enjoyed (*i.e.* the occupation of the house) does not in itself entrench on the gift of the cash. Put another way, the point is that the Revenue may be able to establish that Jason has received a benefit from the associated operation made by his daughter (namely the purchase of the property) but they also have to show that the gifted property (*i.e.* the cash) is not enjoyed to the entire exclusion of any benefit to Jason. Unless the cash gift was conditional or Laos was estopped from using the cash in any other way, Jason does not enjoy a benefit from the cash as such. The purchase of a property and allowing him to live there benefit him but this is still not a benefit from the cash itself which has now gone.

[2] [1954] A.C. 257.
[3] [1958] S.L.T. 198.

Revenue's Approach

25–06

In the Advanced Instruction Manual[4] the Revenue accepts that the tracing rules do not apply to an absolute gift of a sum of money. This is qualified in two ways:

(a) if the absolute cash gift is itself subject to a reservation then the sum of money will be taxable; and

(b) "a gift which initially seems to be of cash may in reality be a GWR, by associated operations, of other property". The example given involves A giving £100,000 cash to B which B uses to buy A's residence (worth £100,000) in which A continues to reside. The Revenue comments that "this is a GWR, by associated operations, of the residence."

As already noted, it is difficult to see how the associated operations rules can be used to re-characterise a gift as being of property rather than of cash. Of course, the specific example involves a circular arrangement in which the actual cash may never have changed hands. The weakness of the argument appears underlined by the subsequent comments (under the heading "What to do").

> "You should not normally raise any enquiries to see if a gift which appears to be of cash may be a gift, by associated operations, of other property. Only ask questions if there is a positive reason for doing so, *e.g.* where
>
> ● the gift is of an odd amount, such as £49,563.15, which suggests it may be related to a purchase by the donee,
>
> or
>
> ● there is specific information that the gift was related to the acquisition by the donee of property, especially if the acquisition is from the donor."

Conclusion on the IHT position

In conclusion, it does not follow that all benefits referable to a gift will come within s.102. It is not sufficient to take the situation as a whole and find that the donor has continued to enjoy substantial advantages which have **some relation** to the gifted property. Each advantage must be considered separately to determine whether it is a benefit within the statute.[5]

25–07

---

[4] This is currently being updated and revised. The relevant section is at D61, *et seq.*
[5] *Oakes v Stamp Duties Commissioner of New South Wales* [1954] A.C. 57 at 72 and see *St Aubyn v AG* [1952] A.C. 15.

25–08 Given that Jason's gift is not caught by the reservation of benefit rules, it will fall within the Regime so that he will suffer an income tax charge from April 6, 2005.[6] The following points may be noted:

    (i) Paragraph 3 applies given that Jason is in occupation of the property and that the contribution condition is met.

    (ii) If Laos had provided some of the purchase price for the "Crow's Nest", para.4(2) will require an apportionment of DV to determine such part of the value of the relevant land as may be attributed to the consideration provided by Jason.

    (iii) Although Jason is not in sole occupation, no allowance appears to be made for this in fixing the rental value of "Crow's Nest".

Jason should consider electing for the reservation of benefit rules to apply[7] in order to avoid the income tax charge. He may consider whether it will then be advantageous to pay full consideration for his occupation (calculated on the basis that it is not "exclusive") in order to cause the reservation to come to an end.[8] Obviously this will depend on what (if anything) Jason can afford to pay and the calculation of the benefit under para.3 (of which he will suffer up to 40 per cent in income tax) as against "full consideration" under the Sch. 20 rules.

The seven-year defence[9]

25–09 If the facts are varied so that Jason made the gift to his daughter in March 1998 and only returns to England in April 2005 when he occupies the property for the first time, then as a result of FA 2004, Sch.15, para.10(2)(c),[10] the pre-owned asset charge will not apply.

The introduction of this seven-year defence (which occurred when the legislation was amended at Committee Stage) is somewhat curious—the explanation for its introduction presumably being the

---

[6] It was a major goal of the Regime to catch such arrangements: see the Consultation Document issued in December 2003 (in Appendix II).

[7] See Chapter 11.

[8] This will result in Jason making a deemed PET under FA 1986, s.102(4): see 11–09, et seq.

[9] See 5–09.

[10] The arrangement is an excluded transaction.

need to impose some limit on the operation of the contribution condition.[11] Of course the seven-year period echoes:

(i) the PET period in the IHT legislation: once the donor has survived his gift by this period it is exempt. In the same way a donor is free to enjoy the use of property purchased with his gifted cash once that period is up; and

(ii) in the anti-*Ingram* legislation there is no reservation if the carve-out is effected at least seven years before the interest in land is given away.[12]

[11] See *Taxation*, May 6, 2004, p.13, (Bruce Sutherland).
[12] See 14–10.

CHAPTER 26

SELLING THE FAMILY HOME—PLANNING OPTIONS

Introduction

26–01 One of the curious features about the Regime is the approach taken to sales of land and chattels. Unlike the reservation of benefit legislation, the Regime can apply even when no gift has been made. Any disposal of land which the disponer continues to occupy can, in principle, be caught by the Regime unless it comes within a specific exemption.

Sale worse than gift!

26–02 Consider the following example:

Rose and Emily are sisters and have lived together for some years. Rose alone owns the house worth £800,000. She decides to sell for full consideration a *half* share in the property to Emily. (She may want the cash to supplement her lifestyle or may wish to give it away to other relatives.)

Emily pays £400,000 for a 50 per cent share in the property. (There is no discount given when they agree the price for the fact that Rose is in occupation.) Despite the fact that Rose has certainly not made Emily a gift or made a transfer of value for inheritance tax purposes, Rose is *prima facie* caught by the Regime. A disposal has been made and Rose continues in occupation. By contrast if Rose had *given* away a half share to Emily, she would have no Regime charge due to the protection of para.11(5)(c) (see Chapter 11 and also Chapter 22 for full discussion).

This transaction is not protected by any of the exclusions or exemptions. Rose will pay income tax on any interest generated by the cash of £400,000 plus a POA charge on the appropriate rental value.[1] The cash of £400,000 is also part of Rose's estate for IHT purposes and similarly a half share in the property is part of Emily's estate. The fact that Emily has paid full consideration for her share does not help Rose—the sale is not protected under para.10(1)(a) because it is not a sale of the whole interest in the land and the pre-owned assets charge cannot be reduced under the non-exempt sale provisions because, again, these require a transfer of the whole interest in land.

Can one argue that the exemption in para.11(1)(b) applies on the basis that Rose's estate includes property which derives its value from the relevant property? Her estate does after all include cash but is this "other property which derives its value from the relevant property and whose value so far as attributable to the relevant property is not substantially less than the value of the relevant property."

It is not thought that para.11(1) is designed to apply to this sort of **26–03** transaction.[2] The difficulty is that the value of the cash does not derive its value from the land. Paragraph 11(1)(b) was intended to deal with cases where a person wholly owns a company which in turn owns the relevant land. In these circumstances, the company shares derive their value from the land.

The question of sales of part of the disponer's interest in land was raised several times in the Parliamentary Debates and one might have expected the Paymaster General to clarify the position if para.11(1)(b) exemption did indeed apply here. The same point applies equally to exchanges, *e.g.* where Blackacre worth £1 million is exchanged for Whiteacre worth £500,000 (this is discussed in Chapter 3).

In arriving at the POA charge on Rose, allowance will be made for the 50 per cent interest in the land which she retains (see 3–12 and note that there may be valuation difficulties in arriving at the DV figure).

Reverter to settlor trust

Could Emily (donee) settle her share on reverter to settlor trusts for **26–04** Rose? Then the property is back in Rose's estate for IHT purposes so that the para.11(1)(a) exemption would apply. The property would not be subject to inheritance tax on Rose's death provided at that

---

[1] As defined in Sch.15, para.4(2). See Chapter 3.
[2] It is to be hoped that the guidance notes to be published later this year will deal with this point.

point it reverted to Emily or her spouse.[3] The fact that there is no IHT charge on Rose's death does not mean that the relevant property is outside para.11(1)(a) protection for Regime purposes. This relief is discussed further in Chapter 23.

At present there is an undertaking from the Paymaster General to consider part sales further and to receive representations from interested parties. The Revenue clearly views with suspicion sales of part for full value between connected parties, presumably on the basis that it is difficult to value such interests. However, it is bizarre that such sales should be in a worse tax position under the Regime than gifts.

Equity release schemes

26–05 Persons who may have entered into equity release schemes with commercial providers may also find themselves caught by the Regime if, as is normally the case, only part of the interest in the house is sold.

> ***Example:***
> Mary needed to raise cash in 2003. After taking financial advice she decided to enter into an equity release scheme and sold 40 per cent of her interest in the property to Mortgage International. She is entitled to go on living there until she moves to a nursing home or dies.
>
> She has received the cash which has generated interest on which she is paying income tax. However, despite the fact that she has carried out no IHT tax planning she is caught by Sch.15 assuming para.11(1) cannot apply.

The response from the Revenue and Ministers has been along the lines that very few people take out equity release schemes and therefore evidence is required that there is a real problem before they will correct it! As noted above, there is also general suspicion that sales of part are more commonly done between members of the family and should not have any protection.

It is hard to see how this approach can be justified. If an elderly person wishes to raise cash from their house why should taking out a loan as opposed to selling equity have such different tax effects? A loan is not caught by Sch.15 because there is no disposal of land; an equity release scheme on the other hand does involve a disposal. Similarly, if an individual borrows cash from his son and charges

---

[3] See IHTA 1984, s.54(2).

property as security he is not caught by the Regime but if the son buys an interest in the house the Regime applies.

Sales for full consideration

Equally curious is the fact that what are arguably more controversial **26–06** arrangements do not appear to be caught by the Regime. The starting point for any planning depends on using the exclusion given in para.10(1)(a). This provides a complete protection from the POA charge if the disposal is "of his *whole* interest in the property *except for any right expressly reserved by him* over the property either by a transaction made at arm's length with a person not connected with him or by a transaction such as might be expected to be made at arm's length between persons not connected with each other" (see 5–08).

Sale of the whole house

One option that has been used in the past (and is still available) is for **26–07** the *whole* home to be sold by the individual to a member of the family for full market value. The member of the family can then allow the vendor to live there free of charge. There is no gift so the reservation of benefit provisions do not apply. The cash is part of the vendor's estate for inheritance tax purposes and he can give it away in due course.

This apparently simple transaction does, however, pose a number of problems. Whilst acceptable for IHT purposes, there are difficulties if the purchaser does not have sufficient cash to pay the purchase price. In those circumstances, he might want the vendor to agree to leave the purchase price outstanding as a long-term loan (in which case any subsequent gift of the debt by the vendor would be more problematic for IHT purposes).

In order to ensure that the para.10(1)(a) exclusion is available, the terms of the loan have to be the same as those offered by any bank or building society, *i.e.* the loan would have to be on reasonable terms, interest bearing with interest being paid not rolled up,[4] secured and with some deposit paid. One has to demonstrate that it is a transaction "such as might be expected to be made at arm's length between persons not connected with each other."

SDLT will be payable—in the past the transaction often rested in contract to avoid Stamp Duty but this is no longer possible.

---

[4] Rolled-up interest was common in home loan arrangements—see Chapter 17.

Another objection is that the purchaser will end up suffering capital gains tax because the donor who occupies the property does not own it. Sometimes this problem has been solved by the donee settling the house on reverter to settlor trusts—see Chapter 23—but care is needed if this route is adopted.

Sale of freehold reversion subject to lease: inheritance tax position

26–08 Given the difficulties involved in finding sufficient cash to pay for the purchase of the whole house a further scheme was developed for IHT purposes under which the donor would first carve out a lease for himself for a fixed term or possibly for life at a nil or nominal rent, and would then sell the freehold interest (subject to that lease) for full market value. There was no gift by the vendor, and therefore the disposal was not caught by s.102A of the FA 1986. However, the vendor had devalued the freehold reversion by carving out the lease in his own favour. The purchaser had to pay far less for the freehold reversion—on a 15-year lease one might expect the freehold value to be devalued by as much as one half. Such an arrangement is acceptable for IHT purposes, although it is critical to ensure that the proper price is paid. The valuations are difficult, not least because the transaction is not a common one. The difficulty is that there is almost certainly a loss of marriage value; the value of the freehold subject to the lease and the value of the lease are together unlikely to be equal to the vacant possession value. Should the children pay for the marriage value as well as for the freehold reversion? If so, that would cause a problem under the Regime—it is not the sort of transaction that would be made between parties at arms length—see para.10(1)(a)(ii).

If, instead, the vendor sells the reversion for a price equal to the value it has in the hands of the children and they pay nothing for loss of marriage value, the vendor's estate has been diminished for IHT purposes. However, such a transaction may not be a transfer of value if there was no intention to confer a gratuitous benefit on the children.[5] Even if the vendor has made a transfer of value, the argument would be that he has not made a gift within the meaning of FA 1986, s.102(1) or s.102A(1).[6] The question that remains is whether such a transaction can qualify for para.10(1)(a)(ii) protection from the POA charge. In a commercial transaction between unconnected parties (such as an equity release scheme) it would be

---

[5] Section 10 of the IHTA 1984.
[6] For the difference between a transfer of value and a gift, see 16–14 *et seq.*

common for the vendor to lose the marriage value rather than for the purchasers to pay for it.

Assuming therefore that this valuation problems can be overcome, it is necessary to define the proprietary interest retained by the vendor with sufficient precision to ensure that one can then value the freehold. Whilst there is some question as to whether a lease for life or a lease for a term of years should be granted, the better view is that a lease for life should be avoided because of s.43(3) of the IHTA 1984: it is hard to argue that the lease has been acquired for full consideration.[7]

The capital gains tax problems mentioned above are still an issue. The vendor will obtain principal private residence relief in respect of the lease but the purchaser will find that the freehold reversion is an appreciating asset in his estate and will not qualify for principal private residence relief under s.222 of the TCGA 1992.

Reverter to settlor trusts

To deal with this problem, one option is for the children to settle the **26–09** purchased freehold interest on a reverter to settlor trust for the vendor.[8] By doing this the children can, with care, achieve a base cost uplift to market value on the vendor's death (see 23–07), thus eradicating any gain on the freehold which has occurred during his lifetime. This route, however, would not achieve principal private residence relief on any sale or disposal of the freehold during the vendor's lifetime because he is occupying the property by virtue of his leasehold interest not by virtue of his freehold interest under the trust. Accordingly, the vendor may not be able to move house without a capital gains tax disadvantage.

Funding the purchase price

Despite the reduced purchase price, difficulties can remain: suppose **26–10** the child still has insufficient cash to fund the purchase? He cannot borrow from the bank and give security on the property itself because the child only owns the reversion and receives no rent. Can the

---

[7] Although the Revenue accepted this in the *Advanced Instruction Manual* at E–15. Under IHTA 1984, s.43(3), a loan for life, unless submitted for full consideration, is treated as creating a settlement with the lessee treated as entitled to an interest in possession in the property.

[8] Alternatively the cash might be settled and then used by the trustees to acquire the freehold.

vendor give cash to his child to enable the child to fund the purchase?

As noted in Chapter 25, the reservation of benefit provisions substituted property rules does not apply to non-settled cash (Sch.20, para.2(2)(b)), assuming that the gift of cash was not made conditional on the purchase of the freehold reversion by the child.

The Regime

26–11 How does all this fit in with the Regime? If the transaction is a straightforward sale of the whole interest and the cash is provided by the children and was not previously gifted by the vendor there is no problem—para.10(1)(a) will provide protection. All that must be done is to ensure that the transaction is at a fully arm's length basis.

If the sale is of a freehold reversion subject to a lease in favour of the vendor the position is more difficult. Assuming that the lease has been carved out first, it should be "a right expressly reserved over the property" and therefore qualify for para.10(1)(a) protection. Is it though a transaction "such as might be expected to be made at arm's length" within para.10(1)(a)(ii)? The difficulties in valuation have already been indicated at 26–08, above. It would certainly be important for the sale price actually to be paid by the children, and not, for example, to be left outstanding by way of loan. However, difficulties in the marriage value remain.

What is the position if the children are purchasing the property using cash previously gifted to them by their parents? As we have seen, this does not generally cause reservation of benefit problems but it would appear to cause pre-owned asset problems. The point is that the contribution condition has been breached because consideration, namely cash, has been paid by the purchaser for the acquisition of an interest in the land that the vendor occupies and that consideration has been directly or indirectly provided by the vendor.[9]

The position, however, would be different if the property is purchased by the children from their own resources and then subsequently the vendor makes a gift of the cash.

Example:
Barry sells his freehold reversion to David and David pays the full market price having sufficient cash in his own right not derived from gifts made previously to him by Barry. Barry then decides to give the cash to, say, David's children. This would

---

[9] On the para.3 charge, see generally Chapter 3.

not appear to fall foul of para.3(3): the consideration for the acquisition of the land has not been directly or indirectly provided by Barry. Even if Barry gives back the cash to David, assuming that David did not borrow on the understanding that he would get the cash back again, this would not appear to be caught by the Regime.

Conclusions

In summary, IHT planning involving sales of the house (or chattels) **26–12** to members of the family are still possible even under the Regime but considerable care is needed to ensure that the more stringent conditions in Sch.15, para.10(1)(a) are satisfied. It is unlikely that the Revenue will accept that sales of freehold reversions subject to a retained lease are within the protection of para.10(1)(a) without some clear valuation evidence, and great care must be taken if the cash is given back. SDLT will increase the costs and CGT issues remain a problem if the vendor wishes to move. In practice, this route is likely to have only limited use for the tax planner.

Chapter 27

BUSINESSES AND FARMS

BACKGROUND

27-01 This is an area of considerable importance and some difficulty. The importance derives from the value frequently attributed to the business or farm and, in many cases, to the availability of 100 per cent relief from IHT.[1] The difficulty arises from the relatively complex structures that are often employed: a business may operate as a sole trade; partnership or as an incorporated entity.

Many businesses are family run and frequently adjustments are made to the ownership and running of the business, classically with parents handing over control and ownership to their children.

APPLICATION OF THE RESERVATION OF BENEFIT RULES

27-02 These are as capable of applying to gifts of business and agricultural assets as to gifts of any other assets. There is no blanket exclusion which applies. However, the following may be noted.

Full consideration let out

27-03 Take the case where father farms land and decides to take the son into partnership, giving him (say) a 50 per cent interest in the land and an accompanying 50 per cent share of all profits. In such a case, the full

---

[1] See IHTA 1984, Pt V, Ch.1 (business property) and Chapter 2 (agricultural property). Agricultural property relief takes precedence over business relief: see IHTA 1984, s.114(1).

consideration let out in FA 1986, Sch.20, para.6[2] may apply so that there is no reservation of benefit in that gift.

This analysis depends upon the father furnishing full consideration for his continued use of the land. This is not the usual straightforward analysis with the donor paying a full rent for continued use of gifted property. It involves looking at the matter in the round and saying that the benefits in the form of profits should be consistent with the contributions that father and son make in the form of capital and labour. With this in mind the sharing arrangements should stack up commercially.[3]

Shared occupation

Broadly speaking if Dad gives Son a share in his land which they   **27–04** both occupy and Dad receives no benefit, other than a negligible one, from Son, which is for some reason connected with the gift, then there is no reservation in the gifted property.[4]

Application of relief if there is a reservation

Business (and agricultural) property which is caught by the reserva-   **27–05** tion of benefit rules is treated as comprised in the donor's estate for IHT purposes at his death if the reservation is continuing. Alternatively, if the reservation ceases *inter vivos* he makes a PET.[5] In both cases, relief may be available to reduce the value of the property subject to charge.[6] The requirements are complex but two sets of conditions need to be satisfied:

(i) **at the time of the gift** the property has to qualify for relief either as relevant business property or as agricultural property[7]; and

(ii) **at the time of the tax charge** the property has to satisfy a number of conditions, the basis of which is the concept of a **notional transfer by the donee.**[8]

---

[2] The legislation is in Appendix I.

[3] For the Revenue's views in this area, see *Advanced Instruction Manual* at D29. See also *Dymond's Capital Taxes* at 9.300 and *AG v Boden* [1912] 1 K.B. 539.

[4] See FA 1986, s.102B(4). See Chapter 22 for a detailed consideration of this exemption.

[5] This is the effect of FA 1986, s.102(3) and s.102(4).

[6] See FA 1986, Sch.20, para.8.

[7] *ibid.*, para.8(1).

[8] *ibid.*, para.8(1A)(b).

In deciding whether the business property relief ownership condition is met,[9] ownership by the donor prior to the gift is treated as ownership by the donee[10] and if the donee dies before the donor (or before the reservation of benefit charge), his personal representatives or his beneficiaries under his Will or intestacy are treated as if they were the donee.[11]

In general, if the conditions are met the rate of relief is then decided by reference to the notional transfer by the donee. This is, however, subject to the qualification that whether certain stocks and shares are relevant business property is to be decided on the basis that they remained owned by the donor.[12] (This has the effect of preventing aggregation with other property of the donee: however, the restriction is of reduced importance given the availability of 100 per cent for minority shareholdings). Similar rules apply in the case of agricultural property relief: for instance, ownership and occupation by the donor before the gift is treated as that of the donee and in the case of the occupation condition, occupation by the donor **after** the gift is also treated as that of the donee.[13]

Take the example of Dan who gives his farm (which he has owned and farmed for many years) to his son Phil. Dan continues in occupation until his death 18 months later. The analysis is as follows:

(i) Dan has made a gift which is caught by the reservation of benefit rules and which will be subject to IHT on his death.

(ii) At the time of the gift the property qualified for agricultural property relief.

(iii) At the time of Dan's death, Phil is treated as making a notional transfer of value and has satisfied the ownership/occupation requirement for agricultural property relief to be available.

Reasonable remuneration

27–06 A question that frequently arises in the context of a gift of shares in the family business is whether the donor can safely continue to be remunerated for working in the business or whether such payment gives rise to a reservation of benefit. The views of the Revenue were published in letters dated February 19, 1987 and May 18, 1987. They

[9] See IHTA 1984, s.106.
[10] See FA 1986, Sch.20, para.8(2)(a).
[11] *ibid.*, para.8(5).
[12] *ibid.*, para.8(1A)(a).
[13] *ibid.*, para.8(2).

make the key point that "the continuation of reasonable commercial arrangements in the form of remuneration and other benefits for the donor's services to the business entered into prior to the gift would not, by itself, amount to a reservation provided that the benefits were in no way linked to or affected by the gift."[14]

IMPACT OF THE PRE-OWNED ASSETS CHARGE

There are no provisions in FA 2004, Sch.15 that deal specifically **27–07** with businesses and farms. Accordingly, the application of the Regime depends on general principles.

In considering the application of the Regime it will be important to identify the property gifted. For instance:

   (i) a gift of shares will only be a problem if the para.8 charge is in point (*i.e.* because the shares become held in a settlor interested trust); and

  (ii) a gift of a partnership share, as for instance when father gives part of his capital account to his son, in a case where land is a partnership asset is a gift of the share (*chose in action*) and not of an interest in land. Again, therefore, there will only be a problem if the para.8 charge could apply.

In cases where the full consideration let out prevents the reservation of benefit rules from applying to land and chattels, the pre-owned assets charge is equally inapplicable.[15]

Default election

If the Regime would otherwise apply, the election is available to the **27–08** taxpayer to opt into reservation of benefit.[16] As a result:

  (a) no income tax will be payable, **and**

  (b) the asset may attract business or agricultural property relief on the death of the taxpayer or earlier cessation of the reservation.[17]

---

[14] The problems posed by this statement are many: what for instance is "reasonable" in the context of remuneration? Why must the arrangements pre-date the gift if the rationale for the statement lies in the commerciality of the services? Note that FA 1986, Sch.20, para.6(1)(a) is limited to land and chattels but does the donor receive a benefit within FA 1986, s.102(1)(b) if the consideration represents no more than a fair commercial payment for his services?

[15] See Sch.15, para.11(5)(d). See Chapter 7.

[16] See Chapter 11 for a consideration of the election.

[17] See 27–05, *et seq.*

CHAPTER 28

WILL DRAFTING

28–01 This chapter is concerned with drafting IHT efficient Wills. In recent years the availability of a range of lifetime planning opportunities meant that Wills had become of diminished significance. All that has now changed and for many married couples the Will is now a principal tool in the battle to save Inheritance Tax.[1]

This chapter will concentrate on the traditional family Will and to simplify the discussion will consider what would be an appropriate Will for Ted who is married to Violet with two adult children and grandchildren. Further, it will be assumed that it is Ted who will die first and that Ted and Violet's combined estate is such that IHT is an issue.

USE OF IHT NIL BAND

28–02 Ted's Will should make use of his IHT nil rate band: in tax year 2004/5 that is worth £105,200 (£263,000 × 40 per cent). This may be utilised:

(i) by making gifts to chargeable persons (children/grandchildren). But if it is felt that Violet (the survivor) may need the use of all the assets in Ted's estate; then

(ii) by establishing a discretionary trust (the classic nil rate band discretionary trust) under which Violet, as one of the beneficiaries, is entitled to benefit. She can, for instance, be paid at the trustees' discretion all the income of the trust if appropriate.

---

[1] See generally Chapter 21 for a consideration of the current tax planning climate. Unmarried tax payers will not find the Will an especially attractive tax planning vehicle. Same-sex couples may in due course enjoy the advantages of a married couple when the Civil Partnership Legislation is enacted.

It is important that nothing is done which would result in Violet becoming entitled to an interest in possession in the trust fund since were that to occur the value of the trust fund would be taxed on her death[2] with the result that Ted's nil rate band will have been wasted.

A practical problem is to select appropriate assets to go into the trust. At first blush, stocks and shares would seem to be ideal but the income tax treatment of dividends distributed as income to beneficiaries of such a trust produces an unacceptably high income tax rate. The ideal is therefore assets producing an income return in some other form: *e.g.* interest bearing securities or let property.

Of course, in many typical estates the reason for the IHT problem is that the couple own a house which has soared in value. Apart from that, a few investments and pensions the couple will have no other assets. In this case, the question of what assets should be put into the discretionary trust can be reduced to the choice between putting Ted's share of the house into the trust (or at least a portion of it up to the value of the IHT nil rate band) or using what is popularly known as the "debt scheme".

THE MATRIMONIAL HOME

Assume that the decision is taken to put Ted's 50 per cent share of the **28–03** matrimonial home into the discretionary trust given that its value[3] equates with his available IHT nil band and there are no other assets in his estate. Assume that Violet survives for a further six years during which time she continues to occupy the property as her main residence. Given that she is entitled to a 50 per cent share in the equity (as well as being the sole legal owner/trustee) it may be thought that when she dies all that will be taxed is her 50 per cent beneficial share with an appropriate discount. Concerns have been expressed, however, that in a case like this, the Revenue may successfully argue that by virtue of her sole occupation of the property she enjoys an interest in possession in the share of the property held in the discretionary trust.[4]

The Revenue argument outlined above might be strengthened if the original house was sold and a replacement bought, again for Violet's sole use. Instead of an argument relying to some extent of trustees' inertia, it might now be said that the trustees have exercised their powers to purchase a property for Violet's use and have

---

[2] See IHTA 1984, s.49(1).

[3] For the value of joint property owned by husband and wife, see *IRC v Arkwright* [2004] EWHC 1720 (Ch).

[4] The authors are not convinced by such arguments and believe that, if raised, they should be fiercely resisted.

therefore given her an immediate right to immediate possession, the hallmark of an interest in possession.[5]

A further point to bear in mind is the future CGT position when, after Violet's death, the property is sold. Given that she did not enjoy an interest in possession in the moiety held in trust, there will be no CGT death uplift and the availability of CGT principle private residence relief will depend on whether she is occupying the property under the terms of the settlement.[6]

Use of reverter to settlor trust

28–04 A possible way round the problem is for Ted's share of the property to be left outright to the children who, after his death, settle it on reverter to settlor trusts for the benefit of their mother. This topic is considered in detail in Chapter 23. Ted should not express in his will a wish that this settlement be created since otherwise he might be considered to have created a precatory trust within IHTA 1984 which would nullify the tax planning.

Loan schemes

28–05 These have come popular in recent years and spawned a voluminous literature.[7] In brief, the discretionary trust is constituted by a debt owed to the trustees by Violet who receives all the assets of Ted's estate. For many couples the practical results of this arrangement are ideal since Violet enjoys the benefit of all the couple's assets whilst Ted has used up his nil rate band on death.

A number of issues need to be addressed before opting for the loan trust, such as:

(i) Will the trust be vulnerable to attack as a "sham" or as one in which Violet enjoys an interest in possession?[8]

(ii) What are the terms of Violet's debt? It can be repayable on demand but should it carry interest (rolled up and so only

---

[5] See Lightman J. in *IRC v Eversden* [2002] S.T.C. 1109 quoted at 16–10.

[6] See TCGA 1992, s.225; *Sansom v Peay* [1976] 3 All E.R. 375 and S.P. 10/79. It is a difficult balancing exercise to obtain the best of both worlds: *i.e.* no IHT charge but CGT relief.

[7] See for instance, the *Encyclopaedia of Forms and Precedents*, col.42(1), [2003 Reissue], Chapter 11.

[8] See *Taxation* April 29, 2004, p.116. In practice it is not thought that this will create a problem provided that the trustees act in a trustee-like manner.

payable with the principal on her death) or be index-linked?

(iii) If Ted's estate includes an interest in land, will SDLT be in point on the basis that Violet is, through the debt, acquiring that interest? The current approach of the Revenue is to argue that duty is payable in all cases (*i.e.* whether or not the arrangement is a simple debt or one in which the executors charge the property in favour of the nil rate band trustees).

(iv) Whether FA 1986, s.103 is capable of operating to disallow the debt on Violet's death. Specifically it is feared that this may be the case if she had made gifts to Ted during his lifetime which she is, in effect, buying back.[9]

BUSINESS AND AGRICULTURAL PROPERTY

If Ted's estate includes property which attracts IHT relief at 100 per **28–06** cent, then simply leaving that property to Violet will be a "waste" in that the spouse exemption will result in the business relief having been wasted.

Rather this property should be specifically gifted (in addition to the nil rate sum) to chargeable persons (children/grandchildren) or put into a discretionary trust, and in many cases the latter option is likely to prove the most attractive.[10]

DEALING WITH RESIDUE

Having used up his nil rate band (and in appropriate cases made sure **28–07** that 100 per cent relievable property has been satisfactorily dealt with), the residue of Ted's estate should be left to Violet in order to take advantage of the spouse exemption.[11]

It is important to realise that this exemption is available whether the residue is given absolutely to Violet or on flexible life interest

---

[9] The section is reproduced in Appendix I.

[10] The simple Will—leaving the nil rate band (being the available amount on death) to a trust and the residue to the surviving spouse produces interesting results if the estate includes 100 per cent relievable property: see IHTA 1984, s.39A (broadly speaking the benefit of the relief is apportioned between trust and residue).

[11] See IHTA 1984, s.18. Even if Violet does not need this property it should not be left to the children on Ted's death given that it will attract a 40 per cent IHT charge. Better to leave it to Violet and for her to make lifetime gifts (PETs) to the children.

trusts. If IHT planning for Violet will be desirable **the advice must now be to leave the property on flexible interest in possession trusts.**

Drafting the Trusts

28–08 Suitable clauses are included at the end of this chapter (**Precedent 1**). Note in particular:

- (i) that under the trusts in default Violet enjoys a life interest (see **cl.3(i)**);
- (ii) that the trustees have power to advance capital to her (see **cl.3(ii)**); and
- (iii) that the above provisions are subject to an overriding power of appointment (see **cl.2**) which can be exercised to bring Violet's interest to an end

  - in whole or in part; and
  - in specific cases

  and the trustees can exercise the power to establish continuing trusts (including discretionary trusts) or to make outright appointments of property: *e.g.* to children.

Exercising the overriding power

28–09 If the overriding power is exercised (*e.g.* to appoint assets absolutely to the children: see **Precedent III**) then Violet will make a PET. Bear in mind that if the assets cease to be settled property a CGT "exit" charge may arise.[12]

Link up with reservation of benefit and the pre-owned asset regime

28–10 Assume that the trustees exercise their power of appointment to create a small (value £263,000) discretionary trust under which the family (including Violet) can benefit (see **Precedent II**). What is the tax analysis?

---

[12] See TCGA 1992, s.71.

(i) the termination of Violet's life interest will be a chargeable transfer not a PET but given that she has not used up her nil rate band no IHT will be payable (notice that although Violet is not the settlor, it is her nil rate band which is relevant given that she makes the transfer of value: see IHTA 1984, s.80(1)); and

(ii) whilst the IHT legislation provides that Violet makes a "deemed" transfer of value[13] it is not considered that she makes a "gift" as required if the reservation of benefit rules are to apply nor is it thought that she makes a disposal of property or settles property for the purposes of the pre-owned asset legislation.[14]

The upshot is that the discretionary trust so established can be used at the trustees' discretion as a vehicle to benefit Violet during her life without the trust being subject to IHT on her death (it is exactly comparable to the nil rate band discretionary trust set up on Ted's death). Violet therefore has the comfort of knowing that assets to a value of £526,000 are available for her use but will not attract an IHT charge on death.

Had Violet been left the residue absolutely, then if she had set up such a discretionary trust of her nil band under which she was capable of benefitting, the gift would be caught by the reservation of benefit rules and the property taxed as part of her estate on death.

The main residence

"*Ingram* schemes" involving a main residence and effected by **28–11** trustees under overriding powers are considered in Chapter 24. If Ted was the sole owner of the matrimonial home then such schemes may prove attractive and should certainly be considered.

In cases where the residue comprises only a share in the house, such arrangements are problematic. The trustees could, however, appoint (say) a 45 per cent share in the house on continuing trusts leaving Violet with a continuing interest in possession in 5 per cent with a view to the trust continuing to qualify for principal private residence relief on their entire 50 per cent share in the event of the house being sold.

---

[13] See IHTA 1984, s.52(1) and 16–14.
[14] These matters are explored in greater detail in Chapter 24.

Posthumous rearrangements

28–12 If Violet has been left an absolute interest in residue, she should consider establishing flexible trusts along the lines of Precedent I by an instrument of variation falling within IHTA 1984, s.142(1).

Concluding comments

28–13 Both the reservation of benefit rules and pre-owned assets charge are concerned with lifetime tax planning. They have no application to the disposition of property on death and, as discussed in this chapter, Wills offer an opportunity for a married couple to set up a tax efficient structure for the benefit of the survivor.

MY TRUSTEES shall hold my residuary estate and the income thereof (hereinafter referred to as "the Trust Fund") upon the following trusts and with the following powers:

1. Definitions

In this clause where the context so permits the following expressions shall have the following meanings:

    (i) "the Discretionary Beneficiaries" shall mean:

        (aa) my said husband/wife
        (bb) my children and remoter issue
        (cc) the spouses widows and widowers of the persons mentioned in (bb)

    (ii) "the Trust Period" shall mean the period commencing with the date of my death and ending Eighty years thereafter and such period of Eighty years shall be the perpetuity period applicable to the disposition made by this clause PROVIDED THAT my Trustees may declare by irrevocable deed that the Trust Period (but not the said perpetuity period) shall terminate on such date as they may specify therein (such date of termination to be earlier than the end of the said period of Eighty years but the same as or later than the date of such deed)

    (iii) "the accumulation period" shall mean the period commencing with the date of my death and ending Twenty-one years thereafter or on the earlier termination of the Trust Period

2. Discretionary Trusts

    (i) My Trustees shall have power to appoint the whole or any part of the capital and/or income of the Trust Fund upon trust for or for the benefit of such of the Discretionary Beneficiaries at such ages or times in such shares upon such trusts which may include discretionary or protective powers or trusts and in such manner generally as my Trustees shall in

---

[1] These follow on from a general clause providing for the residuary estate to be held on trust for sale with provision for the payment of debts/legacies, etc.

their discretion think fit. Any such appointment may include such powers and provisions for the maintenance education or other benefit of the Discretionary Beneficiaries or for the accumulation of income and such administrative powers and provisions as my Trustees think fit

(ii) No exercise of the power conferred by sub-clause 2(i) shall invalidate any prior payment or application of all or any part of the capital or income of the Trust Fund made under any other power conferred by my Will or by law

(iii) Any trusts and powers created by an appointment under sub-clause 2(i) may be delegated to any extent to any person whether or not including my Trustees or any of them

(iv) Any exercise of the power of appointment conferred by sub-clause 2(i) shall:

(aa) be subject to the application if any of the rule against perpetuities and the law concerning excessive accumulations of income and

(bb) be by deed revocable during the Trust Period or irrevocable and executed during the Trust Period

3. Trusts in default

The provisions of this sub-clause shall apply until subject to and in default of any appointment under sub-clause 2(i)

(i) The income of the Trust Fund shall be paid to my said husband/wife during his/her lifetime

(ii) My Trustees may at any time during the Trust Period pay or apply the whole or any part of the Trust Fund in which my said husband/wife is then entitled to an interest in possession to him/her or for his/her advancement or otherwise for his/her benefit in such manner as my Trustees shall in their discretion think fit. In exercising the powers conferred by this sub-clause my Trustees shall be entitled to have regard solely to the interests of my said husband/wife and to disregard all other interests or potential interests under my Will

(iii) My Trustees shall hold the capital and income of the Trust Fund for such of my children (in this sub-clause referred to as Beneficiaries) as shall survive me and if more than one in equal shares absolutely **PROVIDED THAT** if any Beneficiary is already dead or predeceases me the share of my residuary estate to which such Beneficiary would be entitled if he or she survived me and attained a vested interest shall be

held in trust for such of his or her children and remoter issue
(if any) as shall be living at my death and shall attain the age
of eighteen [18] years or marry under that age such issue to
take through all degrees according to their stocks if more than
one in equal shares and so that no issue shall take whose
parent is living at my death and so capable of taking

4. Administration of Estate incomplete

My Trustees may exercise any or all of the powers contained in this
Will notwithstanding that the administration of my estate may then
be incomplete and my residuary estate not by then established and
notwithstanding that probate of this Will may not have been
granted

5. Exclusion of the self dealing rule

Any of my Trustees may join in exercising the powers and discre-
tions conferred by this Will notwithstanding that such trustee may be
personally interested as a beneficiary provided that such powers shall
not be exercisable by a sole trustee who is my said husband/wife

PRECEDENT II: Deed terminating spouse's life interest and creating a "nil rate band" discretionary trust

THIS DEED OF APPOINTMENT is made the day of 2004 by [*insert details of Trustees*] ("the Appointors")

SUPPLEMENTAL to [*insert details of the Will*] ("the Will")

WHEREAS

1. By clause [ ] of the Will ("the Will") the Deceased's residuary estate (as therein defined) was held on trusts under which the trustees were given wide powers of appointment subject to which income therefrom was to be paid to the Deceased's surviving spouse for life.

2. The Trustees are now desirous of exercising the said power of appointment as set out below

3. The "Appointed Fund" comprises part of the Trust Fund

4. The Appointors are the present trustees of the Will

NOW THIS DEED WITNESSES

Definitions

1. In this Deed the following expressions shall where the context permits have the following meaning

   (a) **"Appointed Fund"** means the assets specified in the First Schedule hereto
   (b) **"Beneficiaries"** means [*include surviving spouse*]
   (c) **"Trust Period"** and **"Accumulation Period"** have the meanings given in the Will

Exercise of power of appointment

2. In exercise of the power of appointment conferred on them by clause [ ] of the Will and of all other powers (if any) them enabling the Appointors hereby appoint that the Trustees shall hold the capital and income of the Appointed Fund upon such trusts for all or any one or more to the exclusion of the others or other of the Beneficiaries at such age or time or respective ages or times if more than one in such shares and with such

trusts for their respective benefit and such provisions for their respective advancement maintenance education or benefit and all such other dispositions charges and powers whether contained in the Will or conferred by this Deed or by law of or in relation to the capital and income of the Appointed Fund or any part of it as an absolute owner beneficially entitled to the same could lawfully make or confer of or in relation to the same as the Trustees not being less than two in number or a trust corporation may at any time or from time to time before the expiration of the Trust Period by any deed with or without power of revocation (without infringing the rule against perpetuities) appoint and in particular and without prejudice to the generality of the above provision the Trustees not being less than two in number or a trust corporation may by any deed do the following:

   (i) delegate in any manner and to any extent to any persons or corporations whatsoever or wheresoever resident or situated the exercise at any time within the Trust Period of the power of appointment conferred by this clause

  (ii) extinguish or otherwise restrict in any way and to any extent the future exercise of all or any of the powers contained in this clause PROVIDED that such extinguishment or restriction shall in no way operate by itself so as to invalidate any past performance or exercise of any of the trusts or powers contained in the Will or this Deed

 (iii) provide for the appointment or remuneration of trustees or nominees in any part of the world upon any terms and conditions.

 (iv) create any protective discretionary or other trusts and powers to be executed or exercised in favour of any one or more of the Beneficiaries by any like persons or corporations

  (v) transfer or cause to be transferred to any like persons or corporations as the Trustees or to the trustees of any other settlement in which any of the Beneficiaries may for the time being be entitled to benefit the capital and income of the Appointed Fund or any part or parts of it and so that the receipt of any such other trustees shall be a good discharge to the Trustees

PROVIDED that no exercise of any power contained in or conferred by this clause shall operate to make ineffective any prior payment or application of the capital or income of the Appointed Fund whether made by this Deed or by law

3 Trusts of Income

3.1 In default of and until and subject to any and every appointment made under the power or powers conferred by clause 2
above the income of the Appointed Fund shall during the
Trust Period be held by the Trustees upon trust to pay or apply
or (in the case of a minor) allocate the same to or for the
maintenance support or otherwise for the benefit in any
manner of all or any one or more exclusively of the others or
other of the Beneficiaries for the time being in existence and
if more than one in such shares and in such manner in all
respects as the Trustees shall in their absolute discretion
without being liable in any such case to account for the
exercise of such discretion think fit.

3.2 PROVIDED always that the Trustees shall not be bound to
apply or allocate the whole or any part of the income accruing
to the Appointed Fund during the Accumulation Period but
shall during the Accumulation Period pay apply or allocate
only so much of the income as the Trustees shall in their
absolute discretion think fit and shall accumulate the surplus
(if any) of such income by investing the same and the
resulting income from it in any of the investments authorised
by this settlement and shall hold such accumulations as an
accretion to (and as one fund with) the capital of the
Appointed Fund.

Exclusion of apportionment

3. Insert standard clause

IN WITNESS etc

SCHEDULE

("the Appointed Fund")

insert assets to a value not exceeding the spouse's available IHT nil
rate band

PRECEDENT III: Deed of appointment terminating flexible life interest trusts—appointments in favour of adult beneficiary absolutely and in favour of minor beneficiary contingently on his attainment of specified age[1]

THIS DEED OF APPOINTMENT is made the ... ... day of ...
... ... by *(trustees)* of *(addresses)* ('the Trustees')
WHEREAS

(1) This deed is supplemental to the will of *(testator)* late of *(address)* dated *(date)* ('the Will')

(2) The Trustees are the present trustees of the Will

(3) The property now subject to the trusts of the Will consists of the investments [and cash] set out in the schedule

(4) The Trustees intend by this deed to exercise the power of appointment given to them by clause *(number)* of the Will

NOW THIS DEED WITNESSES as follows:

1 Exercise of power

1.1 The Trustees in exercise of their power of appointment conferred by clause *(number)* of the Will and of all other powers them enabling [irrevocably *or* subject to clause 1.4 below][2] appoint the property set out in the schedule as and

---

[1] Trustees holding property on flexible trusts may wish to terminate those trusts by appointing the trust property amongst all or some of the beneficiaries. They can do this if the document creating the trusts enables them to do so and this precedent is for use when the trustees are acting under powers in the will and assumes that the trustees wish to terminate the trust once and for all. Of course they may wish to make appointments in respect of part only of the Trust Fund: in which case the relevant property ("the Appointed Fund") will be identified in the Schedule. Alternatively they may wish to appoint part of the fund onto discretionary trusts.

This Precedent presupposes that the trust property is still in the form of investments and that these are being appointed *in specie* amongst beneficiaries some of whom are not yet of age. So far as adult beneficiaries are concerned, the effect of the Precedent is that they become absolutely entitled to the shares appointed to them, and these shares can then be transferred to them by the trustees in exchange for formal receipts.

[2] Where some of the interests appointed are contingent (*e.g.* the interest appointed by clause 1.1.2, above), the appointors can reserve power to revoke the relevant trusts. In such a case, the first option in square brackets should be omitted and clause 1.4, above included in the Precedent. The reservation of a power of revocation would mean that the relevant trusts did not qualify (for inheritance tax purposes) as accumulation and maintenance and hence the property would be held on non-interest in possession trusts.

from the date of this deed to be held upon the following trusts:

    1.1.1 as to the property set out in Part I of the schedule upon trust as to both capital and income for *(adult beneficiary)* absolutely

    1.1.2 as to the property set out in Part II of the schedule upon trust as to both capital and income for *(minor beneficiary)* but contingently upon his attaining the age of [18 *or* 21] years

    1.1.3 *(set out trusts (if any) in favour of other beneficiaries)*

1.2 PROVIDED that if any person named in clause 1.1.2 [and clause 1.1.3][3] above shall die before attaining a vested interest but leaving a child or children living at his death then such child or children shall take absolutely and if more than one in equal shares so much of the trust property and the income of it as that person would have taken had he attained a vested interest[4]

1.3 [PROVIDED also that if at any time the trusts declared by clause 1.1.2 [and clause 1.1.3] above read in conjunction with clause 1.2 above shall fail then from the date of failure the property which was the subject of those trusts and the income from it shall be held upon trust *(set out alternative trusts)*

or

PROVIDED also that if at any time the trusts declared by clause 1.1.2 [and clause 1.1.3] above in conjunction with clause 1.2 above in respect of a share of the trust property shall fail then from the date of such failure that share (and any part of the trust property which may already have accrued to it under this provision) shall accrue to the other share or shares (and equally if more than one) the trusts of which shall not at that date have failed and be held upon the trusts from time to time affecting such other share or shares][5]

---

[3] The clause numbers of those clauses appointing contingent interests should be set out.

[4] The interests of the children mentioned in clause 1.2, above are not made contingent on their attaining a specified age and so are vested from the outset. This is partly to make the trusts declared in their favour less likely to infringe the perpetuity rule, and partly to safeguard their families if they should die young leaving a wife or children.

[5] Clause 1.3, above is a longstop provision. The trustees could name here an adult beneficiary who (or whose estate) they would wish to benefit in these circumstances. Alternatively, they could provide that property of which the trusts failed (*e.g.* because a minor died before attaining a vested interest and without leaving children) should accrue to property the trusts of which had not failed, in which case the second of the two alternative forms of clause 1.3 should be used.

250

[1.4 PROVIDED also that the Trustees or other the trustees or trustee for the time being of the Will shall have power at any time or times by deed or deeds wholly or partially to revoke or otherwise vary those trusts declared by this deed which create contingent interests and by the same deed to declare such other trusts (concerning the same) as may be authorised by clause *(number)* of the Will][6]

2 Powers of maintenance and advancement

The trusts contained in clause 1.1.2 [and clause 1.1.3] above shall carry the intermediate income and the statutory powers of maintenance accumulation and advancement contained in the Trustee Act 1925 Sections 31 and 32 (as amended by the Family Law Reform Act 1969 by the Trusts of Land and Appointment of Trustees Act 1996 and by the Trustee Act 2000) shall apply to them with the following variations:

2.1 in the case of the said Section 31 the substitution in subsection (1)(i) of the words 'the trustees in their absolute discretion think fit' for the words 'may in all the circumstances be reasonable' and the omission of the proviso to subsection (1) and

2.2 in the case of the said Section 32 the omission of the words 'one-half of' from proviso (a) to subsection (1)

3 Administrative provisions

The administrative provisions of the Will which are contained in clauses *(specify clauses)* shall apply to the trusts declared by this deed in the same way as they applied to the trusts of the Will itself so far as the same are not inconsistent with the trusts and provisions above declared and contained [save only for the following modifications: *(specify)*][7]

---

[6] See n.2, above.

[7] By this clause the trustees give themselves administrative powers (*e.g.* of investment, charging, insurance, etc). Their power to do this, and its extent, depends on the wording of the power of appointment contained in the original will. It is assumed in the present case that the trustees have power, and wish to give themselves the same powers as they had under the original will. They may also be able to give themselves other powers, for instance, a wide power of advancement which may not have been included in the original will or settlement: if the trustees wish to do this, they should so provide in this deed.

[4 Exclusion of apportionment

All income of the property set out in Part I and Part II of the schedule received by or on behalf of the Trustees or other trustees or trustee for the time being of the Will from and after the date of this deed shall be treated as if it had arisen wholly after such date and the Apportionment Act 1870 shall not be applicable to it][8]

IN WITNESS etc

SCHEDULE

Part I

(describe property to be held on trust for beneficiary specified in clause 1.1.1 above)

Part II

(describe property to be held on trust for beneficiary specified in clause 1.1.2 above)
(continue with further parts as appropriate)[9]

---

[8] This clause should be included if it is wished to exclude the operation of the Apportionment Act 1870 to accruing income. If further parts are added to the schedule the clause should be amended as appropriate.

[9] The schedule should set out all the trust property (or the relevant parts) and will be divided into as many parts as there are beneficiaries in whose favour an appointment is made.

CHAPTER 29

POSTHUMOUS ARRANGEMENTS

If a beneficiary varies the dispositions of property comprised in a **29–01** deceased's estate in accordance with the conditions laid down in IHTA 1984, s.142(1), then "this Act shall apply as if the variation had been effected by the deceased." It is commonly said that the terms of the variation are "read back" into the deceased's Will.[1]

Link-up with Reservation of Benefit

The Revenue accepts that "this Act" includes all the IHT legislation **29–02** which therefore encompasses the reservation of benefit legislation in FA 1986. Hence a redirection of property will not be caught by these rules even if the beneficiary continues to derive a benefit from the property.

> ### Example:
> On her husband's death, Joyce is left the entire estate including the couple's seaside cottage ("Fishnets") worth £250,000. By deed of variation falling within s.142(1), she transfers this property to her son Barney. Joyce continues to use the property on a regular basis.

Tax analysis

1. The variation is read back into her husband's Will and falls **29–03** within his hitherto unused IHT nil rate band.

---

[1] Of course it should be remembered that variations are not confined to the situation where the deceased left a will but also apply to alter dispositions of property occurring under the intestacy rules and to redirect property passing by survivorship under a beneficial joint tenancy.

2. Joyce should also consider whether to elect for CGT purposes: this will be desirable if the property has increased in value since her husband's death by more than Joyce's annual exemption.[2]

3. Although Joyce continues to derive a benefit from the use of the property she is not within the reservation of benefit rules given that, because of read-back, she has never made a gift of the property.

Impact of the pre-owned assets regime

29–04 It is expressly provided[3] that a disposition is disregarded for the purposes of this charge if, by virtue of s.17 of the IHTA 1984, it is not treated as a transfer of value by the chargeable person. That section provides that a variation to which s.142 applies is not a transfer of value, and hence in the above example, Joyce will not be caught by the pre-owned asset charge.[4]

In cases where the residue of the estate is left to the surviving spouse absolutely, there may be attractions in that person effecting a variation to create flexible life interest trusts.[5] In that event, whilst the variation would fall within s.142(1)—since it involves a redirection of property—it would not involve any transfer of value by the surviving spouse. Hence s.17 is wholly redundant in such cases. Does that mean that the Regime (because the exemption is based on s.17) is capable of applying? On balance, the authors are of the opinion that the Regime will not apply to such variations: this point is discussed at 7–25.

Concluding remarks

29–05 Instruments of variation remain a valuable planning tool in the taxpayer's armoury conferring the three advantages that the relevant beneficiary does not make any transfer of value; that the reservation of benefit rules will not apply even if he continues to use or enjoy the redirected property; and that they are outside the pre-owned assets charge.

---

[2] The CGT provisions are in TCGA 1992, s.62(6)–(10). The "reading-back" is more limited in its effect under the CGT legislation: see *Marshall v Kerr* [1994] S.T.C. 638 (HL).

[3] See Sch.15, para.16 ("change in distribution of deceased's estate").

[4] Section 17 of the IHTA 1984 performs something of a "belt and braces" function in that it says that Joyce does not make a transfer whilst s.142 deems the disposition to have been made by the deceased. Had s.142 stood alone, it might have been argued that Joyce had still made a transfer of value.

[5] The advantages of such trusts in terms of future IHT planning are considered at 28–07 *et seq.*

APPENDIX I: THE LEGISLATION

A. FA 1986, s.102, 102A–C; 103; Sch.20 (as amended).

B. FA 2004, Sch.15.

C. The Inheritance Tax (Double Charges Relief) Regulations 1987.

APPENDIX II: MATERIAL ISSUED BY THE INLAND REVENUE

A. Press Release of December 10, 2003 ("Tackling Tax Avoidance").

B. Consultation Document of December 11, 2003 ("Tax Treatment of Pre-Owned Assets").

C. Budget Press Release of March 17, 2004 ("Tax Treatment of Pre-Owned Assets": REV BN 40).

D. Consultation on the Tax Treatment of Pre-Owned Assets: Summary of Responses.

E. Consultation Document of August 16, 2004 ("Taxation of Pre-Owned Assets: Further Consultation").

APPENDIX 1: THE LEGISLATION

A. FINANCE ACT 1986

102 Gifts with reservation

AppI–A1

(1) Subject to subsections (5) and (6) below, this section applies where, on or after 18th March 1986, an individual disposes of any property by way of gift and either—

(a) possession and enjoyment of the property is not bona fide assumed by the donee at or before the beginning of the relevant period; or

(b) at any time in the relevant period the property is not enjoyed to the entire exclusion, or virtually to the entire exclusion, of the donor and of any benefit to him by contract or otherwise;

and in this section "the relevant period" means a period ending on the date of the donor's death and beginning seven years before that date or, if it is later, on the date of the gift.

(2) If and so long as—

(a) possession and enjoyment of any property is not bona fide assumed as mentioned in subsection (1)(a) above, or

(b) any property is not enjoyed as mentioned in subsection (1)(b) above,

the property is referred to (in relation to the gift and the donor) as property subject to a reservation.

(3) If, immediately before the death of the donor, there is any property which, in relation to him, is property subject to a reservation then, to the extent that the property would not, apart from this section, form part of the donor's estate immediately before his death, that property shall be treated for the purposes of the 1984 Act as property to which he was beneficially entitled immediately before his death.

(4) If, at a time before the end of the relevant period, any property ceases to be property subject to a reservation, the donor shall be treated for the purposes of the 1984 Act as having at that time made a disposition of the property by a disposition which is a potentially exempt transfer.

(5) This section does not apply if or, as the case may be, to the extent that the disposal of property by way of gift is an exempt transfer by virtue of any of the following provisions of Part II of the 1984 Act,—

(a) section 18 (transfers between spouses)[, except as provided by subsections (5A) and (5B) below]³;

(b) section 20 (small gifts);

(c) section 22 (gifts in consideration of marriage);

(d) section 23 (gifts to charities);

(*e*) section 24 (gifts to political parties);

[(*ee*) section 24A (gifts to housing associations);][1]

(*f*) section 25 (gifts for national purposes, etc);

(*g*) [...][2];

(*h*) section 27 (maintenance funds for historic buildings); and

(*i*) section 28 (employee trusts).

[(5A) Subsection (5)(*a*) above does not prevent this section from applying if or, as the case may be, to the extent that—

(*a*) the property becomes settled property by virtue of the gift,

(*b*) by reason of the donor's spouse ("the relevant beneficiary") becoming beneficially entitled to an interest in possession in the settled property, the disposal is or, as the case may be, is to any extent an exempt transfer by virtue of section 18 of the 1984 Act in consequence of the operation of section 49 of that Act (treatment of interests in possession),

(*c*) at some time after the disposal, but before the death of the donor, the relevant beneficiary's interest in possession comes to an end, and

(*d*) on the occasion on which that interest comes to an end, the relevant beneficiary does not become beneficially entitled to the settled property or to another interest in possession in the settled property.][3]

[(5B) If or, as the case may be, to the extent that this section applies by virtue of subsection (5A) above, it has effect as if the disposal by way of gift had been made immediately after the relevant beneficiary's interest in possession came to an end.][3]

[(5C) For the purposes of subsections (5A) and (5B) above—

(*a*) section 51(1)(*b*) of the 1984 Act (disposal of interest in possession treated as coming to end of interest) applies as it applies for the purposes of Chapter 2 of Part 3 of that Act; and

(*b*) references to any property or to an interest in any property include references to part of any property or interest.][3]

(6) This section does not apply if the disposal of property by way of gift is made under the terms of a policy issued in respect of an insurance made before 18th March 1986 unless the policy is varied on or after that date so as to increase the benefits secured or to extend the term of the insurance; and, for this purpose, any change in the terms of the policy which is made in pursuance of an option or other power conferred by the policy shall be deemed to be a variation of the policy.

(7) If a policy issued as mentioned in subsection (6) above confers an option or other power under which benefits and premiums may be increased to take account of increases in the retail prices index (as defined in section 8(3) of the 1984 Act) or any similar index specified in the policy, then, to the

extent that the right to exercise that option or power would have been lost if it had not been exercised on or before 1st August 1986, the exercise of that option or power before that date shall be disregarded for the purposes of subsection (6) above.

(8) Schedule 20 to this Act has effect for supplementing this section.

Amendments—
[1] Sub-s (5)(*ee*) inserted by FA 1989, s 171(5), (6) with respect to transfers of value made after 13 March 1989.
[2] Sub-s (5)(*g*) repealed by FA 1998 Sch 27 Part IVwith respect to any disposal made on or after 17 March 1998.
[3] Words in sub-s (5) inserted, and sub-ss (5A)–(5C) inserted, by FA 2003 s 185 with effect for disposals made after 19 June 2003.

[102A Gifts with reservation: interest in land][1]

[(1) This section applies where an individual disposes of an interest in land **AppI–A2** by way of gift on or after 9th March 1999.

(2) At any time in the relevant period when the donor or his spouse enjoys a significant right or interest, or is party to a significant arrangement, in relation to the land—

(*a*) the interest disposed of is referred to (in relation to the gift and the donor) as property subject to a reservation; and

(*b*) section 102(3) and (4) above shall apply.

(3) Subject to subsections (4) and (5) below, a right, interest or arrangement in relation to land is significant for the purposes of subsection (2) above if (and only if) it entitles or enables the donor to occupy all or part of the land, or to enjoy some right in relation to all or part of the land, otherwise than for full consideration in money or money's worth.

(4) A right, interest or arrangement is not significant for the purposes of subsection (2) above if—

(*a*) it does not and cannot prevent the enjoyment of the land to the entire exclusion, or virtually to the entire exclusion, of the donor; or

(*b*) it does not entitle or enable the donor to occupy all or part of the land immediately after the disposal, but would do so were it not for the interest disposed of.

(5) A right or interest is not significant for the purposes of subsection (2) above if it was granted or acquired before the period of seven years ending with the date of the gift.

(6) Where an individual disposes of more than one interest in land by way of gift, whether or not at the same time or to the same donee, this section shall apply separately in relation to each interest.][1]

Amendments—
[1] This section inserted by FA 1999 s 104 with effect from 27 July 1999 for disposals made after 8 March 1999.

[102B Gifts with reservation: share of interest in land][1]

AppI–A3 [(1) This section applies where an individual disposes, by way of gift on or after 9th March 1999, of an undivided share of an interest in land.

(2) At any time in the relevant period, except when subsection (3) or (4) below applies—

(a) the share disposed of is referred to (in relation to the gift and the donor) as property subject to a reservation; and

(b) section 102(3) and (4) above shall apply.

(3) This subsection applies when the donor—

(a) does not occupy the land; or

(b) occupies the land to the exclusion of the donee for full consideration in money or money's worth.

(4) This subsection applies when—

(a) the donor and the donee occupy the land; and

(b) the donor does not receive any benefit, other than a negligible one, which is provided by or at the expense of the donee for some reason connected with the gift.][1]

Amendments—
[1] This section inserted by FA 1999 s 104 with effect from 27 July 1999 for disposals made after 8 March 1999.

[102C Sections 102A and 102B: supplemental][1]

AppI–A4 [(1) In sections 102A and 102B above "the relevant period" has the same meaning as in section 102 above.

(2) An interest or share disposed of is not property subject to a reservation under section 102A(2) or 102B(2) above if or, as the case may be, to the extent that the disposal is an exempt transfer by virtue of any of the provisions listed in section 102(5) above.

(3) In applying sections 102A and 102B above no account shall be taken of—

(a) occupation of land by a donor, or

(b) an arrangement which enables land to be occupied by a donor, in circumstances where the occupation, or occupation pursuant to the arrangement, would be disregarded in accordance with paragraph 6(1)(*b*) of Schedule 20 to this Act.

(4) The provisions of Schedule 20 to this Act, apart from paragraph 6, shall have effect for the purposes of sections 102A and 102B above as they have effect for the purposes of section 102 above; and any question which falls to be answered under section 102A or 102B above in relation to an interest in land shall be determined by reference to the interest which is at that time treated as property comprised in the gift.

(5) Where property other than an interest in land is treated by virtue of paragraph 2 of that Schedule as property comprised in a gift, the provisions of section 102 above shall apply to determine whether or not that property is property subject to a reservation.

(6) Sections 102 and 102A above shall not apply to a case to which section 102B above applies.

(7) Section 102A above shall not apply to a case to which section 102 above applies.]¹

Amendments—
¹ This section inserted by FA 1999 s 104 with effect from 27 July 1999.

103 Treatment of certain debts and incumbrances

(1) Subject to subsection (2) below, if, in determining the value of a person's **AppI–A5** estate immediately before his death, account would be taken, apart from this subsection, of a liability consisting of a debt incurred by him or an incumbrance created by a disposition made by him, that liability shall be subject to abatement to an extent proportionate to the value of any of the consideration given for the debt or incumbrance which consisted of—

   (*a*) property derived from the deceased; or

   (*b*) consideration (not being property derived from the deceased) given by any person who was at any time entitled to, or amongst whose resources there was at any time included, any property derived from the deceased.

(2) If, in a case where the whole or a part of the consideration given for a debt or incumbrance consisted of such consideration as is mentioned in subsection (1)(*b*) above, it is shown that the value of the consideration given, or of that part thereof, as the case may be, exceeded that which could have been rendered available by application of all the property derived from the deceased, other than such (if any) of that property—

   (*a*) as is included in the consideration given, or

   (*b*) as to which it is shown that the disposition of which it, or the property which it represented, was the subject matter was not made with reference to, or with a view to enabling or facilitating, the giving of the consideration or the recoupment in any manner of the cost thereof,

no abatement shall be made under subsection (1) above in respect of the excess.

(3) In subsections (1) and (2) above "property derived from the deceased" means, subject to subsection (4) below, any property which was the subject matter of a disposition made by the deceased, either by himself alone or in concert or by arrangement with any other person or which represented any of the subject matter of such a disposition, whether directly or indirectly, and whether by virtue of one or more intermediate dispositions.

(4) If the disposition first-mentioned in subsection (3) above was not a transfer of value and it is shown that the disposition was not part of associated operations which included—

(*a*) a disposition by the deceased, either alone or in concert or by arrangement with any other person, otherwise than for full consideration in money or money's worth paid to the deceased for his own use or benefit; or

(*b*) a disposition by any other person operating to reduce the value of the property of the deceased,

that first-mentioned disposition shall be left out of account for the purposes of subsections (1) to (3) above.

(5) If, before a person's death but on or after 18th March 1986, money or money's worth, is paid or applied by him—

(*a*) in or towards the satisfaction or discharge of a debt or incumbrance in the case of which subsection (1) above would have effect on his death if the debt or incumbrance had not been satisfied or discharged, or

(*b*) in reduction of a debt or incumbrance in the case of which that subsection has effect on his death,

the 1984 Act shall have effect as if, at the time of the payment or application, the person concerned had made a transfer of value equal to the money or money's worth and that transfer were a potentially exempt transfer.

(6) Any reference in this section to a debt incurred is a reference to a debt incurred on or after 18th March 1986 and any reference to an incumbrance created by a disposition is a reference to an incumbrance created by a disposition made on or after that date; and in this section "subject matter" includes, in relation to any disposition, any annual or periodical payment made or payable under or by virtue of the disposition.

(7) In determining the value of a person's estate immediately before his death, no account shall be taken (by virtue of section 5 of the 1984 Act) of any liability arising under or in connection with a policy of life insurance issued in respect of an insurance made on or after 1st July 1986 unless the whole of the sums assured under that policy form part of that person's estate immediately before his death.

SCHEDULE 20

GIFTS WITH RESERVATION

Section 102

Interpretation and application

1—(1) In this Schedule—   **AppI–A6**

"the material date", in relation to any property means, in the case of property falling within subsection (3) of the principal section, the date of the donor's death and, in the case of property falling within subsection (4) of that section, the date on which the property ceases to be property subject to a reservation;
"the principal section" means section 102 of this Act; and
"property subject to a reservation" has the same meaning as in the principal section.

(2) Any reference in this Schedule to a disposal by way of gift is a reference to such a disposal which is made on or after 18th March 1986.

(3) This Schedule has effect for the purposes of the principal section and the 1984 Act.

Substitutions and accretions

2—(1) Where there is a disposal by way of gift and, at any time before the **AppI–A7** material date, the donee ceases to have the possession and enjoyment of any of the property comprised in the gift, then on and after that time the principal section and the following provisions of this Schedule shall apply as if the property, if any, received by the donee in substitution for that property had been comprised in the gift instead of that property (but in addition to any other property comprised in the gift).

(2) This paragraph does not apply if the property disposed of by the gift—

(*a*) becomes settled property by virtue of the gift; or

(*b*) is a sum of money in sterling or any other currency.

(3) In sub-paragraph (1) above the reference to property received by the donee in substitution for property comprised in the gift includes in particular—

(*a*) in relation to property sold, exchanged or otherwise disposed of by the donee, any benefit received by him by way of consideration for the sale, exchange or other disposition; and

(*b*) in relation to a debt or security, any benefit received by the donee in or towards the satisfaction or redemption thereof; and

265

(*c*) in relation to any right to acquire property, any property acquired in pursuance of that right.

(4) Where, at a time before the material date, the donee makes a gift of property comprised in the gift to him, or otherwise voluntarily divests himself of any such property otherwise than for a consideration in money or money's worth not less than the value of the property at that time, then, unless he does so in favour of the donor, he shall be treated for the purposes of the principal section and sub-paragraph (1) above as continuing to have the possession and enjoyment of that property.

(5) For the purposes of sub-paragraph (4) above—

(*a*) a disposition made by the donee by agreement shall not be deemed to be made voluntarily if it is made to any authority who, when the agreement is made, is authorised by, or is or can be authorised under, any enactment to acquire the property compulsorily; and

(*b*) a donee shall be treated as divesting himself, voluntarily and without consideration, of any interest in property which merges or is extinguished in another interest held or acquired by him in the same property.

(6) Where any shares in or debentures of a body corporate are comprised in a gift and the donee is, as the holder of those shares or debentures, issued with shares in or debentures of the same or any other body corporate, or granted any right to acquire any such shares or debentures, then, unless the issue or grant is made by way of exchange for the first-mentioned shares or debentures, the shares or debentures so issued, or the right granted, shall be treated for the purposes of the principal section and this Schedule as having been comprised in the gift in addition to any other property so comprised.

(7) In sub-paragraph (6) above the reference to an issue being made or right being granted to the donee as the holder of shares or debentures shall be taken to include any case in which an issue or grant is made to him as having been the holder of those shares or debentures, or is made to him in pursuance of an offer or invitation made to him as being or having been the holder of those shares or debentures, or of an offer or invitation in connection with which any preference is given to him as being or having been the holder thereof.

3—(1) Where either sub-paragraph (3)(*c*) or sub-paragraph (6) of paragraph 2 above applies to determine, for the purposes of the principal section, the property comprised in a gift made by a donor—

(*a*) the value of any consideration in money or money's worth given by the donee for the acquisition in pursuance of the right referred to in the said sub-paragraph (3)(*c*) or for the issue or grant referred to in and said sub-paragraph (6), as the case may be, shall be allowed as a deduction in valuing the property comprised in the gift at any time after the consideration is given, but

(*b*) if any part (not being a sum of money) of that consideration consists of property comprised in the same or another gift from the donor and treated for the purposes of the 1984 Act as forming part of the donor's

266

estate immediately before his death or as being attributable to the value transferred by a potentially exempt transfer made by him, no deduction shall be made in respect of it under this sub-paragraph.

(2) For the purposes of sub-paragraph (1) above, there shall be left out of account so much (if any) of the consideration for any shares in or debentures of a body corporate, or for the grant of any right to be issued with any such shares or debentures, as consists in the capitalisation of reserves of that body corporate, or in the retention by that body corporate, by way of set-off or otherwise, of any property distributable by it, or is otherwise provided directly or indirectly out of the assets or at the expense of that or any associated body corporate.

(3) For the purposes of sub-paragraph (2) above, two bodies corporate shall be deemed to be associated if one has control of the other or if another person has control of both.

Donee predeceasing the material date

4—Where there is a disposal by way of gift and the donee dies before the **AppI–A8** date which is the material date in relation to any property comprised in the gift, paragraphs 2 and 3 above shall apply as if—

(a) he had not died and the acts of his personal representatives were his acts; and

(b) property taken by any person under his testamentary dispositions or his intestacy (or partial intestacy) were taken under a gift made by him at the time of his death.

Settled gifts

5—(1) Where there is a disposal by way of gift and the property comprised **AppI–A9** in the gift becomes settled property by virtue of the gift, paragraphs 2 to 4 above shall not apply but, subject to the following provisions of this paragraph, the principal section and the following provisions of this Schedule shall apply as if the property comprised in the gift consisted of the property comprised in the settlement on the material date, except in so far as that property neither is, nor represents, nor is derived from, property originally comprised in the gift.

(2) If the settlement comes to an end at some time before the material date as respects all or any of the property which, if the donor had died immediately before that time would be treated as comprised in the gift,—

(a) the property in question, other than property to which the donor then becomes absolutely and beneficially entitled in possession, and

(b) any consideration (not consisting of rights under the settlement) given by the donor for any of the property to which he so becomes entitled, shall be treated as comprised in the gift (in addition to any other property so comprised).

(3) Where property comprised in a gift does not become settled property by virtue of the gift, but is before the material date settled by the donee, sub-paragraphs (1) and (2) above shall apply in relation to property comprised in the settlement as if the settlement had been made by the gift; and for this purpose property which becomes settled property under any testamentary disposition of the donee or on his intestacy (or partial intestacy) shall be treated as settled by him.

(4) Where property comprised in a gift becomes settled property either by virtue of the gift or as mentioned in sub-paragraph (3) above, any property which—

(*a*) on the material date is comprised in the settlement, and

(*b*) is derived, directly or indirectly, from a loan made by the donor to the trustees of the settlement,

shall be treated for the purposes of sub-paragraph (1) above as derived from property originally comprised in the gift.

(5) Where, under any trust or power relating to settled property, income arising from that property after the material date is accumulated, the accumulations shall not be treated for the purposes of sub-paragraph (1) above as derived from that property.

Exclusion of benefit

AppI–A10 **6**—(1) In determining whether any property which is disposed of by way of gift is enjoyed to the entire exclusion, or virtually to the entire exclusion, of the donor and of any benefit to him by contract or otherwise—

(*a*) in the case of property which is an interest in land or a chattel, retention or assumption by the donor of actual occupation of the land or actual enjoyment of an incorporeal right over the land, or actual possession of the chattel shall be disregarded if it is for full consideration in money or money's worth;

(*b*) in the case of property which is an interest in land, any occupation by the donor of the whole or any part of the land shall be disregarded if—

(i) it results from a change in the circumstances of the donor since the time of the gift, being a change which was unforeseen at that time and was not brought about by the donor to receive the benefit of this provision; and

(ii) it occurs at a time when the donor has become unable to maintain himself through old age, infirmity or otherwise; and

(iii) it represents a reasonable provision by the donee for the care and maintenance of the donor; and

(iv) the donee is a relative of the donor or his spouse;

(*c*) a benefit which the donor obtained by virtue of any associated operations (as defined in section 268 of the 1984 Act) of which the disposal by way of gift is one shall be treated as a benefit to him by contract or otherwise.

(2) Any question whether any property comprised in a gift was at any time enjoyed to the entire exclusion, or virtually to the entire exclusion, of the donor and of any benefit to him shall (so far as that question depends upon the identity of the property) be determined by reference to the property which is at that time treated as property comprised in the gift.

(3) In the application of this paragraph to Scotland, references to a chattel shall be construed as references to a corporeal moveable.

7—(1) Where arrangements are entered into under which— **AppI–A1**

(a) there is a disposal by way of gift which consists of or includes, or is made in connection with, a policy of insurance on the life of the donor or his spouse or on their joint lives, and

(b) the benefits which will or may accrue to the donee as a result of the gift vary by reference to benefits accruing to the donor or his spouse (or both of them) under that policy or under another policy (whether issued before, at the same time as or after that referred to in paragraph (a) above),

the property comprised in the gift shall be treated for the purposes of the principal section as not enjoyed to the entire exclusion, or virtually to the entire exclusion, of the donor.

(2) In sub-paragraph (1) above—

(a) the reference in paragraph (a) to a policy on the joint lives of the donor and his spouse includes a reference to a policy on their joint lives and on the life of the survivor; and

(b) the reference in paragraph (b) to benefits accruing to the donor or his spouse (or both of them) includes a reference to benefits which accrue by virtue of the exercise of rights conferred on either or both of them.

Agricultural property and business property

8—(1) [This paragraph applies where][1] there is a disposal by way of gift of **AppI–A1** property which, in relation to the donor, is at that time—

(a) relevant business property within the meaning of Chapter I of Part V of the 1984 Act, or

(b) agricultural property, within the meaning of Chapter II of that Part, to which section 116 of that Act applies, or

(c) shares or securities to which section 122(1) of that Act applies (agricultural property of companies),

and that property is property subject to a reservation . . . [2]
    [(1A) Where this paragraph applies—

(*a*) any question whether, on the material transfer of value, any shares or securities fall [within paragraph (*b*), (*bb*) or (*cc*) of section 105(1) of the 1984 Act (certain shares or securities qualifying for relief)]⁴ shall be determined, subject to the following provisions of this paragraph, as if the shares or securities were owned by the donor and had been owned by him since the disposal by way of gift; and

(*b*) subject to paragraph (*a*) above, any question whether, on the material transfer of value, relief is available by virtue of Chapter I or Chapter II of Part V of the 1984 Act and, if relief is available by virtue of Chapter II, what is the appropriate percentage for that relief, shall be determined, subject to the following provisions of this paragraph, as if, so far as it is attributable to the property comprised in the gift, that transfer were a transfer of value by the donee.]³

(2) For the purpose only of determining whether, on the transfer of value which, by virtue of [sub-paragraph (1A)(*b*)]¹ above, the donee is assumed to make, the requirement of section 106 or, as the case may be, section 117 of the 1984 Act (minimum period of ownership or occupation) is fulfilled,—

(*a*) ownership by the donor prior to the disposal by way of gift shall be treated as ownership by the donee; and

(*b*) occupation by the donor prior to the disposal and any occupation by him after that disposal shall be treated as occupation by the donee.

(3) Where the property disposed of by the gift consists of shares or securities falling within paragraph (*c*) of sub-paragraph (1) above, [relief shall not be available by virtue of Chapter II of Part V of the 1984 Act on the material transfer of value]¹ unless—

(*a*) section 116 of the 1984 Act applied in relation to the value transferred by the disposal, and

(*b*) throughout the period beginning with the disposal and ending on the material date, the shares or securities are owned by the donee,

and for the purpose only of determining whether, on the transfer of value which, [by virtue of sub-paragraph (1A)(*b*) above]¹, the donee is assumed to make, the requirements of subsection (1) of section 123 of the 1984 Act are fulfilled, it shall be assumed that the requirement in paragraph (*b*) of that subsection (as to the ownership of the shares or securities) is fulfilled.

(4) In this paragraph, "the material transfer of value" means, as the case may require,—

(*a*) the transfer of value under section 4 of the 1984 Act on the death of the donor; or

(*b*) the transfer of value under subsection (4) of the principal section on the property concerned ceasing to be subject to a reservation.

(5) If the donee dies before the material transfer of value, then, as respects any time after his death, any reference in the preceding provisions of this paragraph to the donee shall be construed as a reference to his personal

representatives or, as the case may require, the person (if any) by whom the property, shares or securities concerned were taken under a testamentary disposition made by the donee or under his intestacy (or partial intestacy).

Amendments—
[1] Words in sub-paras (1), (2), (3) substituted by FA 1987 s 58 and Sch 8 para 18 in relation to transfers of value made or other events occurring after 16 March 1987.
[2] Words in sub-para (1) repealed by FA 1987 s 58, Sch 8 para 18 and Sch 16 Pt IX in relation to transfers of value made or other events occurring after 16 March 1987.
[3] Sub-para (1A) inserted by FA 1987 s 58 and Sch 8 para 18 in relation to transfers of value made or other events occurring after 16 March 1987.
[4] Words in sub-para (1A)(*a*) substituted for the words "within paragraph (*b*) or paragraph (*bb*) of section 105(1) of the 1984 Act (which specify shares and securities qualifying for 50 per cent relief)" by F(No 2)A 1992 Sch 14 paras 7, 8 in relation to transfers of value and other events occurring after 9 March 1992 but subject to F(No 2)A 1992 Sch 14 para 9.

B. FINANCE ACT 2004

SCHEDULE 15

Section 84

CHARGE TO INCOME TAX ON BENEFITS RECEIVED BY FORMER OWNER OF PROPERTY

Introductory

1 In this Schedule—   **AppI–B1**

"IHTA 1984" means the Inheritance Tax Act 1984 (c. 51);
"the 1986 Act" means the Finance Act 1986 (c. 41);
"chattel" means any tangible movable property (or, in Scotland, corporeal movable property) other than money;
"excluded transaction" has the meaning given by paragraph 10;
"intangible property" means any property other than chattels or interests in land;
"interest in land" has the same meaning as in Chapter 4 of Part 6 of IHTA 1984;
"land" has the same meaning as in IHTA 1984;
"prescribed" means prescribed by regulations;
"property" has the same meaning as in IHTA 1984;
"regulations" means regulations made by the Treasury under this Schedule;
"settlement" and "settled property" have the same meanings as in IHTA 1984.

2 Section 839 of the Taxes Act 1988 (connected persons) applies for the purposes of this Schedule, but as if in that section "relative" included uncle, aunt, nephew and niece and "settlement", "settlor" and "trustee" had the same meanings as in IHTA 1984.

Land

3 (1) This paragraph applies where—   **AppI–B2**

(a) an individual ("the chargeable person") occupies any land ("the relevant land"), whether alone or together with other persons, and

(b) the disposal condition or the contribution condition is met as respects the land.

(2) The disposal condition is that—

(a) at any time after 17th March 1986 the chargeable person owned an interest—

    (i) in the relevant land, or

    (ii) in other property the proceeds of the disposal of which were (directly or indirectly) applied by another person towards the acquisition of an interest in the relevant land, and

(b) the chargeable person has disposed of all, or part of, his interest in the relevant land or the other property, otherwise than by an excluded transaction.

(3) The contribution condition is that at any time after 17th March 1986 the chargeable person has directly or indirectly provided, otherwise than by an excluded transaction, any of the consideration given by another person for the acquisition of—

(a) an interest in the relevant land, or

(b) an interest in any other property the proceeds of the disposal of which were (directly or indirectly) applied by another person towards the acquisition of an interest in the relevant land.

(4) For the purposes of this paragraph a disposition which creates a new interest in land out of an existing interest in land is to be taken to be a disposal of part of the existing interest.

(5) Where this paragraph applies to a person in respect of the whole or part of a year of assessment, an amount equal to the chargeable amount determined under paragraph 4 is to be treated as income of his chargeable to income tax.

4 (1) For any taxable period the chargeable amount in relation to the relevant land is the appropriate rental value (as determined under sub-paragraph (2)), less the amount of any payments which, in pursuance of any legal obligation, are made by the chargeable person during the period to the owner of the relevant land in respect of the occupation of the land by the chargeable person.

(2) The appropriate rental value is—

$$R \times \frac{DV}{V}$$

where—

R is the rental value of the relevant land for the taxable period,
DV is—

    (a) in a case falling within paragraph 3(2)(a)(i), the value as at the valuation date of the interest in the relevant land that was disposed of as mentioned in paragraph 3(2)(b) by the chargeable person or, where the disposal was a non-exempt sale, the appropriate proportion of that value,

    (b) in a case falling within paragraph 3(2)(a)(ii), such part of the value of the relevant land at the valuation date as can reasonably be attributed to the property originally disposed of by the chargeable person or, where the original disposal was a non-exempt sale, to the appropriate proportion of that property, and

(c) in a case falling within paragraph 3(3), such part of the value of the relevant land at the valuation date as can reasonably be attributed to the consideration provided by the chargeable person, and

V is the value of the relevant land at the valuation date.

(3) The "rental value" of the land for the taxable period is the rent which would have been payable for the period if the property had been let to the chargeable person at an annual rent equal to the annual value.

(4) The disposal by the chargeable person of an interest in land is a "non-exempt sale" if (although not an excluded transaction) it was a sale of his whole interest in the property for a consideration paid in money in sterling or any other currency; and, in relation to a non-exempt sale, "the appropriate proportion" is—

$$\frac{MV - P}{MV}$$

Where—

MV is the value of the interest in land at the time of the sale;
P is the amount paid.

(5) Regulations may—

(a) in relation to any valuation date, provide for a valuation of the relevant land or any interest in the relevant land by reference to an earlier valuation date to apply subject to any prescribed adjustments, and

(b) in relation to any year of assessment, provide for a determination of the rental value of the land by reference to any earlier year of assessment to apply subject to any prescribed adjustments.

(6) In this paragraph—

"the taxable period" means the year of assessment, or part of a year of assessment, during which paragraph 3 applies to the chargeable person;
"the valuation date", in relation to a taxable period, means such date as may be prescribed.

5 (1) For the purposes of paragraph 4 the annual value of the relevant land is the rent which might reasonably be expected to be obtained on a letting from year to year if—

(a) the tenant undertook to pay all taxes, rates and charges usually paid by a tenant, and

(b) the landlord undertook to bear the costs of the repairs and insurance and the other expenses (if any) necessary for maintaining the property in a state to command that rent.

(2) For the purposes of sub-paragraph (1) that rent—

(a) is to be taken to be the amount that might reasonably be expected to be so obtained in respect of a letting of the land, and

(b) is to be calculated on the basis that the only amounts that may be deducted in respect of services provided by the landlord are amounts in respect of the cost to the landlord of providing any relevant services.

(3) In this paragraph "relevant service" means a service other than the repair, insurance or maintenance of the premises.

Chattels

AppI–B3 6 (1) This paragraph applies where—

(a) an individual ("the chargeable person") is in possession of, or has the use of, a chattel, whether alone or together with other persons, and

(b) the disposal condition or the contribution condition is met as respects the chattel.

(2) The disposal condition is that—

(a) at any time after 17th March 1986 the chargeable person had (whether alone or jointly with others) owned—

  (i) the chattel, or
  (ii) any other property the proceeds of the disposal of which were (directly or indirectly) applied by another person towards the acquisition of the chattel, and

(b) the chargeable person disposed of all or part of his interest in the chattel or other property otherwise than by an excluded transaction.

(3) The contribution condition is that at any time after 17th March 1986 the chargeable person had directly or indirectly provided, otherwise than by an excluded transaction, any of the consideration given by another person for the acquisition of—

(a) the chattel, or

(b) any other property the proceeds of the disposal of which were (directly or indirectly) applied by another person towards the acquisition of the chattel.

(4) For the purposes of this paragraph, a disposition which creates a new interest in a chattel out of an existing interest in a chattel is to be taken to be a disposal of part of the existing interest.

276

(5) Where this paragraph applies to a person in respect of the whole or part of a year of assessment, an amount equal to the chargeable amount determined under paragraph 7 is to be treated as income of his chargeable to income tax.

7 (1) For any taxable period the chargeable amount in relation to any chattel is the appropriate amount (as determined under sub-paragraph (2)), less the amount of any payments which, in pursuance of any legal obligation, are made by the chargeable person during the period to the owner of the chattel in respect of the possession or use of the chattel by the chargeable person.

(2) The appropriate amount is—

$$N \times \frac{DV}{V}$$

where—

N is the amount of the interest that would be payable for the taxable period if interest were payable at the prescribed rate on an amount equal to the value of the chattel as the valuation date,

DV is—

(a) in a case falling within paragraph 6(2)(a)(i), the value as at the valuation date of the interest in the chattel that was disposed of as mentioned in paragraph 6(2)(b) by the chargeable person or, where the disposal was a non-exempt sale, the appropriate proportion of that value,

(b) in a case falling within paragraph 6(2)(a)(ii), such part of the value of the chattel at the valuation date as can reasonably be attributed to the property originally disposed of by the chargeable person or, where the original disposal was a non-exempt sale, to the appropriate proportion of that property, and

(c) in a case falling within paragraph 6(3), such part of the value of the chattel at the valuation date as can reasonably be attributed to the consideration provided by the chargeable person, and

V is the value of the chattel at the valuation date.

(3) The disposal by the chargeable person of an interest in a chattel is a "non-exempt sale" if (although not an excluded transaction) it was a sale of his whole interest in the chattel for a consideration paid in money in sterling or any other currency; and, in relation to a non-exempt sale, "the appropriate proportion" is—

$$\frac{MV - P}{MV}$$

where—

MV is the value of the interest in the chattel at the time of the sale;
P is the amount paid.

(4) Regulations may, in relation to any valuation date, provide for a valuation of the chattel or any interest in the chattel by reference to an earlier valuation date to apply subject to any prescribed adjustments.

(5) In this paragraph—

"the taxable period" means the year of assessment, or part of a year of assessment, during which paragraph 6 applies to the chargeable person;

"the valuation date", in relation to a taxable period, means such date as may be prescribed.

Intangible property comprised in settlement where settlor retains an interest

AppI–B4   8 (1) This paragraph applies where—

(a)   the terms of a settlement, as they affect any property comprised in the settlement, are such that any income arising from the property would be treated by virtue of section 660A of the Taxes Act 1988 (income arising under settlement where settlor retains an interest) as income of a person ("the chargeable person") who is for the purposes of Part 15 of that Act the settlor,

(b)   any such income would be so treated even if subsection (2) of that section did not include any reference to the spouse of the settlor, and

(c)   that property includes any property as respects which the condition in sub-paragraph (2) is met ("the relevant property").

(2) The condition mentioned in sub-paragraph (1)(c) is that the property is intangible property which is or represents property which the chargeable person settled, or added to the settlement, after 17th March 1986.

(3) Where this paragraph applies in respect of the whole or part of a year of assessment, an amount equal to the chargeable amount determined under paragraph 9 is to be treated as income of the chargeable person chargeable to income tax.

9 (1) For any taxable period the chargeable amount in relation to the relevant property is N minus T where—

N is the amount of the interest that would be payable for the taxable period if interest were payable at the prescribed rate on an amount equal to the value of the relevant property at the valuation date, and

T is the amount of any income tax or capital gains tax payable by the chargeable person in respect of the taxable period by virtue of any of the following provisions—

(a)   section 547 of the Taxes Act 1988,

(b)   section 660A of that Act,

(c)   section 739 of that Act,

(d)   section 77 of the Taxation of Chargeable Gains Act 1992 (c. 12), and

(e)   section 86 of that Act,

278

so far as the tax is attributable to the relevant property.

(2) Regulations may, in relation to any valuation date, provide for a valuation of the relevant property by reference to an earlier valuation date to apply subject to any prescribed adjustments.

(3) In this paragraph—

> "the taxable period" means the year of assessment, or part of a year of assessment, during which paragraph 8 applies to the chargeable person;
> "the valuation date", in relation to a year of assessment, means such date as may be prescribed.

Excluded transactions

10 (1) For the purposes of paragraphs 3(2) and 6(2) (the disposal condition), **AppI–B5** the disposal of any property is an "excluded transaction" in relation to any person ("the chargeable person") if—

(a) it was a disposal of his whole interest in the property, except for any right expressly reserved by him over the property, either—

> (i) by a transaction made at arm's length with a person not connected with him, or
> (ii) by a transaction such as might be expected to be made at arm's length between persons not connected with each other,

(b) the property was transferred to his spouse (or where the transfer has been ordered by a court, to his former spouse),

(c) it was a disposal by way of gift (or, where the transfer is for the benefit of his former spouse, in accordance with a court order), by virtue of which the property became settled property in which his spouse or former spouse is beneficially entitled to an interest in possession,

(d) the disposal was a disposition falling within section 11 of IHTA 1984 (dispositions for maintenance of family), or

(e) the disposal is an outright gift to an individual and is for the purposes of IHTA 1984 a transfer of value that is wholly exempt by virtue of section 19 (annual exemption) or section 20 (small gifts).

(2) For the purposes of paragraphs 3(3) and 6(3) (the contribution condition) the provision by a person ("the chargeable person") of consideration for another's acquisition of any property is an "excluded transaction" in relation to the chargeable person if—

(a) the other person was his spouse (or, where the transfer has been ordered by the court, his former spouse),

(b) on its acquisition the property became settled property in which his spouse or former spouse is beneficially entitled to an interest in possession,

(c) the provision of the consideration constituted an outright gift of money (in sterling or any other currency) by the chargeable person to the other person and was made at least seven years before the earliest date on which the chargeable person met the condition in paragraph 3(1)(a) or, as the case may be, 6(1)(a),

(d) the provision of the consideration is a disposition falling within section 11 of IHTA 1984 (dispositions for maintenance of family), or

(e) the provision of the consideration is an outright gift to an individual and is for the purposes of IHTA 1984 a transfer of value that is wholly exempt by virtue of section 19 (annual exemption) or section 20 (small gifts).

(3) A disposal is not an excluded transaction by virtue of sub-paragraph (1)(c) or (2)(b), if the interest in possession of the spouse or former spouse has come to an end otherwise than on the death of the spouse or former spouse.

Exemptions from charge

AppI–B6 11 (1) Paragraph 3 (land), paragraph 6 (chattels) and paragraph 8 (intangible property) do not apply to a person at a time when his estate for the purposes of IHTA 1984 includes—

(a) the relevant property, or

(b) other property—

(i) which derives its value from the relevant property, and
(ii) whose value, so far as attributable to the relevant property, is not substantially less than the value of the relevant property.

(2) Where the estate for the purposes of IHTA 1984 of a person to whom paragraph 3, 6 or 8 applies includes property—

(a) which derives its value from the relevant property, and

(b) whose value, so far as attributable to the relevant property, is substantially less than the value of the relevant property,

the appropriate rental value in paragraph 4, the appropriate amount in paragraph 7 or the chargeable amount in paragraph 9 (as the case may be) is to be reduced by such proportion as is reasonable to take account of the inclusion of the property in his estate.

(3) Paragraphs 3, 6 and 8 do not apply to a person at a time when—

(a) the relevant property, or

(b) any other property—

(i) which derives its value from the relevant property, and
(ii) whose value, so far as attributable to the relevant property, is not substantially less than the value of the relevant property,

falls within sub-paragraph (5) in relation to him.

(4) Where any property which falls within sub-paragraph (5) in relation to a person includes property—

    (a) which derives its value from the relevant property, and

    (b) whose value, so far as attributable to the relevant property, is substantially less than the value of the relevant property,

the appropriate rental value in paragraph 4, the appropriate amount in paragraph 7 or the chargeable amount in paragraph 9 (as the case may be) is to be reduced by such proportion as is reasonable to take account of that fact.

(5) Property falls within this sub-paragraph in relation to a person at a time when it—

    (a) would fall to be treated by virtue of any provision of Part 5 of the 1986 Act (inheritance tax) as property which in relation to him is property subject to a reservation,

    (b) would fall to be so treated but for any of paragraphs (d) to (i) of subsection (5) of section 102 of the 1986 Act (certain cases where disposal by way of gift is an exempt transfer for purposes of inheritance tax),

    (c) would fall to be so treated but for subsection (4) of section 102B of the 1986 Act (gifts with reservation: share of interest in land), or would have fallen to be so treated but for that subsection if the disposal by way of gift of an undivided share of an interest in land had been made on or after 9th March 1999, or

    (d) would fall to be so treated but for section 102C(3) of, and paragraph 6 of Schedule 20 to, the 1986 Act (exclusion of benefit).

(6) Where at any time the value of a person's estate for the purposes of IHTA 1984 is reduced by an excluded liability affecting any property, that property is not to be treated for the purposes of sub-paragraph (1) or (2) as comprised in his estate except to the extent that the value of the property exceeds the amount of the excluded liability.

(7) For the purposes of sub-paragraph (6) a liability is an excluded liability if—

    (a) the creation of the liability, and

    (b) any transaction by virtue of which the person's estate came to include the relevant property or property which derives its value from the relevant property or by virtue of which the value of property in his estate came to be derived from the relevant property,

were associated operations, as defined by section 268 of IHTA 1984.

(8) In determining whether any property falls within sub-paragraph (5)(b), (c) or (d) in a case where the contribution condition in paragraph 3(3) or 6(3) is met, paragraph 2(2)(b) of Schedule 20 (exclusion of gifts of money) is to be disregarded.

(9) In sub-paragraphs (1) to (8) "the relevant property" means—

  (a) in relation to paragraphs 3 and 6—

      (i) where the disposal condition in paragraph 3(2) or 6(2) is met, the property disposed of,

      (ii) where the contribution condition in paragraph 3(3) or 6(3) is met, the property representing the consideration directly or indirectly provided,

  (b) in relation to paragraph 8, the relevant property within the meaning of that paragraph.

(10) Property is not to be treated as falling within sub-paragraph (5)(b) at any time in a case falling within section 102(5)(h) of the 1986 Act unless the property remains subject to trusts which comply with the requirements of paragraph 3 (1) of Schedule 4 to IHTA 1984.

Chargeable person resident or domiciled outside the United Kingdom

AppI–B7 12 (1) This Schedule does not apply in relation to any person for any year of assessment during which he is not resident in the United Kingdom.

(2) Where in any year of assessment a person is resident in the United Kingdom but is domiciled outside the United Kingdom, this Schedule does not apply to him unless the property falling within paragraph 3(1)(a), 6(1)(a) or 8(1)(c) is situated in the United Kingdom.

(3) In the application of this Schedule to a person who was at any time domiciled outside the United Kingdom, no regard is to be had to any property which is for the purposes of IHTA 1984 excluded property in relation to him by virtue of section 48(3)(a) of that Act.

(4) For the purposes of this paragraph, a person is to be treated as domiciled in the United Kingdom at any time only if he would be so treated for the purposes of IHTA 1984.

Exemption in cases where aggregate notional annual values do not exceed £5,000

AppI–B8 13 (1) This paragraph applies where, in relation to any person who would (apart from this paragraph) be chargeable under this Schedule for any year of assessment, the aggregate of the amounts specified in sub-paragraph (2) in respect of that year does not exceed £5,000.

(2) Those amounts are—

  (a) in relation to any land to which paragraph 3 applies in respect of him, the appropriate rental value as determined under paragraph 4(2),

  (b) in relation to any chattel to which paragraph 6 applies in respect of him, the appropriate amount as determined under paragraph 7(2), and

  (c) in relation to any intangible property to which paragraph 8 applies in respect of him, the chargeable amount determined under paragraph 9.

(3) Where this paragraph applies, the person is not chargeable for that year of assessment under any of the following provisions—

   (a) paragraph 3(5) (land),

   (b) paragraph 6(5) (chattels), or

   (c) paragraph 8(3) (intangible property).

Power of Treasury to confer further exemptions by regulations

14 Regulations may confer further exemptions from the charges to income **AppI–B9**
tax imposed by paragraphs 3, 6 and 8.

Valuation

15 Except as otherwise provided by this Schedule, the value of any property **AppI–B10**
shall for the purposes of this Schedule be the price which the property might
reasonably be expected to fetch if sold in the open market at that time; but
that price shall not be assumed to be reduced on the ground that the whole
property is to be placed on the market at one and the same time.

Changes in distribution of deceased's estate

16 Any disposition made by a person ("the chargeable person") in relation **AppI–B11**
to an interest in the estate of a deceased person is to be disregarded for the
purposes of this Schedule if by virtue of section 17 of IHTA 1984 (changes
in distribution of deceased's estate, etc.) the disposition is not treated for the
purposes of inheritance tax as a transfer of value by the chargeable person.

Guarantees

17 Where a person ("A") acts as guarantor in respect of a loan made to **AppI–B12**
another person ("B") by a third party in connection with B's acquisition of
any property, the mere giving of the guarantee is not to be regarded as the
provision by A of consideration for B's acquisition of the property.

Persons chargeable under different provisions by reference to same property

18 (1) Where, in any year of assessment, a person ("the chargeable person") **AppI–B13**
is (apart from this paragraph) chargeable to income tax both—

   (a) under paragraph 3 (land) or paragraph 6 (chattels) by reason of his
      occupation of any land or his possession or use of any chattel, and

(b) under paragraph 8 (intangible property) by reference to any intangible property which derives its value (whether in whole or part) from the land or the chattel,

he is to be charged to income tax under whichever provision produces the higher chargeable amount in relation to him.

(2) Where sub-paragraph (1) applies, only the amount under the paragraph under which he is chargeable is to be taken into account in relation to the chargeable person for the purposes of paragraph 13(2).

Relationship with Part 3 of Income Tax (Earnings and Pensions) Act 2003

AppI–B14 19 Where, in any year of assessment, a person is (apart from this paragraph) chargeable, in respect of his occupation of any land or his possession or use of any chattel, to income tax both—

(a) under this Schedule, and

(b) under Part 3 of the Income Tax (Earnings and Pensions) Act 2003 (c. 1),

the provisions of that Part shall have priority and he shall not be chargeable to income tax under this Schedule, except to the extent that the amount chargeable under this Schedule exceeds the amount to be treated as earnings under that Part.

Regulations

AppI–B15 20 (1) Regulations under this Schedule may—

(a) make different provision for different cases, and

(b) include transitional provisions and savings.

(2) Any power conferred by this Schedule to prescribe a rate of interest includes power—

(a) to prescribe different rates in relation to property of different descriptions, and

(b) to prescribe a rate by reference to a rate specified in the regulations.

Election for application of inheritance tax provisions

AppI–B16 21 (1) This paragraph applies where—

(a) a person ("the chargeable person") would (apart from this paragraph) be chargeable under paragraph 3 (land) or paragraph 6 (chattels) for any year of assessment ("the initial year") by reference to his enjoyment of any property ("the relevant property"), and

(b) he has not been chargeable under the paragraph in question in respect of any previous year of assessment by reference to his enjoyment of the relevant property, or of any other property for which the relevant property has been substituted.

(2) The chargeable person may elect in accordance with paragraph 23 that—

(a) the preceding provisions of this Schedule shall not apply to him during the initial year and subsequent years of assessment by reference to his enjoyment of the relevant property or of any property which may be substituted for the relevant property, but

(b) so long as the chargeable person continues to enjoy the relevant property or any property which is substituted for the relevant property—

(i) the chargeable proportion of the property is to be treated for the purposes of Part 5 of the 1986 Act (in relation to the chargeable person) as property subject to a reservation, and

(ii) section 102(3) and (4) of that Act shall apply.

(3) In this paragraph, "the chargeable proportion", in relation to any property, means—

$$\frac{DV}{V}$$

where DV and V are to be read in accordance with paragraph 4(2) or 7(2), as the case requires, but as if—

(a) any reference in paragraph 4(2) or 7(2) to the valuation date were a reference—

(i) in the case of property falling within subsection (3) of section 102 of the Finance Act 1986, to the date of the death of the chargeable person, and

(ii) in the case of property falling within subsection (4) of that section, to the date on which the property ceases to be treated as property subject to a reservation, and

(b) the transactions to be taken into account in calculating DV included transactions after the time when the election takes effect as well as transactions before that time.

(4) For the purposes of this paragraph a person "enjoys" property if—

(a) in the case of an interest in land, he occupies the land, and

(b) in the case of an interest in a chattel, he is in possession of, or has the use of, the chattel.

22 (1) This paragraph applies where—

285

(a) a person ("the chargeable person") would (apart from this paragraph) be chargeable under paragraph 8 (intangible property) for any year of assessment ("the initial year") by reference to any property ("the relevant property"), and

(b) he has not been chargeable under that paragraph in respect of any previous year of assessment by reference to the relevant property or any property which the relevant property represents or is derived from.

(2) The chargeable person may elect in accordance with paragraph 23 that—

(a) the preceding provisions of this Schedule shall not apply to him during the initial year and subsequent years of assessment by reference to the relevant property or any property which represents or is derived from the relevant property, but

(b) so long as the conditions in sub-paragraph (3) are satisfied—

   (i) the relevant property and any property which represents or is derived from the relevant property shall be treated for the purposes of Part 5 of the 1986 Act (in relation to the chargeable person) as property subject to a reservation, and

   (ii) section 102(3) and (4) of the 1986 Act shall apply.

(3) The conditions referred to in sub-paragraph (2)(b) are—

(a) that the relevant property or the property which represents or is derived from the relevant property remains comprised in the settlement, and

(b) that any income arising under the settlement would be treated by virtue of section 660A of the Taxes Act 1988 as income of the chargeable person.

23 (1) In this paragraph—

"election" means an election under paragraph 21 or 22;
"the relevant filing date" means 31st January in the year of assessment that immediately follows the initial year within the meaning of paragraph 21 or (as the case requires) paragraph 22.

(2) The election must be made in the prescribed manner.

(3) The election must be made on or before the relevant filing date, unless the chargeable person can show a reasonable excuse for the failure to make the election by that date.

(4) Where the chargeable person can show reasonable excuse for the failure to make the election on or before the relevant filing date, the election must be made on or before such later date as may be prescribed.

(5) The election may be withdrawn or amended, during the life of the chargeable person, at any time on or before the relevant filing date.

(6) Subject to sub-paragraph (5), the election takes effect for the purposes of inheritance tax from the beginning of the initial year within the meaning of paragraph 21 or (as the case requires) paragraph 22 or, if later, the date on

which the chargeable person would (but for the election) have first become chargeable under this Schedule by reference to the property to which the election relates.

C. THE INHERITANCE TAX (DOUBLE CHARGES RELIEF) REGULATIONS 1987

SI 1987/1130

The Commissioners of Inland Revenue, in exercise of the powers conferred on them by section 104 of the Finance Act 1986,[1] hereby make the following Regulations.

Citation and commencement

1. These Regulations may be cited as the Inheritance Tax (Double Charges **AppI–C1** Relief) Regulations 1987 and shall come into force on 22 July 1987.

Interpretation

2. In these Regulations unless the context otherwise requires— **AppI–C2**

"PET" means potentially exempt transfer;
"property" includes part of any property;
"the 1984 Act" means the Inheritance Tax Act 1984[2]
"the 1986 Act" means Part V of the Finance Act 1986;
"section" means section of the 1984 Act.

Introductory

3. These Regulations provide for the avoidance, to the extent specified, of **AppI–C3** double charges to tax arising with respect to specified transfers of value made, and other events occurring, on or after 18 March 1986.

Double charges—potentially exempt transfers and death

4.—(1) This regulation applies in the circumstances to which paragraph **AppI–C4** (a) of section 104(1) of the 1986 Act refers where the conditions ("specified conditions") of paragraph (2) are fulfilled.

(2) The specified conditions to which paragraph (1) refers are—

(a) an individual ("the deceased") makes a transfer of value to a person ("the transferee") which is a PET,

(b) the transfer is made on or after 18 March 1986,

---

[1] 1986 c 41.
[2] 1984 c 51.

289

(c) the transfer proves to be a chargeable transfer, and

(d) the deceased immediately before his death was beneficially entitled to property to which paragraph (3) refers.

(3) The property to which paragraph (2)(d) refers is property—

(a) which the deceased, after making the PET to which paragraph (2)(a) refers, acquired from the transferee otherwise than for full consideration in money or money's worth.

(b) which is property which was transferred to the transferee by the PET to which paragraph (2)(a) refers or which is property directly or indirectly representing that property, and

(c) which is property comprised in the estate of the deceased immediately before his death (within the meaning of section 5(1)), value attributable to which is transferred by a chargeable transfer (under section 4).

(4) Where the specified conditions are fulfilled there shall be calculated, separately in accordance with sub-paragraphs (a) and (b), the total tax chargeable as a consequence of the death of the deceased—

(a) disregarding so much of the value transferred by the PET to which paragraph (2)(a) refers as is attributable to the property, value of which is transferred by the chargeable transfer to which paragraph (3)(c) refers, and

(b) disregarding so much of the value transferred by the chargeable transfer to which paragraph (3)(c) refers as is attributable to the property, value of which is transferred by the PET to which paragraph (2)(a) refers.

(5) (a) Whichever of the two amounts of tax calculated under paragraph (4)(a) or (b) is the lower amount shall be treated as reduced to nil but, subject to sub-paragraph (b), the higher amount shall be payable,

(b) where the amount calculated under paragraph (4)(a) is higher than the amount calculated under paragraph (4)(b)—

(i) so much of the tax chargeable on the value transferred by the chargeable transfer to which paragraph (2)(c) refers as is attributable to the amount of that value which falls to be disregarded by virtue of paragraph (ii) shall be treated as a nil amount, and

(ii) for all the purposes of the 1984 Act so much of the value transferred by the PET to which paragraph (2)(a) refers as is attributable to the property to which paragraph (3)(c) refers shall be disregarded.

(6) Part I of the Schedule to these Regulations provides an example of the operation of this regulation.

Double charges—gifts with reservation and death

5.—(1) This regulation applies in the circumstances to which paragraph **AppI–C5** (b) of section 104(1) of the 1986 Act refers where the conditions ("specified conditions") of paragraph (2) are fulfilled.

(2) The specified conditions to which paragraph (1) refers are—

(a) an individual ("the deceased") makes a transfer of value by way of gift of property,

(b) the transfer is made on or after 18 March 1986,

(c) the transfer is or proves to be a chargeable transfer,

(d) the deceased dies on or after 18 March 1986,

(e) the property in relation to the gift and the deceased is property subject to a reservation (within the meaning of s 102 of the 1986 Act),

(f) (i) the property is by virtue of s 102(3) of the 1986 Act treated for the purposes of the 1984 Act as property to which the deceased was beneficially entitled immediately before his death, or,

(ii) the property ceases to be property subject to a reservation and is the subject of a PET by virtue of section 102(4) of the 1986 Act, and

(g) (i) the property is comprised in the estate of the deceased immediately before his death (within the meaning of section 5(1)) and value attributable to it is transferred by a chargeable transfer (under section 4), or

(ii) the property is property transferred by the PET to which subparagraph (f)(ii) refers, value attributable to which is transferred by a chargeable transfer.

(3) Where the specified conditions are fulfilled there shall be calculated, separately in accordance with sub-paragraphs (a) and (b), the total tax chargeable as a consequence of the death of the deceased—

(a) disregarding so much of the value transferred by the transfer of value to which paragraph (2)(a) refers as is attributable to property to which paragraph (2)(g) refers, and

(b) disregarding so much of the value of property to which paragraph (2)(g) refers as is attributable to property to which paragraph (2)(a) refers.

(4) Where the amount calculated under paragraph (3)(a) is higher than the amount calculated under paragraph (3)(b)—

(a) only so much of that higher amount shall be payable as remains after deducting, as a credit, from the amount comprised in that higher amount which is attributable to the value of the property to which paragraph (2)(g) refers, a sum (not exceeding the amount so attributable) equal to so much of the tax paid—

(i) as became payable before the death of the deceased, and

(ii) as is attributable to the value disregarded under paragraph (3)(a), and

(b) so much of the value transferred by the transfer of value to which paragraph (2)(a) refers as is attributable to the property to which paragraph (2)(g) refers shall (except in relation to chargeable transfers which were chargeable to tax, when made by the deceased, for the purposes of an occasion which occurred before the death of the deceased on which tax was chargeable under section 64 or 65) be treated as reduced to a nil amount for all the purposes of the 1984 Act.

(5) Where the amount calculated under paragraph (3)(a) is less than the amount calculated under paragraph (3)(b) the value of the property to which paragraph (2)(g) refers shall be reduced to nil for all the purposes of the 1984 Act.

(6) For the purposes of the interpretation and application of this regulation section 102 of and Schedule 20 to the 1986 Act shall apply.

(7) Part II of the Schedule to these Regulations provides examples of the operation of this regulation.

Double charges—liabilities subject to abatement and death

AppI–C6   6.—(1) This regulation applies in the circumstances to which paragraph (c) of section 104(1) of the 1986 Act refers where the conditions ("specified conditions") of paragraph (2) are fulfilled.

(2) The specified conditions to which paragraph (1) refers are—

(a) a transfer of value which is or proves to be a chargeable transfer ("the transfer") is made on or after 18 March 1986 by an individual ("the deceased") by virtue of which the estate of the transferee is increased or by virtue of which property becomes comprised in a settlement of which the transferee is a trustee, and

(b) at any time before his death the deceased incurs a liability to the transferee ("the liability") which is a liability subject to abatement under the provisions of section 103 of the 1986 Act in determining the value transferred by a chargeable transfer (under section 4).

(3) Where the specified conditions are fulfilled there shall be calculated, separately in accordance with sub-paragraphs (a) and (b), the total tax chargeable as a consequence of the death of the deceased—

(a) disregarding so much of the value transferred by the transfer—

(i) as is attributable to the property by reference to which the liability falls to be abated, and

(ii) as is equal to the amount of the abatement of the liability, and

(b) taking account both of the value transferred by the transfer and of the liability.

(4) (a) Whichever of the two amounts of tax calculated under paragraph (3)(a) or (b) is the lower amount shall be treated as reduced to nil

but, subject to sub-paragraph (b), the higher amount shall be payable,

(b) where the amount calculated under paragraph (3)(a) is higher than the amount calculated under paragraph (3)(b)—

    (i) only so much of that higher amount shall be payable as remains after deducting, as a credit, from that amount a sum equal to so much of the tax paid—

        (a) as became payable before the death of the deceased, and

        (b) as is attributable to the value disregarded under paragraph (3)(a), and

        (c) as does not exceed the difference between the amount of tax calculated under paragraph (3)(a) and the amount of tax that would have fallen to be calculated under paragraph (3)(b) if the liability had been taken into account, and

    (ii) so much of the value transferred by the transfer to which paragraph (2)(a) refers—

        (a) as is attributable to property by reference to which the liability is abated, and

        (b) as is equal to the amount of the abatement of the liability,

shall (except in relation to chargeable transfers which were chargeable to tax, when made by the deceased, for the purposes of an occasion which occurred before the death of the deceased on which tax was chargeable under section 64 or 65) be treated as reduced to a nil amount for all the purposes of the 1984 Act.

(5) Where there is a number of transfers made by the deceased which are relevant to the liability to which paragraph (2)(b) applies the provisions of this regulation shall apply to those transfers taking them in reverse order of their making, that is to say, taking the latest first and the earliest last, but only to the extent that in aggregate the value of those transfers does not exceed the amount of the abatement to which paragraph (2)(b) refers.

(6) Part III of the Schedule to these Regulations provides examples of the operation of this regulation

Double Charges—chargeable transfers and death

7.—(1) This regulation applies in the circumstances specified (by this **AppI–C7** regulation) for the purposes of paragraph (d) of section 104(1) of the 1986 Act (being circumstances which appear to the Board to be similar to those referred to in paragraphs (a) to (c) of that subsection) where the conditions ("specified conditions") of paragraph (2) are fulfilled.

(2) The specified conditions to which paragraph (1) refers are—

(a) an individual ("the deceased") makes a transfer of value to a person ("the transferee") which is a chargeable transfer,

(b) the transfer is made on or after 18 March 1986

(c) the decreased dies within 7 years after that chargeable transfer is made, and

(d) the deceased immediately before his death was beneficially entitled to property to which paragraph (3) refers.

(3) The property to which paragraph (2)(d) refers is property—

(a) which the deceased, after making the chargeable transfer to which paragraph (2)(a) refers, acquired from the transferee otherwise than for full consideration in money or money's worth,

(b) which was transferred to the transferee by the chargeable transfer to which paragraph (2)(a) refers or which is property directly or indirectly representing that property, and

(c) which is property comprised in the estate of the deceased immediately before his death (within the meaning of section 5(1)), value attributable to which is transferred by a chargeable transfer (under section 4).

(4) Where the specified conditions are fulfilled there shall be calculated, separately in accordance with sub-paragraphs (a) and (b), the total tax chargeable as a consequence of the death of the deceased—

(a) disregarding so much of the value transferred by the chargeable transfer to which paragraph (2)(a) refers as is attributable to the property, value of which is transferred by the chargeable transfer to which paragraph (3)(c) refers, and

(b) disregarding so much of the value transferred by the chargeable transfer to which paragraph (3)(c) refers as is attributable to the property, value of which is transferred by the chargeable transfer to which paragraph (2)(a) refers.

(5) (a) Whichever of the two amounts of tax calculated under paragraph (4)(a) or (b) is the lower amount shall be treated as reduced to nil but, subject to sub-paragraph (b), the higher amount shall be payable,

(b) where the amount calculated under paragraph (4)(a) is higher than the amount calculated under paragraph (4)(b)—

(i) only so much of that higher amount shall be payable as remains after deducting, as a credit, from the amount comprised in that higher amount which is attributable to the value of the property to which paragraph (2)(d) refers, a sum (not exceeding the amount so attributable) equal to so much of the tax paid—

(a) as became payable before the death of the deceased, and

(b) as is attributable to the value disregarded under paragraph (4)(a), and

(ii) so much of the value transferred by the chargeable transfer to which paragraph (2)(a) refers as is attributable to the property to which paragraph (3)(c) refers shall (except for the purposes of an occasion which occurred before the death of the deceased on which tax was chargeable under section 64 or 65) be treated as reduced to a nil amount for all the purposes of the 1984 Act.

(6) Part IV of the Schedule to these Regulations provides an example of the operation of this regulation.

Equal calculations of tax—special rule

8. Where the total tax chargeable as a consequence of death under the two **AppI–C8** separate calculations provided for by any of regulation 4(4), 5(3), 6(3) or 7(4) is equal in amount the first of those calculations shall be treated as producing a higher amount for the purposes of the regulation concerned.

Schedule and saving

9. The Schedule to these Regulations shall have effect only for providing **AppI–C9** examples of the operation of these Regulations and, in the event of any conflict between the Schedule and the Regulations, the Regulations shall prevail.

SCHEDULE

Regulation 9

INTRODUCTORY

1 This Schedule provides examples of the operation of the Regulations.
2 In this Schedule:

"cumulation" means the inclusion of the total chargeable transfers made by the transferor in the 7 years preceding the current transfer;

"GWR" means gift with reservation;

"taper relief" means the reduction in tax provided under s 7(4) of the 1984 Act, inserted by para 2(4) of Sched 19 to the 1986 Act.

3 Except where otherwise stated, the examples assume that: tax rates and bands remain as at 18 March 1987;

the transferor has made no other transfers than those shown in the examples;

no exemptions (including annual exemption) or reliefs apply to the value transferred by the relevant transfer; and

"grossing up" does not apply in determining any lifetime tax (the tax is not borne by the transferor).

Part I

Regulation 4: Example

Jul 1987	A makes PET of £100,000 to B.
Jul 1998	A makes gift into discretionary trust of £95,000. Tax paid £750
Jan 1989	A makes further gift into same trust of £45,000. Tax paid £6,750
Jan 1990	B dies and the 1987 PET returns A.
Apr 1991	A dies. His death estate of £300,000 includes the 1987 PET returning to him in 1990, which is still worth £100,000

First calculation under reg 4(4)(a)
Charge the returned PET in A's death estate and ignore the PET made in 1987.

		Tax
Jul 1987	PET £100,000 ignored	NIL
Jul 1988	Gift £95,000	
	Tax £1,500 less £750 already paid	£750
Jan 1989	Gift £45,000 as top slice of £140,000	
	Tax £13,500 less £6,750 already paid	£6,750
Apr 1991	Death estate £300,000 as top slice of £440,000	£153,000
	*Total tax due as result of A's death	£160,500

* In first calculation the tax of £153,000 on death estate does not allow for any successive charges relief (under s 141 IHTA 1984) that might be due in respect of 'the returned PET' by reference to any tax charged on that 'PET' in connection with B's death.

Second calculation under reg 4(4)(b)
Charge the 1987 PET and ignore the value of the returned PET in A's death estate.

		Tax
Jul 1987	PET £100,000. Tax with taper relief	£2,400
July 1988	Gift £95,000 as top slice of £195,000	
	Tax £34,000 less £750 alread paid	£33,250
Jan 1989	Gift £45,000 as top slice of £240,000	
	Tax £20,000 less £6,750 already paid	£13,250
Apr 1991	Death estate £200,000 as top slice of	
	£440,000	£111,000
	Total tax due as result of A's death	£159,900

Result*

First calculation gives higher amount of tax. So PET reduced to nil and tax on other transfers is as in first calculation.

* If, after allowing any successive charges relief, the second calculation gives higher amount of tax, 1987 PET will be charged and tax on other transfers will be as in second calculation.

Part II

Regulation 5: Example 1

Jan 1988	A makes PET of £150,000 to B.	
March	A makes gift of land worth	
1992	£200,000 into a discretionary trust of which he is a potential beneficiary. The gift is a "GWR".	Tax paid £19,500
Feb 1995	A dies without having released his interest in the trust. His death estate valued at £400,000, includes the GWR land currently worth £300,000.	

First calculation under reg 5(3)(a)

Charge the GWR land in A's death estate and ignore the GWR.

		Tax
Jan 1988	PET (now exempt)	NIL
Mar 1992	GWR ignored	NIL
Feb 1995	Death estate £400,000	
	Tax £144,000 less £19,500 already paid on GWR*	£124,500
	Total tax due as result of A's death	£124,500

* Credit for the tax already paid cannot exceed the amount of the death tax attributable to the value of the GWR property. In this example the tax so attributable is £108,000 (ie 144,000/400,000´300,000). So credit is given for the full amount of £19,500.

Second calculation under reg. 5(3)(b)

297

Charge the GWR and ignore the GWR land in the death estate.

		Tax
Jan 1988	PET (now exempt)	NIL
Mar 1992	GWR £200,000	
	Tax £39,000 less £19,500 already paid	£19,500
Feb 1995	Death estate £100,000 (ignoring GWR	
	property) as topslice of £300,000	£48,000
	Total tax due as a result of A's death	£67,500

Result

First calculation yields higher amount of tax. So the value of the GWR transfer is reduced to nil and tax on death is charged as in first calculation with credit for the tax already paid.

Part II

Regulation 5: Example 2

Apr 1987	A makes gift into discretionary trust of £150,000	Tax paid £9,500
Jan 1988	A makes further gift into same trust of £50,000	Tax paid £10,000
Mar 1993	A makes PET of shares valued at £150,000 to B	
Feb 1996	A dies. He had continued to enjoy the income of the shares he had given to B (the 1993 PET is a GWR). His death estate, valued at £300,000, includes those shares currently worth £200,000	

First calculation under reg 5(3)(a)

Charge the GWR shares in the death estate and ignore the PET.

Apr 1987	Gift £150,000. No adjustment to tax as gift made more than 7 years before death	NIL
Jan 1988	Gift £50,000. No adjustment to tax as gift made more than 7 years before death	NIL
Mar 1993	PET £150,000 now reduced to NIL	NIL
Feb 1996	Death estate including GWR shares £300,000.	
	No previous cumulation	£87,000
	Total tax due as result of A's death	£87,000

Second calculation under reg 5(3)(b)

Charge the PET and ignore the value of the GWR shares in the death estate.

		Tax
Apr 1987	Gift £150,000. No adjustment to tax as gift made more than 7 years before death	NIL
Jan 1988	Gift £50,000. No adjustment to tax as gift made more than 7 years before death	NIL
Mar 1993	GWR £150,000 as top slice of £350,000 (ie previous gifts totalling £200,000 + £150,000)	£75,000
Feb 1996	Death estate (excluding GWR shares) £100,000 as topslice of £250,000 (the 1987 and 1988 gifts drop out of cumulation)	£43,000
	Total tax due as result of A's death	£118,000

Result
Second calculation yields higher amount of tax. So tax is charged by reference to the PET and the value of the GWR shares in the death estate is reduced to NIL.

Part III

Regulation 6: Example 1

Nov 1987	X makes a PET of cash of £95,000 to Y
Dec 1987	Y makes a loan to X of £95,000
May 1988	X makes a gift into discretionary trust of £20,000
Apr 1993	X dies. His death estate is worth £182,000. A deduction of £95,000 is claimed for the loan from Y.

First calculation under reg 6(3)(a)
No charge on November 1987 gift, and no deduction against death estate.

		Tax
Nov 1987	PET ignored	NIL
May 1988	Gift £20,000	NIL
Apr 1993	Death estate £182,000 as top slice of £202,000	£39,800
	Total tax due as result of X's death	£39,800

Second calculation under reg 6(3)(b)

Charge the November 1987 PET, and allow the deduction against the death estate.

		Tax
Nov 1987	PET £95,000. Tax with taper relief	£600
May 1988	Gift £20,000 as top slice of £115,000	
	Tax with taper relief	£3,600
Apr 1993	Death estate (£182,000–loan of	
	£95,000) £87,000 as topslice of	
	£202,000	£32,300
	Total tax due as result of X's death	£36,500

Result

First calculation gives higher amount of tax. So debt is disallowed against death estate, but PET of £95,000 is not charged.

Part III

Regulation 6: Example 2

Aug 1988	P makes a PET of cash of £100,000 to Q.	
Sept 1988	Q makes a loan to P of £100,000.	
Oct 1989	P makes gift into discretionary trust of £98,000.	Tax paid £1,200
Nov 1992	P dies. Death estate £110,000 less allowable liabilities of £80,000 (which do not include the debt of £100,000 owed to Q).	

First calculation under reg 6(3)(a)

No charge on August 1988 PET, and no deduction against death estate for the £100,000 owed to Q.

		Tax
Aug 1988	PET ignored	NIL
Oct 1989	Gift £98,000	
	Tax (with taper relief) £1,920 less	
	£1,200 already paid	£720
Nov 1992	Death estate £30,000 as top slice of	
	£128,000	£9,000
	Total tax due as result of P's death	£9,720

Second calculation under reg 6(3)(b)

Charge the August 1988 PET, and allow deduction against death estate for the £100,000 owed to Q.

		Tax
Aug 1988	PET £100,000. Tax with taper relief	£1,800
Oct 1989	Gift £98,000 as top slice of £198,000 Tax (with taper relief) £28,100 less £1,200 already	
	Paid	£26,900
Nov 1992	Death estate £30,000–£100,000 (owed to Q)	NIL
	Total tax due as result of P's death	£28,700

Result

Second calculation gives higher amount of tax. So the PET to Q is charged, and deduction is allowed against death estate for the debt to Q.

Part III

Regulation 6: Example 3

1 May 1987	A makes PET to B of £95,000.	
1 Jan 1998	A makes PET to B of £40,000	
1 Jul 1988	A makes gift into discretionary trust of £100,000.	Tax paid £1,500
1 Jan 1989	A makes PET to B of £30,000.	
1 Jul 1989	B makes a loan to A of £100,000.	
1 Dec 1990	A dies. Death estate £200,000, against which deduction is claimed for debt of £100,000 due to B.	

First calculation under reg 6(3)(a)

Disallow the debt and ignore corresponding amounts (£100,000) of PETs from A to B, starting with the latest PET.

		Tax
1 May 1987	PET now reduced to £65,000	NIL
1 Jan 1988	PET now reduced to NIL	NIL
1 Jul 1988	Gift into trust £100,000 as top slice of £165,000	
	Tax £25,000 less £1,500 already paid	£23,500
1 Jan 1989	PET now reduced to NIL	NIL
1 Dec 1990	Death estate £200,000 as top slice of £365,000	£98,000
	Total tax due as result of A's death	£121,500

Second calculation under reg 6(3)(b)

Allow the debt and charge PETs to B in full.

		Tax
1 May 1987	PET £95,000. Tax with taper relief	£1,200
1 Jan 1988	PET £40,000 as top slice of £135,000	£12,000
1 July 1988	Gift into trust £100,000 as top slice of £235,000	
	Tax £41,000 less £1,500 already paid	£39,500
1 Jan 1989	PET £30,000 as top slice of £265,000	£15,000
1 Dec 1990	Death estate £100,000 as top slice of £365,000	£53,500
	Total tax due as result of A's death	£121,200

Result

First calculation yields higher amount of tax. So the debt is disallowed and corresponding amounts of PETs to B are ignored in determining the tax due as a result of the death.

Part III

Regulation 6: Example 4

1 Apr 1987	A makes gift into discretionary trust of £100,000. Tax paid £1,500
1 Jan 1990	A makes PET to B of £60,000.
1 Jan 1991	A makes further gift into same trust of £50,000. Tax paid £8,000
1 Jan 1992	Same trust makes a loan to A of £120,000.
1 Jun 1994	A dies. Death estate is £220,000, against which Deduction is claimed for debt of £120,000 due to the trust.

First calculation under reg 6(3)(a)

Disallow the debt and ignore corresponding amounts (£120,000) of gifts from A to trust, starting with the latest gift.

		Tax
1 Apr 1987	Gift now reduced to £30,000. No adjustment to tax already paid as gift made more than 7 years before death	NIL
1 Jan 1990	PET £60,000 as top slice of £90,000	NIL
1 Jan 1991	Gift now reduced to NIL. No adjustment to tax already paid	NIL
1 Jun 1994	Death estate £220,000 as top slice of £280,000 (the 1987 gift at £30,000 drops out of cumulation)	£77,000

	Less credit for tax already paid	
	£1,500 + £8,000	£9,500
	Total tax due as result of A's death	£67,500

Second calculation under reg 6(3)(b)
Allow the debt and no adjustment to gifts into the trust.

		Tax
1 Apr 1987	Gift £100,000. No adjustment to tax already paid as gift made more than 7 years before death	NIL
1 Jan 1990	PET £60,000 as top slice of £160,000. Tax with taper relief	£12,000
1 Jan 1991	Gift £50,000 as top slice of £210,000 Tax (with taper relief) £16,000 less £8,000 already Paid	£8,000
1 June 1994	Death estae £100,000 as top slice of £210,000. (The 1987 gift drops out of cumulation. No credit for tax paid on that gift.)	£37,000
	Total tax due as result of A's death	£57,000

Result
First calculation yields higher amount tax. So the debt is disallowed and corresponding amounts of gifts into trust are ignored in determining the tax due as a result of the death.

Part IV

Regulation 7: Example

May 1986	S transfers into discretionary trust property worth £150,000. Immediate charge at the rates then in force.	Tax paid £13,750
Oct 1986	S gives T a life interest in shares worth £85,000. Immediate charge at the rates then in force.	Tax paid £19,500
Jan 1991	S makes a PET to R of £20,000.	
Dec 1992	T dies, and the settled share return to S who is the settlor and therefore no tax charge on the shares on T's death.	

303

Aug 1993   S dies. His death estate includes
             the shares returned from T which
             are currently worth £75,000, and
             other assets worth £144, 000.

First calculation under reg 7(4)(a)
Charge the returned shares in the death estate and ignore the October 1986
gift. Tax rates and bands are those in force at the date of S's death.

May 1986	Gift into trust made more than 7 years before death. So no adjustment to tax already paid but the gift cumulates in calculating tax on other gifts	NIL
Oct 1986	Gift ignored and no adjustment to tax already paid	NIL
Jan 1991	PET of £20,000 as top slice of (£150,000 + £20,000) £170,000	£8,000
Nov 1993	Death estate £219,000 as top slice of £239,000 Tax £56,500 less £19,350 (part of tax already paid)*	£37,150
	Total tax due as result of S's death	£45,150

* £19,350 represents the amount of the death tax attributable to the value of the
returned shares, and is lower than the amount of the lifetime tax charged on those
shares. So credit against the death charge for the tax already paid is restricted to the
lower amount.

Second calculation under reg 7(4)(b)
Charge the October 1986 gift and ignore the returned shares in the death
estate. Tax rates and bands are those in force at the date of S's death.

		Tax
May 1986	Gift into trust made more than 7 years before death. So no adjustment to tax already paid but the gift is taken into account in calculating the tax on the other gifts	NIL
Oct 1986	Gift of £85,000 as top slice of £235,000 Tax (with taper relief) £7,100 less £19,500 already Paid	NIL*
Jan 1991	PET of £20,000 as top slice of £225,000	£10,000
Aug 1993	Death estate (excluding the returned shares) £144,000 as top slice of £249,000	

304

<table>
<tr><td>(85,000 + £20,000 + £144,000)</td><td>£57,000</td></tr>
<tr><td>Total tax due as a result of S's death</td><td>£67,000</td></tr>
</table>

* Credit for the tax already paid restricted to the (lower) amount of tax payable as result of the death. No repayment of the excess.

Result

Second calculation gives higher amount of tax. So tax is charged as in second calculation by excluding the shares from the death estate.

APPENDIX 2: MATERIAL ISSUED BY THE INLAND REVENUE

A. PRESS RELEASE OF DECEMBER 10, 2003

2003 PRE-BUDGET REPORT

PN 6
10 December 2003

TACKLING TAX AVOIDANCE

A series of measures to protect tax revenues from fraud, evasion and **AppII–A1**
avoidance were outlined in the Pre-Budget Report today.

Paymaster General Dawn Primarolo said:

> "The measures announced today demonstrate the Government's deter-
> mination to tackle tax avoidance and create a fair environment for
> all."

DETAILS

Trusts

From 6 April 2004 the tax rate paid on the income and capital gains of trusts
will increase from 34 per cent to 40 per cent (and the corresponding dividend
trust rate from 25 per cent to $32\frac{1}{2}$ per cent). This removes a distortion that
provides avoidance opportunities for some higher rate taxpayers, but will not
affect the position of tax payers not liable at the higher rate who receive
income from a trust, who will continue to be able to reclaim any excess
income tax paid by the trustees on their behalf.

In order to reduce compliance burdens for small trusts, the Government
will be consulting on a modernised income and capital gains tax regime for
trusts. In particular the Government will aim to reduce the tax burdens on
smaller trusts and to ensure that trusts established to protect the vulnerable
are not disadvantaged by the tax system. The Inland Revenue will publish
details of the modernisation proposals tomorrow.

With immediate effect, the capital gains "gifts relief" legislation will be
amended to counter tax avoidance schemes that involve the transfer of assets
into a trust. Draft clauses for this change are being published today on the
Inland Revenue website together with draft Explanatory Notes. This legislation will be included in Finance Bill 2004.

Action will also be taken against avoidance of the Inheritance Tax rules for Gifts with Reservation, where the former owner continues to enjoy the benefits of ownership of an asset. Finance Bill 2004 will legislate to impose a charge on the benefit gained from using the asset, following consultation on the detailed workings of this measure.

B. DECEMBER CONSULTATION DOCUMENT

TAX TREATMENT OF PRE-OWNED ASSETS

General

As part of its wider strategy to protect tax revenues the Government **AppII–B1** announced on 10 December 2003 that income tax will in future be charged on the benefit of people enjoy when they have arranged free continuing use of major capital assets that they once owned. Arrangements like this are often made to get round the IHT gifts with reservation (GWR) rules. Essentially these GWR rules are intended to stop people from giving their assets away, so that for IHT purposes they are out of their estate when they die, while still continuing to enjoy the practical benefits of owning them during their lifetime.

Who is likely to be affected?

People who continue to enjoy the use of assets (free of charge, or at a below- **AppII–B2** market rent) which they formerly owned (or provided the funds to purchase).

General description of the measure

Legislation will be included in Finance Bill 2004 which will provide for: **AppII–B3**

- Income tax to be charged each year (under Case VI of Schedule D) on the benefit of using an asset formerly owned by the user unless it has since been sold to an unconnected party in a bargain at arm's length;

- Extensions to cover cases where one asset is replaced by another, or where the beneficiary originally provided cash to fund the purchase of an asset for their use (rather than providing an asset they already owned);

- Rules for valuing the benefit: subject to points made in the consultation, Ministers envisage that this will be at market rent where market evidence allows (*e.g.* for real property) and at a specified percentage of capital value (*e.g.* calculated at the "official rate" of interest for benefit-in-kind purposes) in other cases (such as art or antiques).

This will be subject to:

- A set-off for any rent actually paid for the benefit;
- An exclusion for incidental use;

- An exclusion for cases where the donor has expressly reserved a right to continued occupation when making the gift;

- A substantial de minimis exclusion set at a cash amount which Ministers will determine in the light of this consultation;

- Any other exclusions or modifications which seem appropriate, given Minister's objective for the charge, in the light of this consultation;

- A power to make further exclusions by statutory instrument.

Operative date

AppII–B4 The charge, will apply whenever a benefit is received in chargeable circumstances in or after the income tax year 2005–06. Arrangements which currently exist to provide benefits for former owners will not be chargeable if they have been dismantled, or the former owner starts to pay a full rent, by 6 April 2005.

Finance Bill 2004-01-22

AppII–B5 The Income Tax (Earnings and Pensions) Act 2003 provides, broadly, that the benefit of the use of assets at no or low cost is subject to income tax when they are provided by reason of the employment. That charge is unaffected by the present proposal (to be included in Finance Bill 2004) for a new source of income falling under the rules of Case VI of Schedule D of the Taxes Act 1988

C. BUDGET PRESS RELEASE

REV BN 40: TAX TREATMENT OF PRE-OWNED ASSETS

Who is likely to be affected?

1. People who have entered into contrived arrangements to dispose of **AppII–C1** valuable assets, while retaining the ability to use them. The main purpose of arrangements subject to the charge is to avoid inheritance tax. There are specific exceptions to the charge which are explained below.

General description of the measure

2. Pre-Budget Report announced that a free-standing income tax charge will **AppII–C2** apply from the 6 April 2005 to the benefit people get by having free or low-cost enjoyment of assets they formerly owned (or provided the funds to purchase). The charge will apply in appropriate circumstances both to tangible assets (with separate provision for land, including living accommodation, and for chattels) and to intangible assets. Broadly following the model of the benefit-in-kind charge on employees, the rules will quantify an annual cash value for the benefits enjoyed by a taxpayer: this will be treated as an addition to their taxable income, subject to a de minimis threshold, and a set-off for any amounts made good by them for the benefit.

Operative date

3. The charge will apply when a benefit is received in chargeable circum- **AppII–C3** stances in or after the income tax year 2005–06.

Current law and proposed revisions

4. The Government is aware that various schemes designed to avoid **AppII–C4** inheritance tax have been marketed in recent years. These use artificial structures to avoid the existing rules about gifts made with reservation. As a result, people have been removing assets from their taxable estate but continuing to enjoy all the benefits of ownership. The Government is determined to block this sort of avoidance and announced in the Pre-Budget Report that people who benefit from these sorts of schemes would be subject to an income tax charge from April 2005, to reflect their additional taxable capacity from receiving these benefits at low or no cost.

5. Following consultation, the Government has confirmed, and proposes to extend, the exclusions outlined in the consultation document published

313

following the Pre-Budget Report. So the proposed charge will not apply to the extent that:

- the property in question ceased to be owned before 18 March 1986;

- property formerly owned by a taxpayer is currently owned by their spouse;

- the asset in question still counts as part of the taxpayer's estate for inheritance tax (IHT) purposes under the existing "gift with reservation" (GWR) rules;

- the property was sold by the taxpayer at an arm's length price, paid in cash: going further than the consultation document, this will not be restricted to sales between unconnected parties;

- the taxpayer was formerly the owner of an asset only by virtue of a will or intestacy which has subsequently been varied by agreement between the beneficiaries; or

- any enjoyment of the property is no more than incidental, including cases where an out-and-out gift to a family member comes to benefit the donor following a change in their circumstances.

6. More generally, the rules for tangible assets will mean that former owners will not be regarded as enjoying a taxable benefit if they retain an interest which is consistent with their ongoing enjoyment of the property. For example, the proposed charge will not arise where an elderly parent formerly owning the whole of their home passes a 50 per cent interest to a child who lives with them.

7. Intangible assets formerly owned by the taxpayer (or derived from other property formerly owned by them) will be treated as giving rise to a taxable benefit, only to the extent that the taxpayer may derive benefits from them, and those benefits would diminish the benefits potentially available to others. So for example, no charge would apply if the taxpayer has funded life insurance policies held on trust and the taxpayer's continuing claims are limited to particular retained benefits, such as the return of the life assurance premium, and the balance of the policy value is held on trust solely for others. But a charge would be due if, say, the whole value of such a life policy was held on discretionary trusts for a class of beneficiaries including the settlor (and the circumstances were such that the trust property was not covered by the existing "gift with reservation" rules).

Territorial scope

AppII–C5 8. The charge will apply to residents of the UK. For taxpayers who are domiciled in the UK (or deemed to be), the charge will apply to their assets anywhere in the world. For taxpayers who are not domiciled in the UK (or not deemed to be), the charge will apply only to their UK assets. For taxpayers who have become domiciled in the UK (or deemed to be), the charge will not apply to any non-UK assets which they ceased to own before they acquired that domicile.

De minimis

9. The consultation document said that there would be a substantial de **AppII–C6** minimis threshold below which the cash value of benefits in a given year would be disregarded. The Government has decided to set this threshold at £2,500 per year.

An election for transitional relief

10. A number of responses in consultation made the point that existing users **AppII–C7** of tax-driven schemes may find it difficult or impossible to dismantle the resulting structure—so eliminating any income tax charge and re-instating the potential IHT charge they originally sought to avoid—although that is, with hindsight, the outcome that many of them would prefer. In response to that, the Government proposes, additionally, that taxpayers involved in existing schemes may choose a special transitional treatment if they elect for this by 31 January 2007. If they elect, they will not be subject to the new income tax charge in relation to property covered by the election, but the property in question will be treated as part of their taxable estate for IHT purposes, while they continue to enjoy it, in essentially the same way as under the existing "gift with reservation" rules. As under those rules, property subject to such an election would be potentially eligible, in due course, for the normal IHT reliefs and exemptions available, for example, to business and agricultural property, and to heritage assets.

Valuation and further consultation

11. The Government has confirmed the approach outlined in the consultation **AppII–C8** document and proposes that the cash value of benefits should be determined by reference to market rentals in the case of land, and by reference to imputed percentages of capital value in the case of chattels and intangible assets. They would welcome further representations, in the light of the decisions now announced, on the detailed arrangements that should apply to valuation and on the rates of return for chattels and intangibles, so they reflect available market evidence while minimising avoidable compliance costs. They therefore propose to settle these matters in secondary legislation following a further round of consultation which the Inland Revenue will undertake later this year.

Further advice

12. If you have any questions about this change, please contact the Probate/ **AppII–C9** IHT Helpline on 0845 3020 900.

www.inlandrevenue.gov.uk

D. SUMMARY OF RESPONSES

CONSULTATION ON THE TAX TREATMENT OF PRE-OWNED ASSETS SUMMARY OF RESPONSES

General

The Inland Revenue published a consultation document on 11 December **AppII–D1**
2003 outlining the Chancellor's proposals for a new income tax charge on
the benefit of "pre-owned assets", first announced in his pre Budget
Statement on 10 December. Comments were invited on the detailed
workings of the income tax charge; this is a summary of the responses.

2. 192 responses were received up to the formal closure of the consultation
period on 18 February (plus a further 22, to date, since that time). Of the
timely responses, 23 were submitted by representative bodies, 98 by
individual firms of advisers and intermediaries, and 71 by individuals.

Process and timing

3. A number of responses commented on the document itself; the end-date **AppII–D2**
for responses; the proposal to legislate in Finance Bill 2004; and/or the
introduction of the charge in the tax year 2005–06. The Chancellor has
confirmed his intention to legislate in Finance Bill 2004 with effect from
2005–06. He regards that as necessary to bring an early end to substantial
risks to the Exchequer, while giving taxpayers and their advisers adequate
notice of the measure in its final form before it comes into effect.

4. The timing of the consultation, and the form of the document, was
designed to meet this timetable while allowing for genuine consultation to be
completed in time for responses to inform Ministers' decisions on the detail
announced in Budget 2004. They were aware, and recognised from the
outset, that this meant a shorter consultation period than the Code of Practice
recommends. Ministers were grateful to all who responded and for the
efforts they made to comment in the time available; this materially assisted
them in finalising their proposals.

General reactions

5. A significant minority of the responses from individuals were clearly **AppII–D3**
responding to second-hand reports of the Chancellor's possible intentions,
and particularly to reports that a charge might apply to situations like gifts
between spouses or to straightforward cash gifts to children. Given that it
was Ministers' objective, confirmed in the Budget, to focus this measure on
tax-driven structures, we have not given further details here where we
believe that the position has been sufficiently clarified by the announcements
in Budget 2004 and the Finance Bill 2004. More generally, we have not spelt
out Ministers' conclusions point-by-point on matters of policy judgement

(for example, whether it is fair to treat this matter as a proper subject for an income tax charge) when the answer is implicit in their decision to proceed with the proposals as announced in Budget 2004. Ministers did, of course, value these responses and take full account of them in finalising their proposals.

6. A number of other responses from individuals stressed that any legislation should not affect the future benefits enjoyed by the respondent under a scheme they had already implemented, but either did not offer further comment or did so in the same terms as a number of other respondents.

7. Of those respondents who offered a reasoned response on the subject matter of the consultation, a majority—whether of representative bodies, firms or individuals—argued against what they saw as a retrospective aspect to the proposals in that it will potentially affect future benefits flowing from structures already implemented. Even so, most of these responses made clear that the structures in question had been adopted for tax-avoidance reasons, and many conceded that it was necessary, or at least proper, for Ministers to counter avoidance using comparable structures in the future.

8. Some of these responses specifically mentioned structures implemented before March 1986 when the current structure of inheritance tax (IHT) was introduced—that is to say, the exemption of most lifetime gifts and the consequent special rules for "gifts with reservation". They saw a distinct case for protecting such transactions, given Ministers' recent perceived objective to counter IHT avoidance: they argued that no pre-1986 transaction could be regarded as avoidance-driven, and made the point that such transactions may well have already suffered tax, up-front, under the rules in force at that time.

9. Many of the responses which were ready to accept the case in principle for anti-avoidance action argued that it should be done, as hitherto, in the form of specific amendment to the IHT code, tackling what the respondents saw as the technical weaknesses underlying recent anti-avoidance activity. Putting a similar point in rather different terms, a number argued that the approach actually proposed by Ministers—regarding recent IHT avoidance as evidence of a systemic weakness, and tackling it by action through the income tax code—was in some way unfair or improper, although responses were not always able to articulate very clearly why this was so.

Feedback on factual issues

AppII–D4 10. Reports following the announcement last December suggested that the proposals might impact on up to 20–30,000 recent users of tax-driven schemes. Formal responses to the consultation document neither confirm nor undermine that assessment. It is clear from responses that "packaged" inheritance-tax-avoidance schemes—usually designed to take the users' homes out of their taxable estates while securing continuing occupation—were widely marketed in the period before the Pre-Budget Report. But responses also confirmed that the proposals potentially affected a wider range of tax planning—involving different structures (such as giftand-leaseback arrangements, and short-term trust interests); a wider range of assets (including valuable chattels and intangible assets such as insurance bonds); and longer time period (extending, as stated above, back to planning implemented under the different tax structures ruling before March 1986).

11. Equally important, responses confirmed that the new proposals were potentially relevant to a much wider range of situations of widely varying size and sophistication, not necessarily—or generally—implemented for tax reasons. These ranged from structures implemented with the aim of avoiding IHT but in fact failing to do so; through structures implemented by potential IHT-payers for non-tax reasons, with the intention that they would be IHT-neutral; to structures which were executed with no "tax-planning" motive by people well below the IHT threshold, either to secure non-tax objectives or simply out of the desire to give a gift.

12. These examples of potential hard cases have informed both the specific exclusions announced in the Budget, and the detailed drafting of the text that appears in the Finance Bill.

Points in relation to "caught" cases

13. Many responses concerned with the effects of these proposals on existing **AppII–D5** planning stressed that it would be difficult, or even impossible, for users of such schemes to fund new income tax liabilities. Many added that it would be impossible, or at best difficult and costly, to unwind the arrangements already made—even though many respondents would evidently have preferred that, failing outright exclusion from the proposed charge. A few representations mentioned that "unwinding" their structures would in itself have tax repercussions (*e.g.* for IHT and/or CGT purposes) under current law: they did not in general make specific proposals about how that might be addressed or indicate that "unwinding" would necessarily be a live option if ever that were done.

14. Ministers concluded from this that there were transitional issues needing to be addressed for caught cases, and that the priority was to focus on options which would not require actual reversal of the structure currently in place: hence the measure announced, in the Budget, for former owners effectively to opt back into IHT liability if they choose, on assets they continue to enjoy.

De minimis

15. The consultation document indicated that Ministers intended a "sub- **AppII–D6** stantial" de minimis exclusion. Responses endorsed this proposal and suggested a range of figures up to and exceeding the IHT nil-rate-band limit (then £255,000). In considering these responses, Ministers saw a link with the scope of any exemptions and abatements for particular circumstances. They do not regard the de minimis relief as affording a "ration of avoidance", and in that perspective would regard a level comparable to the IHT threshold as markedly too high. They believe that transactions of that order of value should be covered by the design of the charge and by express exemptions where they are justified. The de minimis provision is designed to cover the sort of dealing within a family circle which people are already

accustomed to make without particular thought about potential tax complications.

16. They propose a level of £2,500 imputed income, which is equivalent to roughly £50,000 of capital value (taking the "official rate" of 5 per cent as a guide to conversion) which they believe will encompass the transactions which are realistically in reach for the great majority of families.

Territorial scope

AppII–D7 17. A number of responses noted that the territorial scope of the charge would need to be defined; mentioned the particular issues raised for visitors to the UK who might have existing arrangements in place; and noted a read-across to the ongoing consideration of issues of residence and domicile in relation to tax charges more generally. The Chancellor's decisions announced in the Budget responds to those concerns.

Valuation/Quantification/Operational aspects

AppII–D8 18. Some responses commented, mostly in non-specific terms, that compliance with the new charge could involve significant costs and uncertainties, for example in establishing values of unique or unusual assets. Some mentioned that they would be particularly burdensome if, as they understandably inferred might be so, the new rules required the necessary valuations to be redone each year. Other responses, notably in relation to chattels, indicated that some existing arrangements already involve regular revaluation of the assets concerned to a market value standard. The overall impression is that there might be useful scope for avoiding compliance costs without prejudicing Ministers' objectives, but that the representations received to date had not yet provided sufficient input—quite understandably so, given the other priorities that respondents were seeking to address and the wide scope of the initial proposal.

19. Some responses made more fundamental points about the quantification of benefits particularly in relation to arrangements involving valuable chattels. Some argued that arrangements already in place provide for rents at full market levels and should not be regarded as conferring any benefit whatsoever. Others argued that the illustrative rental yield mentioned in the consultative document—*i.e.* the "official rate", currently 5 per cent, which currently applies to "beneficial loans" to employees—was in any event too high. Given that the assets likely to be involved—typically art and antiques—were likely to preserve their value in real terms, they argued that it would be appropriate to use an imputed yield which took account of this.

20. Ministers concluded that the available evidence of "chattel-leasing" between arm's length parties is too slender to support the contention that the current nonarm's-length transactions are at market terms, and that the yields ruling in other markets point to materially higher levels. But they have decided, as announced in the Budget, to launch a further round of consultation later this year to inform the detailed valuation and value-setting rules, and have included appropriate enabling powers in the Finance Bill.

E. AUGUST CONSULTATION DOCUMENT

Background

The Chancellor of the Exchequer announced proposals in his Pre-Budget **AppII–E1**
Report on 10 December 2003 to impose an income tax on the benefit from
enjoyment of "pre-owned assets". Further details were published on 11
December 2003 in an Inland Revenue consultation document ("Taxation of
Pre-Owned Assets") which is available at *http://www.inlandrevenue.gov.uk/
consult_new/taxtreat_preowned_assets.pdf*

2. The Chancellor confirmed his intention to proceed with this proposal at
Budget 2004: further details were published in Inland Revenue Budget Note
BN40 (also "Taxation of Pre-Owned Assets") published on 17 March 2004.
In particular REV BN40 confirmed (paragraph 11) that the taxable benefit
would be calculated broadly as originally announced (that is by reference to
market rentals in the case of land, and by applying an imputed yield to
capital values in the case of chattels and intangible assets); but indicated that
further consultations would follow to settle the applicable rates of yield and
other operational matters. Regulations addressing these matters will then be
made before the charge comes into effect on 6 April 2005.

Scope of this document

3. This consultation seeks your views to help us prepare the draft Regula- **AppII–E2**
tions. It also outlines our expected timetable for completing the regulations
and publishing the guidance on how the charge in Schedule 15, Finance Act
2004 will operate. We would like your comments on the matters to be
covered by this guidance; and your views on how it will operate.

Valuing assets and quantifying the chargeable benefit

4. The rules for establishing the benefit which is chargeable are set out in **AppII–E3**
Schedule 15, Finance Act 2004. The precise machinery—and therefore the
matters to be covered in the forthcoming regulations—depends on the nature
of the assets in question.

5. In the case of land, the "cash equivalent" of enjoyment in a particular
tax year is derived from *market rental* that would be paid for use of the land
over the "taxable period" (that is, the tax year or any shorter period for
which the asset is "caught" by Schedule 15). This figure is then scaled down,
in cases where the taxpayer's "stake" in the caught asset is less than 100 per
cent, in the proportion DV/V, where V is the value of the whole asset on the
"valuation date" for the year, and DV is the value reasonably attributable to
the taxpayer on that date. In many cases, however, we would expect that
taxpayers and their advisors will be able to establish the ratio DV/V from the
surrounding circumstances without necessarily establishing the absolute
amount of V or DV.

6. In the case of *chattels*, the "cash equivalent" of enjoyment in a particular tax year is found by applying a specified rate-of-return, over the "taxable period", to the capital value of the asset as at the "valuation date" for the year. As with land, the cash equivalent may then fall to be scaled down in the proportion DV/V, though again we would generally expect this ratio to be found without the absolute values of DV and V needing to be estimated.

7. In the case of *intangible assets*, the cash equivalent is calculated, as for chattels, by applying a specified rate-of-return, over the "taxable period", to the capital value of the assets as at the "valuation date". There is, however, no provision for scaling down this figure, equivalent to that made for land and for chattels.

Matters that must be covered in regulations

AppII–E4 8. It follows therefore that the following regulations must cover two matters in order for the charge in Schedule 15 to be fully operational at the beginning of tax year 2005–06:

— a valuation date must be specified for all assets in each tax year from 2005–06 onwards;

— a rate-of-return must be specified for chattels and for intangible assets from 6 April 2005 onwards.

In both of these respects, the primary legislation is compatible *either* with a uniform rule for all assets in question, *or* with regulations specifying distinct dates.

The valuation date

AppII–E5 9. As noted above, the capital value of "caught assets" will directly affect the charge in the case of chattels and intangible assets, but not generally in the case of land. So the way that the "valuation date" is fixed is likely to be material in the case of chattels and intangibles rather than land. The relevant considerations differ to some degree between these two cases.

10. Values of the *chattels* most likely to be "caught" by Schedule 15 (for example high-value antiques and art objects) will generally be subject to quite wide margins of uncertainty. These uncertainties are likely to swamp any fluctuations in estimated value arising from the precise way that the "valuation date" is fixed in a given year. For formal purposes, however, we propose that the valuation date should be fixed at the *earliest time* in the tax year when Schedule 15 applies to the asset in question. This has the advantage of relative simplicity, and adopting an early date is likely, other considerations being equal, to give taxpayers a marginally lower nominal value than other dates would.

11. If in practice taxpayers find it more convenient to do their valuation at a later date in the tax year or in the period from the year-end to their filing date, we would not generally expect to challenge the amounts returned to us

unless there is some indication that the date was chosen for tax-saving reasons.

12. Similar considerations may apply to some intangible assets: their values will be subject to a sufficient margin of uncertainty that the precise timing of the valuation date will be relatively immaterial. In other cases, however, intangible assets will be capable of precise valuation and their values may fluctuate materially from day to day—where for example the assets are quoted securities or reflect the value of quoted securities. In such cases we would expect taxpayers to return amounts determined for the particular valuation date specified in the regulations. In the absence of any obvious reason for adopting any other approach, however, we propose that the valuation date should again be the earliest time in the year when Schedule 15 applies: it should be no more burdensome in compliance cost terms than any other date, and as before should, other things being equal, be marginally favourable to the taxpayer.

13. **We would like your views on whether there are any important exceptions to this general picture.** It is conceivable that some assets may have a "natural" valuation date which will not necessarily coincide with a date specified in regulations—for example, where intangibles take the form of a proprietary financial product such as a life policy. We would generally expect such products to be continuously valued, (*e.g.* where they are linked to a unitised fund) so that taxpayers could readily satisfy a standard valuation rule. It is conceivable, however, that arrangements already in place will mean that good valuations are available at relatively low compliance cost at particular times of year—*e.g.* on policy anniversaries.

We would welcome your views on whether such situations are likely to be found often enough to merit special consideration; if so;

(a) **what provision might be possible for them without significant risk to the Exchequer, and**

(b) whether this should be embodied in the regulations or treated as a matter of operational good practice to be covered in the Revenue's guidance?

Consultation Questions

Question 1. Ministers propose that the "valuation date" for purposes of **AppII–E6** Schedule 15 should, as a general rule, be 6 April of the tax year in question, or if later the first day of the "taxable period" for the asset in question. Do you agree that this should be the general rule?

Question 2. If not, what should be the alternative?

Question 3. Are there, in any event, particular cases which call for special treatment, either in the regulations or in guidance?

There could be different rates for different cases. In the interests of **AppII–E7** simplicity, however, Ministers are starting from the presumption that uniform rules will apply to all cases unless they are satisfied, following this consultation, that a case has been made to justify distinct provision for different cases.

Valuation at longer than annual intervals

AppII–E8 14. The basic valuation rule in the primary legislation requires the taxable benefit to be computed afresh each year by reference to values as at the valuation date for that year. The forthcoming regulations may however, but need not, provide for the value for an earlier year to be carried forward (more strictly, the valuation date for an earlier year can be "re-used" to make valuations for a later year: in practice this will generally allow valuations already made to be re-used). Such regulations may, but need not, provide for "old" valuations to be adjusted, *e.g.* by increasing or reducing them in line with intervening movements in an index of prices.

15. This provision was made to address the concerns expressed in earlier consultations that repeated annual valuations could involve substantial compliance costs. But that is not true for all assets subject to Schedule 15. And even where costs are high, invoking this power to "re-use" valuations would itself mean increased complexity and hence extra compliance costs. It could also involve costs to the Exchequer, to the extent that nominal values of assets "caught" by Schedule 15, and the corresponding rental values in the case of land, are likely to increase over time. And it would be positively counter productive in compliance-cost terms if any special valuation regime functioned primarily to allow taxpayers a choice of valuations, so that taxpayers would incur all the compliance costs of applying both possible valuation bases for the purpose of seeing which one gave the lower liability.

16. It follows, therefore, that Ministers will only invoke the power allowing valuations less frequently than annually if they are satisfied following this consultation that to do so would make an overall improvement, taking compliance costs and Exchequer costs together.

17. More particularly, they believe that any special rule for valuation

— should apply only to assets where the compliance costs of valuation are high relative to the tax at stake between one valuation and the next

— should be as simple as possible, consistently with Minister's other objectives; and

— should be focussed on prospective compliance costs, and allow the minimum temptation for taxpayers to fine-tune their decisions, or to change from one valuation rule to another, in order to minimise prospective liability.

Which assets?

AppII–E9 18. For the reasons already noted, the compliance costs of an annual valuation, or an annual assessment of rentals, seem likely to be high for land generally and for chattels generally, but not as a rule for intangible assets.

Question 4. Do you agree that any special valuation regime should be restricted to land and chattels? If so:

(a) should it extend to intangible assets; and

(b) which ones should it apply to; and

(c) why?

A detailed argument in your reply to question 4.c) would help us assess the merits of the case for individual types of asset.

Should extended-interval valuations be compulsory or voluntary?

19. It would be simpler if any special valuation regime applied to all assets **AppII–E10** of an eligible kind which are caught by Schedule 15, and need to be valued for more than one income tax year. But this approach could in some cases involve higher liabilities than a strict annual valuation—and could seem particularly harsh from the taxpayers' perspective if prevailing market prices (or market rents) fell sharply soon after an "actual" valuation having effect for an extended period of years. It would also require taxpayers to keep track of each asset's valuation status (particularly if indexation were required in "non-valuation" years) over an extended period of years.

Question 5. Do you accept that a special valuation regime would be compulsory for eligible assets; or would taxpayers always want the option of a strictly-annual valuation?

20. Even if "extended-interval" valuations were in principle voluntary, we propose that the choice once made for a particular asset should be binding for the whole of a given "cycle". If, for example, the rules permitted an actual value to be used for five years before re-valuation, a taxpayer would have the choice of valuation approach in this scenario to re-use the actual value for year 1 of the charge in their return for year 2 (after adjustment, if that were required): but having done so they would also be obliged to re-use it in years 3, 4 and 5 before the revaluation in year 6. And similarly if they chose to revalue on an actual basis in year 2 they would be obliged to use an actual value in years 3 to 5, as well as year 6—following which the choice would be available again for the next cycle. (This does not, of course, exclude the possibility that the actual value estimated for, say, year 3 might be the same amount as the actual value estimated for year 2.)

21. The significance of the remaining design features obviously depends to some degree on whether the regime as a whole was voluntary. And, they are also inter-related. In particular, if there were a long period between successive valuations, and no provision for indexation of the figures in intervening years, this could involve significant Exchequer cost, and a risk that taxpayers would choose the option (if it were voluntary) primarily for tax-saving reasons. The corollary of that is that requiring indexation of asset values (up or down) in the years between "actual" valuations could allow longer intervals between valuations. But indexation of this kind would in

itself significantly complicate the regime particularly given the difficulty in specifying an index—or different indices for different asset types—which are simultaneously authoritatively easy for taxpayers to find and use, and relevant to the actual assets which fall to be valued.

22. In very broad terms, we see a choice between a scheme which is

— compulsory for all land and chattels; simple, with no indexation of values in years between valuations; and operating over a relatively short cycle of, say, actual valuations every three years; or

— a voluntary system (but with the choice made once-for-all-years in each cycle, as above); possibly with indexation; and possibly therefore operating over a longer cycle of, say, 5 years or more.

23. It is very much for taxpayers and their advisers to judge in the light of their own circumstances if either of these broad approaches offer advantage over an annual revaluation.

Question 6. Are either of these options attractive? If so:

a)   which and why? and

b)   do you have any comments on the design issues discussed here?

Special cases

AppII–E11 24. We have assumed so far that any regime permitting valuation at less-than-annual intervals would operate over a cycle running from the tax year in which the asset in question first becomes chargeable under Schedule 15. That seems the right approach as a general value. But it is conceivable that it could cut across a "natural" cycle of valuation for the asset involved. For example, it is possible that some land covered by Schedule 15 might be subject to rental payments by the former owner (though not, *ex hypothesi*, payments which are high enough to extinguish liability under Schedule 15) and these are subject to revision at regular intervals but less frequently than annually. There might in principle be advantage in synchronising tax calculations with such an existing third-party commitment.

Question 7. Are situations like this likely to arise in practice? If so, how could they be accommodated without risk to the Exchequer, either in the regulations proper or in our operational guidance?

The imputed yield on chattels and intangible assets

AppII–E12 25. It is necessary to specify the rates-of-returns to be used in the calculations at paragraphs 7(2) and 9(1) of Schedule 15.

26. As already noted, the regulations may, but need not, make different provision for different cases. They may also, but again need not, specify the rates in such a way that they vary over time (*e.g.* by following an externally-

determined rate) rather than being determined in particular numerical amounts.

27. In consultation to date, Ministers have taken as their starting point a single rate for both chattels and intangible assets at the level currently applying (and known as the "official rate") to "beneficial loans" to employees. Ministers continue to see this as the right starting point. They see strong arguments on grounds of simplicity for applying a single rate, or the simplest possible structure of multiple rates; and so far as possible to use rates which are already familiar to taxpayers and practitioners. And they think it would be out of place, given the objectives of Schedule 15 and the range of circumstances to be covered, to attempt a close analysis of each case in order to determine the rate to be applied. It is fair to say that the responses generally have not so far commented in detail on the consideration. It has, however, been argued that the rate on intangible assets should be lower than that on chattels. The argument, put shortly, is that the benefit from intangibles is of a different character from that from chattels, or from land. The benefit from intangible assets caught by Schedule 15 is the comfort from these assets being *available* to the taxpayer (but outside the taxpayer's inheritance tax charge): any actual benefit they get by way of income or appointment of capital is already taxable in the normal way. Taxpayers enjoying chattels or land caught by Schedule 15, by contrast, get all the benefits following from actual possession which are properly measured by a full rental value, or a value approximating to that where the "official rate" applies to the capital value.

28. Even if the fundamental distinction were accepted, there is clearly further analysis required to explore what would be an appropriate rate of return for intangible assets.

Question 8. Do you have comments on these issues, or do you have any other points which you think would inform Ministers' judgement on these rates?

Other operational matters

29. Schedule 15 imposes a charge to income tax. Tax returns for the year **AppII–E13** 2005–06 and onwards will make provision for amounts chargeable under Schedule 15, and anyone who finds in due course that they are liable but have not received a return should notify their chargeability to tax in the normal way. We are also preparing the forms that taxpayers will require to make the election contemplated by paragraph 23 of Schedule 15. We expect these to be available for the beginning of the 2005–06 tax year. We are also willing to implement the election through e-mail channels.

30. Once the Schedule 15 charge is fully in force, we expect that taxpayers and their advisers seeking day-to-day advice on the application of the charge will approach our Capital Taxes, Nottingham office which will have overall responsibility for implementing the legislation and carrying out any appropriate compliance checks. That office is currently drafting our guidance on the operation of Schedule 15; we expect to publish it in draft shortly after this consultation closes, and in final form early in the New Year. The guidance in preparation will be informed by the points and problem cases that have

already been put to us in early consultations and during the passage of the legislation, so far as not overtaken by the amendments reflected in the Finance Act as passed.

Question 9. Do you have further points that you would like to see covered by our guidance, or are there any other points that you would like to re-emphasise?

Early responses to this question would be especially helpful —if possible by the end of September 2004. In any event your reply should reach us by 18 November 2004.

Next Steps

AppII–E14 31. We will publish draft regulations and draft guidance shortly after this consultation closes. The regulations will be made, and final guidance will be published, early in the New Year.

INDEX

329

330

Double trust scheme
see under Home loan scheme

Equity release schemes
absence of motive requirement, 1–15
Eversden **case**
discretionary trusts, 2–09
facts, 16–01, 22–02
IIIT spouse exemption, 2–05, 2–09,
2–10, 16–02, 16–14, 16–16
scope of s.49(1), 16–18
transfers of value and gifts, 16–14,
16–15, 16–16, 16–18
Eversden **schemes**
background, 16–01
development, 1–04, 1–05
disadvantages, 16–05
discretionary trusts, 6–13, 16–04,
16–10, 16–11
double taxation, 1–22, 10–03
effect of POT Regime
appointing back house,
16–34—16–37
double inheritance tax charge,
16–35
election by spouse, 16–39
excluded transactions, 16–30
income tax charge, 16–38
options in relation to family home,
16–32
purpose of Regime, 16–28
reverter to settlor exception, 16–35
schemes involving family home,
16–29
spousal exemption, 16–31, 16–33,
16–36, 16–39
example, 3–13
exemptions for transfers of value,
1–08
family home arrangements
analysis of s.12, 16–13
capital gains tax issues, 16–07
effect of POT Regime, 16–29
gift, definition, 16–14, 16–15,
16–16, 24–03
income tax issues, 16–08
interest in possession, 16–10,
16–12, 16–13, 16–16, 16–33
PET regime, 16–09, 16–15
rearrangement of beneficial
interests, 16–07
settlor/life tenant, 16–18
spouse exemption, 16–09, 16–14,
16–16, 16–31, 16–33
structure, 16–06
termination of interest in
possession, 16–06

Eversden **schemes**—*cont.*
family home arrangements—*cont.*
transfers of value and gifts, 16–14,
16–15, 16–16, 16–18, 24–03
Trusts of Land and Appointment
of Trustees Act 1996, 16–10
insurance-based arrangements, 19–06
insurance bonds
appointing interest in possession,
16–44
calculation, 16–42
cashing bond, 16–42
example, 16–41
excluding settlor from benefit,
16–43
inflexibility, 16–04
moving out of intangibles, 16–45
spousal interest not terminated,
16–41
trustees, 16–04, 16–05
types of arrangement, 16–03
under 2003 legislation, 2–25
unscrambling, 16–46
use by home owners, 16–02
Eversden II **schemes**
background, 16–21
disposal by way of gift
avoidance, 16–25
sale at undervalue, 16–24
gift of undivided share in land,
16–27
lacuna in s.102, 16–26
position under Regime, 16–22
powers of trustees, 16–23
property not settled in favour of
spouse, 16–23
restitutionary claims, 16–22
sale at undervalue, 16–24
spousal exemption, 16–23, 16–27
successive spousal interests in
possession, 16–26
Excluded liability provisions
definitions, 7–06
IHT associated operations, 1–19
nullifying home loan schemes, 7–06
Excluded transactions
annual and small gifts, 5–07
arm's length sale, 5–01, 5–08
arm's length transaction test, 5–08
charge on chattels, 5–01
charge on land, 5–01
charge on settled intangible property,
5–01
contribution conditions
not met, 5–01, 5–09
disposal conditions
arm's length sales, 5–08